A Bateman  Family Novel

SAVING Beth

JENNY GLAZEBROOK

With much love to Rob;
my husband, friend, hero,
and inspiration for this story.
You're more than I could have dreamed.

A NOTE FROM JENNY

Dear friend,

Before you read this story, I feel the need to connect with you. As an author, I feel a huge responsibility to value and care for your mind, heart and emotions.

I've always been a bit of a dreamer and a romantic, and when I was a young adult, I suffered devastating loss that shattered my heart and my dreams. However, I never could have imagined how beautifully and completely God would redeem. It still leaves me breathless in wonder.

I want you to know that nothing in *Saving Beth* was written lightly. It's one of the hardest stories I've ever written, because it's based on my own real life experiences of love, loss and redemption. For this reason, it's very close to my heart, but it's also written with you in mind. I want you to always, no matter what you go through, look for God's loving hand, and when you can't see it, trust His heart, and know that redemption is coming.

I have come to learn that God never causes suffering. He is too good, too kind, too loving. But He has also given us the amazing gift of free will, and some of the consequences of that are the pain, loss and suffering we experience in this broken world.

But God is also sovereign, and nothing can compare with the beauty and wonder of His ability to redeem.

This doesn't mean He planned or wanted the pain that led to our redemption.

My prayer is that no matter what happens in your life, you will always surrender every part of it to Him—including any pain or shattered dreams. May you see the wonder of His redemption unfold, and may it be beyond all you could have dreamed possible.

Jenny xx

CHAPTER ONE

Beth glanced at the road ahead, then looked again.

'No, God, please no.' The words came out in a painful, breathless whisper. 'Not now. Not today.'

Her bike wobbled and she dropped one foot to the ground, eyes fixed on the lopsided grey and pink bundle huddled on the side of the road.

Taking a deep breath, she closed her eyes then opened them again. She couldn't change reality. Experience had well and truly taught her that. She could ignore it. Keep riding. She had homework to do. Assignments to finish. Chores to complete.

But it was young, its greyish-pink feathers indicating it was less than a year old. If she helped, it could live at least another fifty years. *God, I can't leave it there. Can I?*

A car whizzed by and the bird toppled sideways. A gust of wind swept through the gum trees, unsettling the leaves and filling Beth with a sense of urgency. Letting her bike drop to the ground, she crept forward. Slowly. Steadily.

Why did it have to be a galah? Was God trying to make her feel worse? Was He testing her?

The galah tilted its head, dark brown eyes watching her every move. Then it attempted a few hops, but one wing dragged on the ground, clearly out of place.

'You're a sweet little guy, aren't you?' She spoke softly, keeping eye contact. 'It's okay, I'm just trying to help.'

She didn't have gloves. Didn't have a towel. This was going to hurt. *Please God, make him fly away. He's supposed to be free. He needs to be free!*

The galah closed its eyes as though shutting out her presence—until she wrapped her fingers around his wings. He fluttered fiercely, and his sharp, curved beak dug into the tender skin between her thumb and forefinger. She bit her lip, holding back a cry, and shifted her hands. It didn't help. The bird twisted his head and hooked his beak in again, clamping down with his pincer-like grip.

She deserved it. She really did. There was something satisfying about the pain. Something right.

She couldn't take him home. Mum would have a fit. No, she would take him to the Cairns' farm. It was a long walk from here, but she and this bird were in it together.

Only he didn't seem to think so.

By the time Beth arrived at the farm, her forehead glistened with sweat, her fingers were pinched and bleeding, and her eyes streamed with tears. So many memories, so many regrets.

Clare raced out the front gate to meet her. 'Beth! What is it?'

Beth held out the bird, and her sister's eyes widened, fixed not on the galah, but on the blood dripping from her fingers. 'Oh Beth, what have you done?'

What had she done? If only she knew. 'Have you got a box? A towel? Somewhere we can keep him until I call Wildlife Rescue?'

Clare raced into the house and called for her fiancé, Phil. Beth heard him jogging down the stairs before he rounded the corner. His eyes widened just the way Clare's had, but then softened with compassion. 'You should have called us. We could have picked you up.'

'I couldn't. I needed both hands for him.' She nodded down at the galah, who struggled again, twisting his neck to find another tender spot to bite.

Clare arrived with a towel and a box and, with great care, Beth placed the bird inside.

'You can't keep him at your place,' Phil said, eyes knowing.

'No, I was going to call Wildlife Rescue.'

'They don't operate in this area. Last time I called, they said I needed to take the bird to a vet to have it put down.'

Beth gasped. 'Why?'

'It's too expensive to fix wings, and they believe they have no quality of life if they can't fly free.'

What? That was so wrong. The bird still had breath and life. True, it was wounded and trapped and would probably never fly free again, but wasn't life of value because God had granted it? She was wounded and trapped too, wasn't she?

She looked down at her hands. Blood blisters and broken skin acknowledged the pain screaming at her. But her heart hurt more. Tears filled her eyes again. 'I can't let them put him down.'

'Always have to be saving someone or something, don't you?' Clare gave her a tender look. Or was it a patronising big sister look? 'Beth, sometimes you have to let nature take its course.'

Unexpected anger heated Beth's chest. 'So nature was right to take Dad and Grandpa?'

Clare froze and Phil winced. Then silence. Complete silence. Beth bit her lip. Why had she said that? How dare she? Nature didn't take Grandpa—her foolish attempt to save a galah just like this one had done that. But she couldn't let Clare guess what she'd done. Couldn't let anyone in the world know that her attempt to save had taken a life. It was a secret she would take to the grave. A secret Grandpa had taken to the grave because she had put him there.

Phil cleared his throat. 'We can keep him at the cottage, in the old chook pen. I can fix it up for you.'

'You would do that?' Hope filled her. Phil and Clare's wedding was in a few weeks, and they would move into Aunty Joy's old cottage. Beth wouldn't have thought they'd want to take on an injured galah.

Phil's eyes met and connected with Clare's and a message passed between them, before Phil faced Beth again. 'You'd need to come out every day to feed and care for him.'

That's if he lived that long. Shock could kill a bird. And a person. Beth knew that too well. She shook away the awful memories. 'You really wouldn't mind?'

Clare gave a small smile. 'I was telling Phil how much I'd miss you when I leave home.' She shrugged. 'This way I'll see you every day.'

A fear Beth had buried deep within, lifted. She wasn't just the tag-along little sister after all. Clare might have been consumed with her fiancé these last few months, but clearly she still liked having her around.

Clare looked at Beth's shaking hands. 'Go and wash off the blood,' she ordered, big sister back in place. 'Then after we've patched you up, we'll go and look at this chook pen.'

It was then that she remembered. 'I left my bike by the side of the road. Near Hayman's corner.'

Phil headed for the door. 'I'll get it. Be back soon.'

Beth watched him go, then went to wash her hands. She scrubbed away the dried blood, wishing she could just as easily wash the stains from her heart. She didn't deserve their kindness. Any of it. She was a hypocrite, and she'd rather die than have them find out.

MUM WAS NOT HAPPY. No surprises there.

'Just how much work is this bird going to be?'

Beth bit her lip. 'Not too much.' She pictured the galah the way she'd left it, sitting on the ground in the chook pen looking scared and lost. Everything within her wanted to bring him home and care for him in her room where she could check he was still breathing every time her overreactive imagination suggested otherwise.

Mum's reaction proved it was not an option. 'How do you expect to keep up with schoolwork if you're traipsing out to the Cairns' farm every afternoon?'

To her relief, Clare cut in with an airy wave of her hand. 'She'll be fine, Mum. She can do her schoolwork out there. Phil can bring us both home. We'll chuck her bike in the back of the farm ute. And then after we're married, you can pick her up after you've finished at the office each night.'

Mum frowned. 'But I don't get home until late.' As evidenced by tonight. Another nine o'clock night at the office with a quick, reheated dinner and an irritated frown at any inconvenient requests made by her daughters—like wanting to care for an injured galah.

Clare wasn't deterred. 'So, it would be better for her to have company and not be here all by herself.' She winked at Beth, and Beth couldn't help smiling in return. Clare would win the argument. She always did. It was nice to have her sister on her side— another sign of the change in Clare since she'd met Philip Cairn and become a Christian.

Mum frowned. 'What about the bike? It won't fit in my car.'

More like Mum wouldn't want a dirty bike touching the beautiful leather of her car seats. Beth pushed down her irritation. 'I'll ride home earlier then. While it's light. And then I can bring in the washing and get dinner. And do the ironing.' That should convince her.

Mum tapped the end of her fork on the table. Gently, so as not to mark the beautiful polished cedar. 'I don't like it …'

Beth bit back her smile, sensing a 'but' was coming. Showing triumph too early would be a mistake.

'But I'll allow it, if you keep up with your schoolwork. However, if your marks drop …'

Clare let out an unladylike snort. 'Well they can't exactly get any higher, can they?' She pointed to Beth's latest book review on the table. The teacher's bright red pen scrawled her results at the the top.

Excellent work, Beth. 20/20.

Mum's eyebrows drew together, and Beth spoke quickly, not willing to lose any ground. 'I'll keep up the marks. I promise.'

Mum's face relaxed and she almost smiled. 'Two weeks. We'll trial it until the wedding. But you must ride straight to the Cairns' farm from school. No stopping on the way. No more rescuing creatures. No talking to strangers.'

Clare rolled her eyes, and Beth grinned. Mum would always be Mum. She'd learned a long time ago it wasn't worth reminding her she was no longer a little girl. Mum treated her adult employees like children, so there was no way she could be expected to treat her real children any different, no matter how old they were. Clare didn't seem to understand that sometimes it wasn't worth the fight. Better to go with the flow and keep under Mum's radar as much as possible.

BETH SAT IN CLASS, wishing the school day was over so she could ride out the the farm and see the galah. She'd been trying to work out a name for him all day. Harry? No, maybe Heathcliff. Or

Darcy. She wrote the name carefully in her notepad, looking at it from every angle. Better to save that name for a rescue animal whose gender she couldn't pick. This galah's dark eyes gave her no doubt he was a boy.

Cooper

She looked at the name she'd written down, then shook head. Where had that come from? She hadn't thought of him in years, and there was no way Clare or Dan would let her live it down if she named a bird after him.

'Who's Cooper?'

Her hand flew across the notepad, her heart sinking as Dara looked over her shoulder. It was impossible to hide anything from Dara McCann. 'I'm trying to come up with a name for my rescue bird.'

Dara let out a hoot of laughter. 'Cooper because you're keeping him in a chicken coop?'

She couldn't help smiling. 'I hadn't thought of that. But no, it's not right for him.'

'What then? Oliver? Cameron? He'd be flattered you know.'

Beth laughed. There was no way she was naming the galah after the class clown. Although … No. It would give people the wrong impression. 'Gilbert,' she said on impulse. She loved L.M Montgomery's novels and she needed to put an end to this conversation.

Dara tilted her head, her gaze watchful. 'Like in *Anne of Green Gables*?'

'Maybe.'

Dara grinned. 'Why not Andy? You and Andy Saunders are like Anne and Gilbert, aren't you? Always competing for Dux.'

Beth winced darted a look around. Dara was way too loud and way too close to the mark. She couldn't afford to let her guess her feelings for Andy. She had a way of trampling anything precious into the ground; especially closely guarded secrets like this one.

'Who's talking about me?'

The deep, cheerful voice had Beth's head whipping around again. Warmth filled her cheeks as she looked up into Andy's sparkling blue eyes. His dark hair flopped over his forehead, curly and out of control.

'I'm looking after an injured galah.' She flipped her notebook shut. 'I've decided to name him Gilbert.'

Dara smirked while Andy's expression softened. 'What happened to him?'

'It looks like he was hit by a car, but he should be fine. I'm keeping him out at the Cairns' until he heals, and then I'll release him.'

Andy's eyes crinkled at the corners. 'Trust you to always believe the best.'

She had to. That's what he didn't understand. There was no other choice. Gilbert couldn't die. Enough lives had been lost at her hands already.

CHAPTER TWO

Tomorrow was the big day. Beth put down her pen with a contented sigh. She could fill her journal with true life romance. Not her own, but Clare's. She glanced back down at her neat, flowing cursive.

Tomorrow my sister Clare is going to marry Philip Cairn, the country farm boy with the singing voice of an angel and a heart of gold. He looks at her with a tenderness born of adversity, overcome through love deeper than any circumstance.

She bit her lip. Was that last sentence original, or did she find it in a book? Sometimes her own thoughts tangled with the thousands of lives she'd lived through novels.

'What are you doing?'

At Clare's voice, she shoved her journal under her pillow.

Clare's eyes sparkled with mischief. 'Writing about Andy?'

Beth tensed. She'd been too slow. 'No.'

Clare stepped into the room, moving toward the hidden journal. 'You won't mind me taking a look, then.'

'Clare.' Beth hated the familiar feelings of helplessness, fear and humiliation rising in her gut.

Clare grinned and lunged for the journal.

Instinctively, Beth held out an arm. 'Don't.'

Something in her voice hit its mark because Clare stopped, the light leaving her face. 'I'm just teasing ...' She didn't finish, instead lowering herself onto the bed beside Beth. 'Dan and I hurt you pretty badly, didn't we?'

Beth couldn't answer. To reveal the extent of her hurt would make her vulnerable once more. Besides, her throat ached, and trying to speak would start a flow of embarrassing tears.

'I'm so sorry, Beth. Dan and I should never have stolen your journal or made fun of you.'

Beth's face heated at the memory. Her brother and sister tossing her journal between them, hooting with laughter at her declaration of feelings for Cooper. Threatening to tell Cooper. And they had. She knew, because from that day Cooper couldn't even look at her. She had lost both a dream and a friend that day, thanks to Clare and Dan.

Clare touched her arm. 'Beth, I really am so sorry. I was so thoughtless. I never meant to hurt you. If I could go back in time, I would do so many things differently.'

Beth nodded, annoyed by the tears stinging her eyes. 'It's okay.'

'It's not okay, but I need you to forgive me anyway. I was horrible to you.'

Beth looked into her sister's beseeching eyes and wondered at the transformation in her. Clare was a completely new person. The old Clare was gone, and in her place was a sensitive, compassionate sister who understood love more than Beth ever had.

'You're forgiven.' Beth winced. If Clare knew what had really happened to Grandpa, she'd realised Beth had no right *not* to forgive.

Clare bit her lip, studying Beth as though trying to work out if she meant it.

'It really is okay, Clare. You're so different. And you believe in love now.'

A relieved smile filled Clare's face. 'Speaking of love, do you want a preview of my wedding dress? The alterations are all done.'

Beth's smile matched Clare's. 'Yes! Put it on.'

Clare laughed. 'It's not that simple. I'll need your help.'

Beth believed it. She'd seen all the clips and buttons and swathes of white satin, tulle and lace. She followed Clare to her room, where the dresses all hung from Clare's window curtain rail, the only rail high enough to keep Clare's dress and train off the floor.

Clare stood on a chair to pull her dress down and they worked together to lay it out on the bed. Clare spun her hand in a circle. 'Turn around while I fight my way into it.'

Beth smiled and turned. She could hear the rustle of fabric as Clare wrestled with the train. Finally, Clare let out a small squeak. 'Help.'

Beth spun to find her in a twisted mess of dress and train. A giggle burst out, and Clare bit her lip, dimples showing. 'I got kind of stuck.'

'You think?' Beth came to her rescue, moving the train into some semblance of order, both of them now giggling uncontrollably.

Clare turned so Beth could do up all the fasteners. 'Do you think Phil will be able to see me? What if I kind of sink into all this material and just become one big dress?'

Beth laughed out loud at the picture that made. 'You'd outshine any dress any day. Everything will be perfect.'

Clare screwed up her nose. 'Mum's made sure of that, hasn't

she? I wanted to get married out on the Cairns' farm in the woolshed.'

Beth laughed. Surely Clare didn't mean that? She couldn't be sure these days. Clare was so different since she'd met the Cairns. But she was also right that everything would be perfect if she and Mum had any say in it.

Her only concern was Dan.

Surely he wouldn't put exploding candles in the church? Or set his mobile phone to go off every five minutes? Or hide a water balloon under the cushion they'd put on great Aunt Shirley's seat for her bad back? He'd threatened that and more.

It was too much to hope her brother would change too. And whatever it took, she had to hide her feelings for Andy during the wedding. If Dan picked up on them ...

She did up the final button and stepped back. Her breath caught and her chin quivered. 'Clare, you look like sunshine on a winter's morning.'

Clare laughed. 'You're such a romantic. Do you think the seam-stress took it up enough?' She twirled, the dress swirling about her, shimmering, alive and almost breathing.

'It's perfect.' Beth sat on the edge of Clare's bed. '*Everything's* perfect. I always knew you'd marry Phil.'

Clare's eyes misted. 'I know. I'm so blessed to have you as my sister. You were the one who dreamed my dreams for me when I was too weary to believe in them anymore.'

Beth's lips lifted in a watery smile. What a poetic thing for the practical Clare to say. 'Careful. You're starting to sound like me.'

'Scary, isn't it?' Clare wiped her eyes, and her dimples peeked through as she pointed up at Beth's bridesmaid dress still hanging on the curtain rail. 'You should try on your dress again.'

Beth hesitated.

'Go on. I want to see you in it.' Her eyes lit up. 'I can't wait for Andy to see you in it.'

'Clare.'

Clare sobered. 'It's okay, Beth, I'd never tell him. This is different. Andy is different. Cooper was … not good enough for you.'

Beth shook her head but didn't say what she was thinking. Andy was too good for her, but she would dream of him just the same. From the day she had met him—the same day she decided to give her life to God—he had been there. His joy at her decision had caused him to pull her into an impulsive, heart-warming hug that made her blush bright red but smile with pleasure at the same time. That youth event had changed her life. It was an eternal moment, as Phil and Clare would say. If only she'd had the courage to confess what was really bothering her; the thing that made her so undeserving of him.

'Beth?' Clare gave the dress a small shake. 'Please? For me?'

With a smile, Beth gave in and reached for her sky-blue bridesmaid dress, taking it from Clare and laying it on the bed.

Clare turned her back, then shuffled outside the door. 'You done?'

'Patience, Clare.' Beth chuckled as she dragged it over her head and slid the zip into place. So much simpler than Clare's dress. 'Done.'

Clare turned. For a moment, she didn't speak. Then her face broke into a wide smile. 'Beautiful,' she breathed.

Beth looked down at herself. The blue was the same colour as Andy's eyes. What would he think? She'd never met anyone else like him. So full of life and fun but so deep and compassionate at the same time. Despite not deserving him, there was still that dream that refused to die; the dream of marrying Andy.

She helped Clare undo the fasteners of her dress, then went back to her own room while she changed.

God really did change people. And God liked happy endings as much as she did. After all, he saved Philip Cairn's life and brought him back from the mission field to marry Clare. It was the perfect love story. Better than any romance novel, because it was real and being lived out perfectly right in front of her.

Smiling, she let herself fall back onto her bed. Then jumped up with a gasp. What would Mum say if she wrinkled the dress? Mum insisted on the most expensive dresses for the wedding and then grumbled about the cost as she spent extra hours at work to pay for it all.

'Besides, now that Adam Cairn has decided to leave to be a missionary in the Madorean Islands, I'm on my own in the office,' she complained. 'I have to work double time to keep up.'

Beth knew the truth. Money wasn't an issue. Mum just needed to escape. She didn't know how to respond to the change in Clare and Beth since they'd become Christians, nor how to react to her best worker moving overseas to become a missionary. And so, she worked harder and longer than she ever had.

She also worked on making Clare's wedding unforgettable. No expense was spared as Mum sought to impress the world with her class and style.

Beth didn't get it. She was the child who bent over backwards to please Mum, but it was Clare—the impish, daring one—Mum was so proud of. Clare had caused no end of trouble in the family, from—

A familiar flashback stole her breath. She closed her eyes to shut out the memory. How could she say Clare caused trouble in the family? Grandpa should be here. He should be the one walking Clare down the aisle tomorrow. It was bad enough losing Dad in a car accident when she was only two years old, but that wasn't her fault. Grandpa, however … She let out a shaky breath. If only she could escape herself.

But that was impossible. All she could do was give everything to make people's lives better, whatever the cost. To somehow make up for what she had done. Only, some days, she got so tired … tired of trying, tired of the struggle and tired of the battle raging in her mind.

THE DAY of Clare's wedding dawned bright and clear. Beth sat with Gilbert in the early morning light, her bike leaning against the chicken pen. The bird still watched her carefully, stretching his good wing, not completely trusting. She didn't blame him. Maybe he sensed what she was like deep down inside. She rubbed her eyes, wishing she'd had a better sleep. Her nightmares were constant and draining. Too many of them included her forgetting to feed and water Gilbert, but she was never going to let that happen in real life. He was dependent on her and she wasn't going to let him down.

She stood, and Gilbert let out a little squawk. She smiled. 'Sorry Gilbert, but I have to go. Clare's getting married today.'

He tilted his head to the side as though trying to understand. If only she had more time to sit here quietly; to let her heart settle. But she had to race home. It was her job to make sure the day was perfect—or as perfect as it could be without Grandpa there to walk Clare down the aisle.

BETH MANAGED to shower and have breakfast before Clare emerged from her room, her smile alive with joy. 'Beth, I'm marrying Phil today. It's actually happening!'

'I know.' Beth beamed back at her. Even in her nightdress with her hair tousled from sleep, Clare was beautiful. Her eyes danced, and everything about her was animated. She remembered Mum's words when she was little. 'You need to eat more, Beth. I think you would have a beautiful heart-shaped face like Clare's if you filled out a bit more.'

She shoved the memory aside. Today was about Clare. 'Mum's

down at the reception hall making sure everything's perfect. She said she'll be back with the car in plenty of time.'

Clare nodded, then stopped short at the bottom of the stairs, her eyes widening in panic. 'We forgot to tell Pete to collect the car keys. I knew we'd forget something.'

Beth pulled out her phone. 'Don't worry. I'll call Andy and ask him to let Pete know.' Pete Saunders was Phil's friend from childhood and would be driving the bride's car.

Clare's shoulders relaxed. 'Thanks Beth. I knew you'd be perfect as chief bridesmaid. What would I do without you?'

Have your grandfather walking you down the aisle.

Beth shut off the thought as she called Andy. His cheerful voice answered. 'Hey Beth, what's up?'

'Clare forgot to tell your brother to get the car keys. They're still here.'

He let out his distinctive laugh—the merry sound she'd grown to love. She didn't think she'd ever seen Andy in a bad mood. 'She's in a bit of a daze, is she? Well, I'll have to come and get them 'cos Pete's down getting his hair and nails done.'

Beth laughed. That was the last thing the blokey Pete would be doing.

LESS THAN TEN MINUTES LATER, Andy wandered up to their front door, looking slightly overwhelmed as he gazed up at their palatial home. Beth opened the door with a wide smile, hoping to put him at ease.

His gaze connected with hers, and his expression relaxed into a cheerful grin. 'So, the big day has arrived.' He kicked off his shoes in the foyer and Beth looked away, embarrassed that Mum expected this of guests.

'Yeah. Finally.'

He chuckled. 'Big build up, isn't it?' He followed her down the main hall and into the formal lounge room where he flopped onto the sofa. 'Where's the bride?'

'In the shower. I'll ask her where she put the keys.'

'No, have a seat. I can wait.' His blue eyes sparkled as he motioned to the seat across from him, and her heart missed a beat. He looked up at the array of dresses now hanging by the stairs. 'So that's what you'll be wearing?'

'Yeah. Clare loves that colour.' And so did she. It matched Andy's eyes.

He smiled. 'Clare loves everything and everyone.'

He had that right. 'Especially Phil.'

'Yeah, I've noticed. They don't leave each other's side, do they? I hope I'm that much in love if I get married someday.'

Beth blinked. 'Of course you will be. Why else would you get married?'

He shrugged. 'Out of loneliness? Or convenience, or money, expectations, or just because. There's plenty of reasons other than being hopelessly in love.'

'I don't see how you could marry without being in love.'

He laughed, a gentle friendly sound. 'Beth, my friend, not all people have the capacity to love the way you do. Lots of people marry for reasons other than *true love*. You can marry for sensible, practical reasons.'

How could he say that like it was okay? What was life without love?

'What does that look mean?' He sounded amused.

What would happen if she told him what she was really think-ing? That love made life worth living. That she would die for it— that she would die for *him*. Because there would never be anyone else she could love more than him. Ever.

A door opened and Clare floated downstairs, towel wrapped around her wet hair. 'I thought I recognised that laugh.'

Andy grinned up at her. 'Nice veil.'

She shot him a fake frown, removed the towel and proceeded to dry her hair. 'The keys are on the bench.'

'I know. I saw them.'

'So why are you still here?'

'Because I wanted to have a chat with Beth … and get a peek at the wedding dress so I can describe it to Pete so he can describe it to Phil.'

Clare shook her head at his teasing. 'I'm not worried. Guys can't describe dresses.'

Andy scooped up the keys from the bench and headed for the door where he slid his shoes back on. 'Don't underestimate me, Clare Bateman. I happen to have a phone in my pocket. Pictures are worth a thousand words, you know.'

Clare merely laughed and closed the door behind him, eyes shining at Beth. 'He didn't, did he?'

She shook her head.

'Didn't think so.'

Two hours and one hairdresser and make-up artist later, Beth stood, transfixed by her sister.

'Clare, you are so beautiful!'

Clare smiled, turning in her flowing white gown, her dark hair braided on top of her head and decorated with a tiara of flowers. 'You are too, Beth.'

Why did people do that—compliment her in return just because it was the nice thing to do? She had a mirror. She knew she didn't have Clare's sweet, heart-shaped face, eyes that sparkled with life and that dancing smile that swept everyone off their feet. Neither did she have the knack of being able to relate to everybody with ease. No wonder Phil loved Clare.

Allie, another of Clare's bridesmaids, came out of the bathroom and stopped. Then she burst into tears before swiping at her cheeks and laughing at herself. 'Sorry, Clare. I just can't believe this is finally happening. You look like a dream. Both of you.'

Beth noticed the way she added the 'both of you' almost as an afterthought.

Pete Saunders appeared in the doorway, broad and handsome in his tux. 'Ready Clare? It's time to head to the church.' His eyes moved to Beth. 'Looking good, Junior Clare.'

She smiled, but irritation welled up. She was going to marry his brother one day, so he needed to learn her name. As much as she admired Clare, she didn't want to live in her sister's shadow.

Pete held out an arm with an arrogant confidence that bugged her. She allowed him to escort her to the car, hoping he realised she was not the type to fall at his feet like other girls. Pete had nothing on his brother. Andy might not be so dashingly good looking, but he was full of personality, life and love. And most of all, he had a faith and godliness she admired.

Phil's father stood waiting at the church with a smile lighting his farm-weathered face. He came and helped ease Clare from the car, ready to give her away. Mr. Cairn was an amazing man, but it still hurt that Dad or Grandpa weren't here to do it.

Dale Cairn bent to speak into Clare's ear, and she smiled and set her eyes on the church. Beth suspected she was desperate to see Phil, just like she was desperate to see Andy. He would be inside, guiding people to their seats, fulfilling his role as usher. Beth had begged Clare to give him that job. It was important he be a part of this big day, considering she wanted him to play the most significant part in hers one day.

Soft music flowed through the church doors, reaching Beth's ears. Her heart pounded and she fought to hold in emotion. It was time.

Allie stepped down the aisle first, her eyes fixed on her fiancé, Scott. He stood down the front of the church beside Phil, and tenderness lit his eyes as he watched Allie's progress. It softened his whole face, and for the first time Beth could see the resemblance between Phil and his older brother.

All eyes settled on Beth. She stepped forward. This was it. How many people could tell she was blushing through her makeup? Was she holding her stomach in tight enough? What if one of her bra straps was showing? She tried not to think of all the phones being held up, capturing the moment forever.

Thankfully, Clare reached the doorway and all eyes focused on her instead. Beth reached the front and turned to see Clare, eyes fastened on Phil who stood tall, looking at his bride in a way that did something to Beth's heart. The perfect love story; love triumphing over all the storms of life.

She searched for Andy. There he was, standing at the back of the church, hands in pockets, dark curls flopping over his forehead in their usual haphazard way. He turned as though sensing her gaze, and grinned. Then he rolled his eyes and shook his head as though he was amused by the whole thing; as though he knew exactly what Beth was thinking. That it was all so romantic and right.

And it was.

WHY DID Andy have to be working again? One of the waiters hadn't turned up for the reception so Mum asked him to fill in. He seemed more than willing to do so, his manner smooth and charming as he served drinks to the guests.

'You're looking beautiful today,' one of Phil's uncles complimented Beth as he walked past.

'Thank you.' She hoped she sounded gracious. It was traditional to say nice things to the bridesmaids, but it made her uncomfortable.

A young man with a pointed nose and intense eyes approached. One of Phil's cousins. 'Would you like to dance?'

She gave him a polite smile. 'No thanks. I like sitting back and watching.'

A flash of something, possibly hurt, darkened his eyes before he nodded and moved away. Guilt niggled. Had he seen her watching Andy?

Clare approached, her beautiful white gown trailing behind. She lowered herself into the empty chair beside Beth, tucking the folds of her dress beneath her. 'Beth, you look like royalty sitting here like this.' She gave her a cheeky, dimpled smile. 'Phil said to tell you to stop being a princess and start dancing.'

Beth glanced to where Phil stood, his gaze never leaving his wife. Maybe she should dance, but Andy was busy, her brother Tim sat to the side looking surly and unapproachable, and Dan was out decorating the car Phil and Clare would take on their honeymoon. At least Dan was occupied and seemed to have forgotten all his other crazy threats to ruin the day. She just hoped he didn't damage the car.

'I'm not being a princess. I'm just enjoying the show.' It wasn't totally true. But she knew what Clare would say if she admitted she was keeping a close eye on everything; making sure nothing went wrong. Clare wouldn't understand why it was her responsibility—why she owed it to her.

Clare's look turned thoughtful, then she nodded. 'Just don't spend your whole life watching, or you'll miss out on actually living.'

Beth laughed, but her heart was heavy. She was living because she was breathing, confined to the small cage she'd made to keep herself and others safe.

THE LONG DAY FINALLY ENDED. If only she'd accepted Andy's offer to dance, but it would have looked way too obvious after she'd refused everyone else. She groaned. She was a master of self-sabotage. She stood with Mum and her brothers as Clare and Phil's car rattled down the road, cans clunking behind.

Tim grunted. 'Well, she's happy.'

Of course she was. She was married to the man of her dreams. Tim had been the only one against the wedding. 'She's too young. It won't last,' he griped. 'She should at least move in with him before she makes such a big decision.'

Beth kept her mouth shut, but wished she had the courage to explain that Christians didn't do that. They believed you should only ever sleep with the one you were committing your life to. But Tim had made it crystal clear he wasn't impressed by Clare and Beth's newfound faith.

Mum glanced around at the mess in the hall and heaved a sigh. 'I just hope she gets more rest than I do. Everyone thinks the work gets done magically by itself.'

Beth frowned. Mum never noticed her. Never noticed the way she desperately tried to help, to take some of her load. Sometimes she wondered if she was actually invisible. Maybe it was better that way.

Guests were leaving, but they didn't take their rubbish. Great Aunt Shirley appeared to have left her cardigan on the back of her chair. Beth moved toward it, grabbing dirty serviettes along the way, and balloons as deflated as she was. This complete exhaustion was a high price to pay for the day. But then she remembered the way Clare and Phil looked at each other and allowed herself to dream that one day her own dreams might come true.

CHAPTER THREE

Beth missed Clare and Phil. If they were back from their honeymoon she wouldn't need to be doing this. She raised her hand to knock on the Saunders' front door, then let it drop again. Why couldn't she just knock? What was wrong with her?

She jumped as a car door slammed. Pete's deep voice called from the driveway. 'Junior Clare! How's it going?'

How did she not hear his car? Oh. It was one of those modern electric ones. The sleek, shiny vehicle suited him. He headed towards her, wearing his work uniform, a smart blue shirt advertising the local electrical company. He'd been lucky to receive an apprenticeship in this small town.

She gave him a tentative smile. 'Home from work?'

He responded with his wide, charming smile so like Andy's but so much less, too. 'I'm never home from work. It follows me wherever I go.'

There was an awkward pause as she searched her mind for what to say. He rescued her.

'You're after Andy?' She nodded, waiting as he juggled his

keys and fumbled with the front door. 'I saw your picture in the paper. Congratulations.'

If Pete saw the picture, Andy probably did too. The long hours alone with Clare away were well spent. It was therapeutic to sit in their backyard beside the chook pen, keeping Gilbert company and sketching. She could express her heart, her greatest hopes and dreams, and help clear her mind at the same time. Talking every-thing through with Gilbert was a bonus. He listened carefully, one wing still drooping, head on the side, dark eyes watching her.

She never expected her art teacher to enter her sketch in a competition, though. And she certainly never imagined she'd win.

Pete dumped his keys on the hall table and called through the house. 'Andy, you've got a visitor.'

Beth took a deep breath. There was no backing out now.

'Beth.' Andy's eyes lit up as he wandered in from the back room. 'Pete always surprises me with what he brings home from work.' He grinned and motioned for her to take a seat. 'Shove the papers out of the way.'

She folded the newspapers scattered across the lounge and placed them on the coffee table, aware of his eyes on her as she sat and crossed her legs, straightening her skirt.

Andy grinned. 'What can I do for you?'

'Well, I won a prize for my Anzac artwork—'

'Yeah I saw. You definitely have a gift.' Warmth crept into her face at his praise. He leaned forward and picked up the local newspaper from the neat pile she'd made on the coffee table. He flipped it open to the second page. 'Here it is.'

Beth wished she could read his thoughts as he studied the photo of her beside her sketch. He folded the paper and dropped it on the lounge beside him. 'Yep, definitely a gift.'

'You understood it?' Hope lit her heart.

'I think so. I definitely see you in the girl who's cleaning up the little boy's scraped knee. You can see the compassion in her expression. I figured you were giving a voice to those stuck at home while their husbands and fathers were at war. And you were showing the power of compassion and understanding—the huge contrast between this scene and the battle scenes of war. Am I right?'

'Yes.' So right. Could this guy be any more perfect? She drew in a deep breath. 'There's a dinner I'm supposed to attend to get my award. I'm supposed to take a guest with me …'

He watched her, waiting, and she mustered up the courage to continue. 'Clare and Phil are still on their honeymoon, and Mum has a business meeting in the city that night.' She forced herself to maintain eye contact. 'I wondered if you're free. It's okay if you're not—but I wondered if you might be able to come? It's Friday night at seven.'

There. She'd done it.

'I can come.'

She couldn't hold back her smile. 'You're sure?'

One corner of his mouth lifted. 'Do I get a free meal?'

'Yes.'

'Then there's no way you can keep me away.'

He was a tease, but she could match him. Before she could second-guess herself, she tapped her chin. 'I could stay home and let you go by yourself if it's just the free meal you want. I mean, I know my company can be a bit trying.'

His eyes sparkled with amusement. 'It can be, but if you promise not to talk all evening, I'll let you come with me.'

She bit her lip to stop a smile. 'Thank you. I will try to control my urge to chatter on.'

'*Yabber*,' Andy corrected. 'The only way to describe the way you go on is *yabber*.'

A snort of laughter escaped before she could stop it. Mortified, she covered her mouth, feeling the colour rising in her cheeks. Mum would be horrified.

Andy's brows lifted. 'Snorting, Beth?' He shook his head. 'If I come with you, there will be no snorting and no giggling either. Got it?'

She bit her lip to hold back her giggle, despite her embarrassment. 'If you come, I promise not to do any of those things.' She couldn't even bring herself to say the word *snort*.

He sat back and his eyes crinkled at the corners. 'I take it back. It's kind of nice to hear you relax enough to snort in my presence.'

Her already warm face heated further under his gaze. The way he was looking at her … She shot to her feet. 'Well I'd better go.' She returned the newspapers on the coffee table to the lounge chair.

'Why?'

She kept her face averted, hoping he couldn't see her burning cheeks. What could she say? The silence lengthened and no sensible response came.

'It's okay, I understand,' Andy teased. 'You probably have to paint a masterpiece or something.'

'Something like that.'

He gave her a long look as though trying to figure her out. She glanced down and self-consciously straightened her skirt. Oliver Cameron from school accused her of dressing more like a businesswoman than a teenager. She knew she wasn't like other girls, but other girls didn't have Veronica Bateman for a mother. Poise and control had been bred into her.

Beth moved toward the door. She hated this awkward feeling that so often overcame her when she realised how she must appear to others. Anxiety blocked all sensible thoughts.

'What should I wear?'

She turned back at Andy's question. 'Mum said to tell you to wear a suit and tie if you have one, but I don't really think it matters if you don't want to.'

'Do *you* want me to?'

Did she? She opened her mouth to answer, then closed it again. She had no idea.

Andy shrugged. 'I'll wear one. Might as well make use of the one I got for Clare's wedding.'

BETH ARRIVED EARLY for the dinner. To her surprise, Andy was already waiting by the door. She glided up the steps, aware of his eyes on her. Thankfully, she was used to heels and could walk gracefully in them. Mum had insisted she buy a new dress, and matching heels were a given. She felt like her mother tonight. Tall, slim and elegant.

'Andy.' She smiled and held out her hand for him to shake. 'You're early.'

He ignored her hand and pulled her into a warm hug. Then he pointed to his tie. 'Am I suitably dressed?'

She stepped back and allowed herself to appreciate his appearance. Her mouth turned dry. He looked even better than at the wedding. Older, broader, stronger. She forced her voice to work. 'Yes. Shall we go and find our seats?'

Andy chuckled and she had the distinct feeling he knew the effect his appearance had on her. Heat filled her face and she headed inside, keeping her face averted. To her relief, it didn't take her long to spot their place cards.

'So here we are.' Andy pulled out their chairs, then plopped into his. 'And don't I feel a bit silly.'

'Silly?' Prickles of dismay unsettled her heart. Was he uncomfortable with her? Was he already not enjoying himself?

He laughed, picked up his place card to glance at it before flipping it back onto the table. 'Well, look at me—all dressed up like I'm someone important when I'm really just here because you couldn't find anyone else.'

Surely he couldn't really think that? Beth straightened his place card. 'I'm grateful you came. You're definitely better company than my mum. And you don't look silly.'

She couldn't look at him. What if he saw what she was really thinking? *There's no one else I'd rather be here with. You're the best looking, kindest, most godly young man I know and I'm seriously in love with you.* She'd say it if she could make her mouth work, but her heart wasn't pounding like a runaway horse.

He straightened in his seat. 'So, when do you get your award?' He ran his fingers through his thick, dark hair, making it stand on end. What would happen if she reached over and smoothed it down?

What was she thinking? 'Um, sorry, what did you ask?'

He let out a wholehearted laugh and everyone at the surrounding tables glanced their way. He leaned toward her, his voice going soft. 'You know what I think, Beth? You're not getting an award at all. You just made the whole thing up to get me into a suit and out on a date with you.'

Her face burned, but she forced herself to match his teasing. 'What if I did?'

'I don't know. Perhaps I'd have to take you out somewhere that requires you to wear jeans and a t-shirt ... and crocs. Or don't you have any?'

'Of course I do.' Well, the jeans and t-shirt, anyway.

'I've never seen you wear them.'

'I've had no reason to wear them.' Beth tilted her chin playfully. 'I move in higher circles than you do.'

He clutched at his chest, but his eyes twinkled. 'Ooh, that hurt.' His hand dropped to the table and he flipped the place card over again. 'But maybe you're right. You are classy. I doubt that you'd ever go out with someone just to get a free meal.'

She gave him a look. 'I doubt that you would either.' Even as the challenge came out, she wanted to snatch it back. Why hadn't she kept the conversation at the comfortable level of light-hearted banter?

She was saved by the chairman of the RSL club coming to the microphone. He cleared his throat. 'If I can just ask you to take your seats, ladies and gentlemen, we will begin the formalities.'

Chairs scraped as people found their places, and suddenly Beth's heart was pounding in her ears. What if she tripped going up the steps? Why had she agreed to heels? What if she slid on the smooth, shiny floor? Why did she invite Andy? Of all the people to witness her humiliation ... Her eyes slid shut. *Just breathe.* She couldn't make out the words being spoken on stage.

A warm hand covered hers, and her eyes flew open to meet with Andy's. They were filled with understanding. He leaned closer and whispered in her ear, 'You'll be fine.'

Taking a deep breath she managed a smile. Calm spread through her body, and when the chairman finally called her name to receive the award for the best Anzac artwork by a high school student, she floated up the steps. She glanced back. Andy was smiling and clapping. Just like in *Anne of Green Gables* when Gilbert clapped for Anne at the poetry recital. She knew his appreciation and pride in her were genuine. And she knew this was a moment she would never forget.

'Thanks for asking me,' he said as the night came to a close.

'I had to. I thought of you with every pencil line I put on that paper.'

His laugh was dubious. 'I'm sure you did.'

She smiled. What would he think if he knew she thought of him almost every moment of every day? In every brilliant sunset, in every starry evening, in every arrival of dawn and in every vision of beauty, she dreamed that someday she would share it with her blue-eyed hero, and they would enjoy its depth and eternal significance together. Forever. In every novel she read, Andy was the hero. Maybe she was a rebel, refusing to accept the author's descriptions, replacing the hero with images of Andy, but it was one area of life she could control.

She may have made a mess of her real life, but at least she could still dream.

CHAPTER FOUR

Beth sat on a rock beside the chook pen, watching Gilbert pull himself up the bird wire to latch onto a perch with his beak. He still wasn't using his wing, and she wished she knew how to strap it. Belinda from Wildlife Rescue in Sydney had texted her instructions, but she was too afraid of doing it wrong and ruining Gilbert's chances of flying free someday.

She heard the screen door of the house bang and smiled as she looked up. It was good to have Phil and Clare back from their honeymoon.

They came down the back steps, heading her way, and Phil leaned in to give Clare a kiss. Beth pretended to be disgusted. 'Oh, stop it, you two.'

Phil grinned. 'What's wrong? Were we supposed to stop showing affection as soon as the honeymoon was over?'

'Yes. Romance novels always end at the wedding. Or at least when the couple finally discover their love for each other.'

Phil threw back his head and laughed. 'Right. And we all know real life is like those stories you read.'

Clare pulled him close and whispered something in his ear while Beth strained to catch the words. 'What are you saying?'

Phil looked away, deliberately gazing straight past her and up at the hills surrounding their home. Beth detected a faint blush in his cheeks. She let him off the hook, but she had no such compassion for Clare. 'Tell me what you said, Clare, or I'll tell Phil every mean thing you ever did to me as a kid.'

Phil's gaze shot to hers. 'Tell me. I'm listening.'

Beth stood and brushed off her jeans. 'Where to begin?'

With a spurt of laughter, Clare held up her hands. 'No need for such drastic measures. I'll tell you. I said that there are some things too good to be expressed in words and some things too private to be shared, okay? That's why novels don't go into the details of marriage.'

Beth's cheeks heated. Why had she asked? 'I still think stories should end later.'

'What, like at the hero's funeral?'

'You are so unromantic. No, like at the thirtieth wedding anniversary.'

Phil ruffled her hair. 'Life is so much more than a story, Beth.' He waved his hand toward the old house and the chairs on the wooden verandah. 'Aunty Joy knew that.' He smiled down at Clare. 'She taught us so much, didn't she?'

Clare nodded, then grabbed Beth's hand. 'Come on, I want to show you our plans for the place.'

Phil took Clare's other hand and together, the three of them made their way up onto the verandah. Clare pointed to the chairs lining the wrap-around verandah. 'We're not changing this. This is where we used to sit—Aunty Joy and Phil and I. We'd watch the sun sink over that hill and talk about life and love and God.'

'And our dreams,' Phil added with a tender smile in Clare's direction.

Clare's laugh was soft as she lowered herself into one of the chairs. 'They weren't dreams, Phil. They were reality, because God gives us the desires of our heart when we walk with Him.' Suddenly, she stopped and poked her fingers down the side of the chair. 'What's this?'

Beth moved over to look.

Phil took the photo from Clare's fingers. 'That's Gus.'

'Gus? Really?' She laughed. 'Not how he looked when I met him.'

Beth tried to see. 'Who's Gus?'

'Phil's friend and another one of Aunty Joy's foster children.' Clare turned the photo so Beth could see. 'She rescued him from his abusive father. Then they found his mother, and he went to live with her.' Her eyes softened. 'He came back when Phil was missing on his mission trip. We prayed for Phil together.'

She passed the photo over to Beth. From what she could see in the old, scratched photo, Gus was a lad of about ten with a large gap between his front teeth. His clothes hung off him. Her heart squeezed with compassion. 'What did his father do to him?'

'Beat him up. Neglected him. Gave him a stupid name that left him wide open to ridicule and bullying.'

Beth looked up. 'What's wrong with *Gus*?'

'Angus Bull was his name. Not a good name to have in a live-stock farming community. His father lost a gambling bet the night he was born, and his mates got to name him. His middle name was rejected by the Registry of Births, Deaths and Marriages, but they still used it. I won't even tell you what it was.'

Anger and disgust heated Beth's chest. 'That's not even funny! What was his father thinking?' She shook her head. 'Where is he now? Is someone caring for him properly?'

Phil laughed softly and patted her shoulder. 'It's okay, Beth, he's fine. He's well and truly left home, and he can definitely look after himself. That photo must be ten years old. He looks nothing like that anymore. He's now Gus Richards and he's just finished an apprenticeship as a builder carpenter.'

'Oh.' Beth handed the photo back to Clare. Her throat burned to imagine what that poor little boy had suffered. She didn't want to think about it. She changed the subject. 'So, what other plans do you have for the place?'

Clare pointed to the garden. 'Right there is where Phil proposed. I want to build one of those pergola things there, or whatever they're called.'

Phil grinned. 'You mean a gondola?'

'No, I don't think that's the word …'

Beth looked between them. Were they serious? 'Do you mean a gazebo? Or a rotunda?'

Phil and Clare chuckled in unison and Phil nodded. 'Yeah. Thanks. That's what we mean. What would we do without you, Beth?'

Clare poked him in the chest. 'We'd be trying to row a gondola in our little duck pond, that's what we'd be doing.'

Phil captured her finger, pulling her closer. 'Doesn't it sound romantic, though?'

Beth clicked her tongue. 'I thought we were discussing your plans for the place.' Their affection was cute but awkward to watch.

Clare's head jerked up. 'Oh. Yeah.' She looked around the garden. 'We are going to weed for a start, and put a nice rockery along the fence. But we're also going to re-paint the bedrooms. Something more cheerful than the dull yellow-green colour Aunty Joy had.' She paused and looked at Beth expectantly.

'What?'

'I just thought you might know the real name for the colour and correct me.'

Was Clare having a go at her? Beth wasn't sure.

Clare shrugged. 'Mum told me its real name is Chartreuse yellow.'

'How does she even know that?'

'I dunno. But she also said we have to keep you outside while we're sanding and painting. She doesn't want dust or fumes getting in your lungs.'

Beth laughed. 'What about *your* lungs?'

'Guess she's not responsible for them anymore.' Was that hurt that passed through her eyes? Clare had always hated Mum's fussing as much as Beth did.

Phil drew Clare to him. 'Well I get to look after you now, so I guess you two have to do the weeding while I do the sanding and painting.' His expression as he looked down at Clare was so warm, tender and protective that it stirred Beth's heart. What would it be like to have someone care for her that way? Not Mum's fussing and controlling, but *real* care?

THE FOLLOWING AFTERNOON, Beth helped Clare in the garden while Phil began washing down the lounge room walls, which he said were actually a pleasant colour underneath all the dust.

Clare sighed as she looked around the yard. 'It's been sadly neglected since Aunty Joy went home.'

Home? Beth knew she meant heaven, but she'd never heard anyone call heaven *home* before.

Clare bent to her knees beside the garden, pulled out a weed and shook the dirt from its roots. 'I know Aunty Joy always believed Phil and I would live here one day, and that just makes it all the more special that we've begun our married life here.'

Beth let go of the milk thistle she'd been working out of the ground, and turned her full attention to Clare. 'Do you think she knew she was going to die?'

'Not that day, no. I think Aunty Joy expected to have a few more years on earth. But in some ways, she always seemed closer to heaven than earth.'

Clare's words hit Beth like an electric jolt. Andy seemed to belong closer to heaven than earth. Surely *he* wouldn't die? And yet, Andy had a longing for heaven like no one else she'd ever known. He looked wistful whenever he talked about heaven and when he prayed, it was like he was already there, face to face with Jesus.

Stop it. Don't think that way. She forced her mind away from Andy.

The garden still looked like a paddock of weeds when Phil's cheerful voice hollered from the house. 'Hey you two, I'm ready for a break. Who wants a cuppa?'

Clare cupped her hands around her mouth and yelled back to him. 'We haven't been working that long yet.'

Beth winced. Clare had become so rough and loud since she'd known the Cairns.

'I know,' Phil called back, 'but I'm lonely in here by myself.'

Clare brushed dirt from her jeans and stood. 'Let's go and keep Phil company.'

They wandered inside and stopped short. The lounge room spotless. Every wall was washed and the old paint glowed, breathing new life into the place.

'No wonder you need a break!' Clare dropped onto the lounge beside Phil. It was covered in a ragged old sheet, and she obviously hadn't noticed it was now splattered with dirty, soapy water. Beth moved to the cleanest looking lounge and gingerly sat down.

'What do you think?' Phil looked pleased with himself.

Clare twisted her head to look around the room and beamed. 'I love it. I wish Aunty Joy could see it like this.'

'She did.' Phil's eyes shone. 'It's only been the last few years Aunty Joy hasn't been up to keeping the house spotless.'

Clare and Phil still spoke of Aunty Joy in the present tense as though she was still alive. Which was true, Beth supposed, but she was in heaven, wherever that might be. And who knew what form the old lady was in now? Did she look like she did when she died, or when she was young? Would anyone even recognise her? Beth tried to shut out the questions that left a heavy feeling in her gut, threatening to rise up and suffocate her.

She jumped at the sound of knuckles pounding on the front door. A gruff voice called through the house. 'Phil, you there?'

Clare bounced off the lounge. 'Rod! What are you doing here?'

Beth tensed. She hated to admit it, but Rod Green intimidated her. The ex-bully, who stunned everyone by committing his life to God, still came across as hard and tough. His square, determined jaw sporting a goatee didn't help his image. Nor the earring through his eyebrow. The rumour going around school said he used to sit in class and pierce his ears and eyebrows with a syringe. Rod never denied the allegation.

Clare opened the door and Rod sauntered through. 'I've got an idea I want to run by you and Phil.'

'What kind of idea?'

'A business idea.'

Clare's eyes twinkled. 'Now Rod, I've told you before, we're not interested in any of your crazy schemes. We're law abiding citizens.'

'Phil,' Rod growled, pushing past Clare and coming into the lounge room. 'What have you been telling her?'

Phil stood and slapped Rod on the back, laughing. 'She too much for you, Rod?'

'No. I'm just too polite to sort out someone else's missus.'

Phil's brows rose. 'Rod Green, polite?'

'Things change, Philip Cairn. Now are you going to offer me a seat, or do I have to stand here like a fence post?'

Phil swept out an arm. 'Be my guest.'

Rod plopped into the seat Phil had just vacated and swung his feet up onto the coffee table. His shoes were dirty, but Beth didn't dare mention it. She shrank back, trying to make herself invisible.

Rod crossed his arms over his chest. 'I'm back home for good.'

'What happened to your Bachelor of Social Work?' Phil took the lounge facing Rod and pulled Clare into his lap.

Rod smirked as he watched Clare settle comfortably against Phil's chest. 'You think I quit, don't you? I never quit. You should know that.'

'So you've finished?'

'Nope. Finished my Diploma of Community Services and I'll finish the rest online. I've got a job case managing.'

'What, at an airport?'

Rod rolled his eyes at the grinning Phil. 'Not suitcases, you ignoramus. Caring for wards of the state. I'm a carer. I have a little guy at the moment who I'm in charge of. Rehabilitating him back in to the normal world, you might say.'

'Rehabilitating? From what?'

Rod shook his head. 'Can't say.'

'You don't know?'

'Of course I know, I just can't tell you. Client confidentiality and all that.'

Rod seemed to enjoy the way he had everyone curious. It irritated Beth. He should just tell them his business plan and have it over with.

He didn't. Instead, his smile grew, and Beth followed his gaze to the shiny wedding ring Phil fiddled with on his finger. Rod waved his hand at Phil and Clare. 'And to think I was beginning to believe every love story doesn't end happily after all.'

Clare's smile was radiant as she slid her arm around Phil's neck. 'Sometimes they don't.'

Rod gasped in mock horror. 'Batesy! How dare you. You knew all along you were going to marry the Cairn man but now you won't give us the same hope that love will conquer all.'

'I'm not Batesy anymore. My name's changed, remember?' Her voice softened. 'And the truth is, I didn't know I was going to marry Phil. I honestly thought I might not see him again this side of heaven. Beth was the only one who never doubted it.'

Rod's eyes flew to Beth as though he'd only just realised she was there. 'So Little Clare's a bit of a romantic, hey?'

Why did everyone think she was merely a replica of her sister?

Rod snorted. 'I would frown too, sis. Those two are way too happy. It's sickening.'

Beth's face heated. 'Too happy? What's your problem?' Her eyes widened. She had blurted out exactly what she was thinking, to Rod Green of all people.

Rod cackled. 'Oh. She speaks.'

Beth retreated into herself at the mocking tone. It reminded her of her brother, Dan. To her relief, Phil came to the rescue.

'So, what's this plan you were talking about when you barged in our door?'

Rod winked at Beth before leaning toward Phil. 'I want you to set up a place here on the farm for delinquent kids coming out of the foster system.'

'What?'

'You heard me. They need to learn skills, to discover who they are. Not all of them fit into Uni, and most of them aren't ready to face the world on their own. They need a place they can call home — somewhere to belong. And I know it's exactly what Aunty Joy would have wanted.'

Beth waited for Phil to shoot down the crazy idea, but a light came to his eyes. 'How would we fund it?'

'It's government funded. I'm in charge of finding a place and setting it up. But I can't do it on my own. I need your help. And your farm. With your family's approval, of course.'

Clare jumped off Phil's lap. 'Hold on a minute. Are you talking about bringing them right here on the property? Like, living here?'

Rod nodded. 'I know, I know, you're newly married and don't want to think outside of yourselves, but these troubled kids need you.'

'I don't understand.'

'What's to understand?' Rod frowned at Clare. 'These are city kids who have come from a world of crime and violence. They stole or dealt in drugs or vandalised until the law caught them.

Now they need to learn how to make an honest living, how to go to school or work. But they can't make the leap from stealing to earning without some skills and time to learn how to fit into everyday society.'

'But what are we supposed to do? We don't know how to rehabilitate kids like that.' Clare expressed Beth's own silent reservations.

'Yes, you do.' Rod shifted his feet on the coffee table. 'Remember how I used to be? And you and Phil, you just made an effort to care about me and be my friend. You showed me the love of God, and that's what these kids need. Now this is how it will work ...'

CHAPTER FIVE

Beth had to admit Rod's enthusiasm was infectious. But when Clare relayed his plans to Mum, she knew it wasn't going to end well. Mum listened in silence, perched carefully on the edge of Clare's lounge chair, hands folded in her lap. Her lips pursed. It was subtle, but Beth knew what it meant.

Clare finished and Mum sniffed, her head tilted ever so slightly. 'You don't know how to handle those types of people, Clare.' She glanced around the untidy room with a disapproving expression, then faced Clare again. 'They need professional help. Not everyone will respond to love. Especially young people who have only ever lived for themselves. They will just take whatever they can get.'

'Perhaps that's because they've never *been* loved.' Clare didn't sound discouraged in the least. 'Remember Rod Green?'

'Who could forget him?' Mum shook her head, and not one strand of her professionally styled hair moved. 'But what about his father?'

Beth drew in a breath. She had a point. Rod's father was her own dad's foster brother. He was in jail somewhere after a lifetime of dealing drugs and substance abuse.

Mum's lips remained pinched. 'Miracles happen occasionally, but you can't count on them. Rod can't assume everyone is like him and that they want to be good people but don't know how.'

'Rod didn't want to be good, Mum,' Clare laughed, 'but God just kept working on his heart until he couldn't help changing.'

Beth wished Clare would give up. Veronica Bateman wouldn't be beaten without a fight. And Beth hated conflict.

Mum tried another tactic. 'What about accommodation?'

'The wards will build it themselves with qualified supervision. It will be part of their training or rehabilitation or whatever you want to call it. Phil's started searching for a builder who will work with them. Dad has already given some of his land for the project.'

Dad? How would Mum feel about Clare calling her father-in-law *Dad*? To Beth's surprise, she didn't bat an eyelid.

'And where will they live until it's built?'

'In the Cairn's house or in the old shearer's quarters. Phil's parents are keen on the idea now they have four empty bedrooms, and Dad desperately needs help on the farm. It's perfect, really.'

Mum shook her head. 'You haven't done any training in this type of thing, Clare. You're not qualified.'

'No, but Rod has, and he's going to oversee it. He's officially in charge and we're just employees. I guess you could call it on-the-job training. Phil and I will do an online course as well.'

'I don't think you realise who you're dealing with. Children in need are different to young adults who are rebellious and don't want to be loved.'

She had a point. For a moment Beth pictured an orphanage out on the farm with cute little children running around. That, she would enjoy being a part of. Maybe some children from Africa could be brought over …

Clare didn't even respond to Mum's argument. Instead, she

jumped up and gave her a hug. Beth felt as awkward as Mum looked.

Clare grinned. 'Don't worry, Mum. Just sit back and watch God's miracles unfold.'

What gave Clare so much confidence? Why didn't she fear disapproval? Was it because she had Phil's love and acceptance or was it something more?

PLANS for the project were underway. Beth sat at Clare and Phil's table doing homework while Phil sat across the other side filling out paperwork for Rod. Clare perched beside him, completing enrolment forms for their social work course.

Clare gnawed her lower lip. 'I honestly don't know how I'm going to do this, Phil. Maybe Mum's right. I'm not academic like you.'

Phil dropped his pen and leaned over to put his arm around her. 'We're working together in this, remember? We're a team now.'

Clare's worried frown relaxed into a smile. Phil smiled back into her eyes. 'We might have to pull out of some things, but it'll be okay.'

Beth's heart sank. 'What might you pull out of? You'll still lead Youth Group, won't you?"

Phil glanced at Clare before looking back at Beth. 'Actually, that's one of the things I thought someone else could take on.'

'Like who?'

'I don't know. Maybe Mr. and Mrs. Holmes.'

What? The staid older couple? They didn't strike Beth as particularly fun people. Or warm or friendly. She'd once heard Mrs. Holmes criticise Andy, saying he laughed too loud. She gathered up the courage to voice her thoughts. 'I don't think that's a good idea.'

Phil gave her his full attention. 'Why?"

Now what should she say? 'Well, I just can't see them relating to teenagers like you do.'

Phil reached over and gave her a brotherly hug. 'Aw, thanks Beth, but I think you're a bit biased. Tell you what, how about you and Andy keep working with us the way you have been and we'll ease Mr. and Mrs. Holmes in slowly? Clare and I will keep going until the first wards arrive.'

Beth sighed. It wasn't worth saying anything. It didn't matter what she thought.

WHERE WAS ANDY? He was supposed to be here half an hour ago for a meeting about Youth Group. Beth worried something had happened to him.

Phil came from the kitchen and placed a plate of biscuits directly under her nose. She pushed it away and smiled. 'What are you doing?'

'Trying to distract you from whatever is making you frown at that spot on the table like it's been calling you offensive names.'

Her laugh caught in her throat as movement through the screen door caught her attention. Andy had arrived. He shot her a cheeky grin and put a finger to his lips as he silently eased the door open and stepped inside. Taking off his hat, he aimed it directly onto the table. It narrowly missed Clare and landed on top of the biscuits. All eyes turned to him.

'Andy!' Phil beamed. 'Glad you finally decided to join us.'

Andy attempted to straighten his tangled hair. 'Yeah, sorry I'm late. I had a few problems getting here. You know how the traffic is down that road of yours.'

Beth laughed. She doubted more than three cars travelled the dusty farm road each day, and most of them were farm vehicles. But then again, her dad had died swerving to miss a kangaroo on that same road.

'What traffic are you thinking of?' Phil challenged.

Andy pulled out the chair beside Beth. 'You know, all those young fellas who don't know Clare's your wife yet.'

Beth lifted Andy's hat from the plate of biscuits, turned it upright and straightened the brim. Andy grinned at her before he sat down and reached for it. He deliberately turned it over, bent the brim and placed it back in front of her, making sure it was lopsided.

Beth met his teasing eyes. *Game on.* She righted the hat and smoothed out the brim with precise, neat movements. As expected, Andy reached across her and turned it again before slapping it back onto the table. Suppressing a laugh, Beth went into battle.

Finally, Andy laughed and reached a hand to stop hers. 'Stubborn, aren't you?' He grabbed his hat and threw it onto the floor. Then his blue eyes looked straight into hers in a challenge.

Okay, now would be the time to say something clever. Nothing came. All she could think of was the way his hand felt on hers, and the way he was looking at her. What would he do if she kissed him? Where had that thought come from? She was clearly reading too many romances.

She sprang forward to retrieve the dirty hat from the floor, but Andy grabbed her around the waist and pulled her back.

She froze, heat rising into her cheeks. She only just heard Phil's voice above the pounding of her heart. 'What's going on between you two?'

Andy's hands relaxed and he released her. 'Just a simple Battle of the Hat.'

'I don't think so, Andy.' Phil winked. 'It takes a lot of energy to do battle on a hot afternoon like this.'

Andy's eyes widened. 'We're good friends, Phil, that's all.'

Phil drew Clare into his arms. 'That's what we used to say, isn't it Clare?'

Clare just smiled.

'Well in this case it's the truth. Beth and I enjoy spending time together, we have good laughs, good times, and some pretty serious discussions, but there's no romance here—isn't that right Beth.'

It was a statement, not a question. Beth swallowed hard and managed to meet Andy's gaze. 'That's right.'

Phil smirked. 'Okay, okay, you don't need to convince me. Just convince yourselves, and then I'll believe you.' He wandered into the kitchen to get a drink.

When he was out of earshot, Beth gave an awkward laugh. 'I wish people wouldn't do that.'

Andy peered at her. 'Do what?'

'Match-make. I find it very uncomfortable.'

He nodded, flipped his hat over one more time and followed Phil into the kitchen.

Clare studied her from across the table. 'Don't take it too seriously, Beth,' she said in her irritating big-sister tone. 'Guys are like that. They don't look as deep into the meanings behind words and actions as we do. Andy will probably totally forget Phil ever said anything.'

Beth frowned. Not likely.

Andy wandered back from the kitchen carrying a can of Coke. 'So, are we going to get this Youth Group program sorted out, or what?'

'You don't come here to organise Youth Group,' Clare teased. 'You just come to help yourself to our fridge.'

Andy opened his mouth to retaliate but a yell from Phil cut him off. 'Fire! There's a fire in the lucerne paddock!'

CHAPTER SIX

Beth couldn't move. So many nightmares over so many years but she'd never dreamed of fire. Clare scrambled to the window, Andy close on her heels.

'Quick!' Phil raced to the door. 'We have to get down there.'

Beth forced words past her dry throat. It felt like a pinecone was trying to make its way down. 'What about the RFS?'

Phil looked back over his shoulder. 'Yes, give them a call. But they're probably still out fighting the fires at Eardman's place.'

'Where are your parents?' Clare called to him as she charged toward the door.

'I think they're in the woolshed.'

Clare took off at a run.

'Keep away from the flames!'

Clare waved to signal she heard, then kept going. Phil turned back to Andy. 'You up to fighting this thing?'

Andy nodded and followed Phil out the door.

Beth tried to steady her shaking hands as she rang triple zero. She could hardly comprehend what she was told. The trucks were all occupied elsewhere, fighting spot fires the hot, gusty wind was spreading. Ayleward could send some trucks, but they were over half an hour away. For now they were on their own.

'Put your fire plan into action and if there aren't enough resources, leave while you can,' the operator instructed. 'Remember, it's not worth risking a human life. For anything.'

Beth couldn't believe it. This was Australia. How could they be abandoned in an emergency like this? Her heart pounded. She was a city girl. She had no idea what to do in a situation like this. A glance out the window told her the flames were taking hold. They needed help from locals. But who?

Please God, stop the fire! She paced the room, unable to think. Her stomach churned and a feeling of complete helplessness overcame her—the same feeling she'd had as she'd watched Grandpa gasp for breath. She wanted to sink to the floor and cry.

Stop it. She spotted the church directory sitting on the table. *Thank you, God!*

She called the first number in the book. Mr. Gordeon, the church secretary. His deep, reassuring voice helped. 'First, I'll get the prayer chain rolling, and then I'll send out some help,' he said. Beth wished he would send the help first. Sure, she believed God could stop the fire, but she didn't have as much confidence in His willingness to do it.

A flock of cockatoos flew over, screaming in alarm. *Gilbert!* If they had to leave, she needed to take him, or he would burn to death. But where could she put him? She tore around the house looking for a box but was interrupted by the sound of a car tearing down the road. It stopped in a cloud of dust outside.

Pete Saunders and his dad raced to the house. 'I grabbed some water on the way,' Pete said, hauling a pack of 600ml bottles of water under his arm. 'Andy asked me to grab all the woollen blankets we can find.'

She stared, her mind blank.

'To beat out the flames.'

Oh. She blushed at her ignorance and dashed to the linen

cupboard. People said she was smart, but she sure didn't feel it. She plucked every blanket she could find from the shelves, checking the tags to see if they were wool, and piling them up to her chin. What could she do about Gilbert? Her mind felt fuzzy, but no wonder; she was breathing in blanket fluff.

Mr. Saunders grabbed the pile from Beth, called to Pete, and the two of them raced back to the car and took off down the road. More cars tore down the road, followed by two utes with fire hoses and tanks on the back. Thank God for neighbouring farmers. Then she spied the bottles of water Pete had left behind. Surely they were needed at the fire scene? She'd have to take them herself. Her eyes darted toward the hills as she hurried down the front path. Despite the heavy weight of the bottles, she was determined to get them to the firefighters. Smoke billowed ominously toward her, the flames like a monster devouring anything in its path. The air tasted gritty, and her throat and eyes stung. She broke into a run. The sun bit into her skin, and the harsh wind tousled her hair. She shook it out of her eyes, then stared in horror at the thick black smoke rising into the air, and the flames racing toward the woolshed. They surged forward with a menacing roar. People held blankets, chasing spot fires and beating them out while others set up hoses from dams, dragging the heavy, snake-like tubes as close to the flames as they dared.

Clare spotted her and ran over. 'It's bad,' she rasped through cracked lips. Beth sensed her fear. This fire was way too close and real. Clare ripped off the plastic around the water bottles and plucked one out. She guzzled down the water then raced back toward the flames. Beth followed, heart stuck in her throat. Phil looked over and called out to Clare.

'Keep away from the flames, Clare. The wind could turn at any moment.' His green eyes were intense as he swiped at the sweat streaming down his face.

Clare continued toward the flames. 'No, Phil, you need my help. I can't let the farm burn down.'

Phil shook his head, frustrated. 'You don't understand fires, Clare.' He took the water bottles from Beth's arms. 'Please—please if you do anything, go back to the main house and bring us some more drinking water. And grab all Mum and Dad's woollen blankets, too.'

Clare hesitated, then grabbed Beth's hand, pulling her toward the main farmhouse Phil's parents lived in. 'Let's get water and blankets. And pray!'

Beth nodded. She had been. With every breath.

BETH FOUND the white brick house eerily peaceful amidst the chaos. Clare raced down the hall. 'I'll find the blankets, you get the water.'

Beth bent to look in the kitchen cupboards. Her hands fumbled as she dragged out a tray, knocking over a pile of plastic plates. Where were the cups?

The screen door banged and footsteps sounded down the hall. 'Want help?'

Andy. Beth breathed a sigh of relief at his voice. He was safe. He came around the corner and she froze. His face was smoke-blackened and his clothes were filthy. He grinned, and his teeth shone white through the grime. 'It's okay. It's me.'

She curbed her horror and waved toward the cupboards. 'I'm trying to find some cups for water.'

'Yeah, Phil said.' He glanced into the recycling bin and dragged out two empty juice bottles. 'You'd be better off using these. Quicker and easier.'

'What? Everyone drink from the same bottle?'

Andy laughed. 'They're not going to care, Beth. They're desperately thirsty and it will be so much quicker and easier.'

She wasn't convinced but took the bottles and began filling

them from the tap. Andy scrabbled around in the cupboards and came up with a few more bottles. At least they appeared clean.

The moment they were filled, she and Andy grabbed an armful and ran back to the firefighters. Smoke permeated the air, making it hard to take in enough oxygen.

Phil was the first to grab a bottle of water. He gulped down a few mouthfuls, gasping for air in-between. Then he looked at Andy. 'Can you get the hose from beside the woolshed? Hose down all around it and get rid of the leaves from under the sheep pens. Find Pete and get him to help.'

Andy bolted toward the sheds and Beth's heart constricted at the sight of him so close to the flames.

Suddenly Phil stopped short, his eyes drilling into Beth's. 'Where's Clare?'

'Finding more blankets.'

He nodded, then called for everyone to come and get a drink.

'Keep an eye on the bottles and fill them as they empty,' he ordered Beth, then raced back to fight the flames.

Andy was right. One by one, hot, smoke-blackened people came to moisten their parched, dry throats, and not one of them cared that they were all drinking from the same recycled juice bottle.

'It doesn't look good,' Phil confided in Beth when he returned a few minutes later for another drink. 'The shearer's quarters have already gone up in flames. It's headed straight toward the woolshed. Dad's not sure what to do next.'

Beth's heart jumped. 'Isn't Andy in the shed?'

Phil's eyes widened. 'You're right.'

Both of them took off at a run, but Phil pulled her back as they neared. 'Don't go inside.'

She stared at him. The flames were bearing down on the shed. How could she just stand and watch? It went against everything inside her.

Phil's deep voice was hoarse but carried as he roared their names. 'Andy! Pete! Get out! Now!'

An ember carried by the wind landed at the base of the shed and lit the dead grass. Flames lapped hungrily at the boards and Beth screamed. Heaven help her, she would drag Andy and Pete out if she had to. There would not be another death on her watch.

Someone shot out of the side door. Pete. But there was no sign of Andy. Cries welled up inside Beth as she prayed for him to appear, bracing herself against the heat and watching the boards smoulder.

'Please God!' she begged. Desperate sobs erupted from her scorched throat and she charged forward, blinded by tears. Strong arms jerked her back, and she struggled. Other firefighters screamed for Andy to get out. Then a horrified silence fell as a tree crashed to the ground and sparks flew up.

Screams erupted from her throat, and she fought with everything in her. Those annoying arms held her, and Phil's deep voice came in her ear. 'Don't, Beth.' His voice cracked. 'Only God can save him now.'

This was it. Andy was going to die. *God, no! Please!* And what about Gilbert? She'd forgotten all about him. It was just like when Grandpa died. She was completely helpless. There was nothing she could do to change this reality.

Suddenly the screaming of sirens filled her ears as trucks sped down the road. One stopped beside them. Men jumped out and unreeled hoses, while Beth felt every heartbeat, every second as it ticked by. Then came the rush of water from the hoses, and the flames around the shed gave one last desperate leap before they sputtered and died, hissing in protest.

Andy bolted out of the shed. He stared at the firefighters, then at the blackened faces of his friends.

'You idiot! Didn't you hear us hollering?' Pete yelled at his younger brother. He let out a shaky breath. 'You scared the life out of me!'

Andy looked dazed. 'You and me both.'

Phil shook the hand of one of the firemen as they prepared to move on and continue fighting the other fire front. 'Thank you, so much. I really thought the shed was gone. We've already lost the shearer's quarters.'

Beth wanted to hit him. What about Andy? He nearly lost his life, and all Phil was concerned about was the replaceable building? She made an effort to suppress her emotions as she picked up a bottle of water and approached Andy. He was on the ground, leaning against a wooden rail, his head between his knees.

She lowered herself onto the ground beside him. 'That was close.' It was impressive how calm she managed to sound.

He wiped his brow with a shaking hand, then looked up, raw shock turning his eyes a dark blue. 'I thought I was gone.'

She let out a long breath. 'So did I.'

'That was a pure miracle the trucks arrived when they did.' He shuddered. 'It was so fast. I saw an ember land, and then whoosh, it was all on.'

Beth nodded, then handed him the bottle of water.

'What a horrible day!' He gulped down a mouthful. 'No, that's not right. No day is bad when God's in control. It's been a hard day, but God has turned it around for good.'

She gritted her teeth, the taste of smoke an awful reminder of the flames. 'What good?'

He rested the bottle of water between his knees. 'Well, now I know for sure that God has more work for me to do. Otherwise He wouldn't have stopped those flames today.'

He questioned that? Surely someone like Andy knew God had a lot for him to do? He was the type she'd expect to end up being a minister or missionary overseas, making the world a better place. God would be crazy to take him.

Andy guzzled down some more water, then heaved himself up from the ground. He held out a blackened hand and helped her up. Their eyes met and she swallowed, locked in the moment. The intensity of her feelings threatened to overwhelm her. For the first time in her life she let go of all caution and threw her arms around him. Her impulsive action startled him, but then he grasped her, holding her tight, clinging with a strength that took her breath away. She felt so drawn to Andy Saunders right now and she knew he felt it too. They belonged together. That's why God didn't allow the fire to extinguish his life.

Thank You, Lord, for saving him!

CHAPTER SEVEN

Beth was disappointed the summer holidays were coming to an end, but the change in weather was a relief. The harsh winds and hot days were settling into cool evening breezes, and local farmers were taking advantage of it. Phil worked late into the evenings and then came home to sit on the verandah with Clare and Beth.

'Summer seems hotter every year,' Clare groaned as they sat on the verandah in the hot and still evening air, looking out at the burnt hills. Small tufts of green peeked through the scorched ground.

Phil stretched his long legs in front of him and looked at Clare. 'You're just living in harsher conditions now. I doubt your mother would ever dream of living without an air conditioner.'

Beth acknowledged he was right. The house in Lydon Estate had the latest temperature control technology. But as she gazed at the orange glow of the sun disappearing behind those black hills, she knew she would choose true love over living in comfort, any day. And she knew Clare would, too.

Phil shot Clare a teasing look. 'Regrets? Thinking of going back to live with your mother?'

'Definitely not!'

He laughed at her vehemence. 'Good.'

She moved closer, but he moved away. 'I'm a bit sticky … and hot.'

'I don't care.'

A soft smile touched his lips before he drew her close. Beth wondered if they remembered she was there. Sometimes they acted like they were the only two people in the world.

Phil now had Clare in his lap, snuggled against his chest. 'I'm glad you prefer the rough life.'

'I didn't say that. If we had a choice between this place and a palace like my mum's, well …'

'But Clare, our way of life is so much more natural. We are inventors, improvisers, good ol' Aussie battlers. We'll never grow fat and lazy.'

Clare sat up and poked his tummy. 'I don't know, I think you've put on weight.'

Beth joined in. 'And I haven't seen you invent or improvise anything.'

Phil put on a wounded look, pushed Clare off his lap and jumped to his feet.

She narrowed her eyes. 'What are you up to?'

'Nothing much.'

Clare stepped away. 'It doesn't look like *nothing much* to me.'

'Come on, I'm just taking you up on your challenge.' He reached a hand toward her, an impish sparkle in his eyes.

'What challenge?'

'We're going to do some exercise and improvise at the same time.'

'What are we improvising?'

Phil pointed to the duck pond. 'A pool.'

'No way!' Clare laughed. 'There's no way you're getting me in there with those ducks. They have … well, they've done their business in there.'

Phil looked sideways at her. 'Business? We only have plain, simple ol' poo here at the Cairns' farm. Come on, Clare, remember you assured me you would never become like your mother? Don't go all proper on me.'

Beth tried not to let her surprise show. They had an issue with Mum? And being proper? What must they think of *her*? She'd made it her life's goal to please Mum and receive her approval. She hated making mistakes and not living up to her standards.

Clare eyed Phil, then, to Beth's horror jumped into the pond filled with *duck business*. There was a loud splash followed by a frenzied flapping and squawking. The ducks scrambled out of the pond and waddled away while Beth stared, open-mouthed.

Phil cracked up. 'Clare, what have you done? You're so … so chaotic!'

Clare bit her lip as she squeezed some of the water out of her shirt and watched it drip back into the pond. 'I didn't think I'd cause such a major reaction.' She looked at Beth and grinned. 'Come on Beth. Join me. It's an amazingly freeing experience.'

There was no way Beth was getting in there. Apart from anything, she felt sorry for those poor nervous ducks. But then, if she had a choice of being like Mum or Clare … On impulse, she kicked off her shoes and made her way into the murky water before she could change her mind.

Clare giggled and nudged her with her elbow. 'Can you imagine what Mum would think if she could see us now?'

Beth refused to think about it.

Phil stepped into the pond and waded toward them. 'It is not fitting for young ladies to be swimming about in a duck pond as though it were an indoor spa,' he said, impersonating Mum. 'And who knows what kind of unmentionable, squelchy substances might be lying at the bottom of that dark, murky water? That water is only suitable for ducks and leeches.'

Beth's heart lurched and she scrambled from the water. 'Are there really leeches?'

Clare headed toward the edge, too, but Phil chuckled and tugged her back in. 'Come on, Clare, I've never seen a leech in here. But if one latches onto you I promise to rescue you. I'm not sharing you with anybody!' He pulled her against his chest, his smile tender.

Clare relaxed against his chest and gazed up at him, her eyes shining. 'I can't imagine my life without you, Philip Cairn. Nothing will ever stop me loving you.'

'I hope not,' he said softly, all teasing gone, 'but there's sure to be times you don't feel as loving toward me as you do now.'

'I doubt that. We've been through too much, grown to love each other too much. I'm determined our marriage is going to be worthy of those romance stories Beth reads.'

Phil chuckled. 'Even romance stories have conflict. Let's make our marriage one that glorifies God. That's all I ask.'

Uncomfortable knowing they were about to kiss, Beth turned and headed back onto the verandah. But she couldn't help smiling.

First day back at school for the year and Beth's stomach churned. Clare wasn't keen to return to work in the school office, either.

'I need to do something more fulfilling,' she confided in Beth as she drove her to school. 'Something eternally significant, something more than filing student records and answering phones. I'm keen to start working with Phil on Rod's project.'

Beth asked God to work it all out soon, not only for Clare's sake, but because the idea was exciting. Clare and Phil were the perfect couple to work with troubled people needing a place to belong. They knew how to make someone feel completely loved and accepted.

The moment Beth walked in the school gate, Dara McCann sidled up to her with the knowing look in her eyes Beth had come to dread. 'I hear you had quite an adventure on the Cairns' farm over the holidays.'

Beth kept walking, refusing to satisfy Dara's thirst for gossip.

'I hear Andy nearly died and that he's severely traumatised.'

Beth bristled. What did Dara know of Andy's feelings? He seemed fine after the initial shock wore off. It was Beth who still had nightmares.

'It was a miracle he escaped,' Dara added, her eyes probing Beth's for confirmation. Then she pouted. 'Why are you secretive about the whole thing?'

'I'm not being secretive. I just don't have anything more to add. You seem to know more about it than I do.'

Dara missed the bristle of irritation in the words and gave a satisfied smile.

BETH MANAGED to avoid sitting next to Dara in the first class. She absently wrote Andy's name on the cover of her notebook while she waited for the teacher. Then realised what she'd done and scribbled it out. If Dara noticed, she would never live it down. Dara already knew too much. She possessed an incredible ability to know any and everybody's business. Most people avoided Dara McCann, but her life was troubled and she needed friends. As much as Beth disliked her, she wanted to help.

'Beth! You have no idea how much I missed you over the holidays.' Cameron Oliver sauntered into the classroom with an impish grin. He knelt down on one knee beside her desk and, with a melodramatic air, held out a cheese ring. 'Marry me, Beth?'

She felt the blush rise into her cheeks and stumbled for something to say. Nothing came.

He set the cheese ring on the desk. 'Tell you what, I'll leave it with you and you can get back to me.' Rising and turning with a flourish, he sauntered off.

Unfortunately, Dara had noticed and was staring, wide-eyed. 'What was that about?'

Beth shrugged, relieved to see the teacher come into the room. 'Just Cameron messing around as usual.'

The tall, skinny teacher with a mouth that looked prone to smiling, was a substitute. However, his expression was serious as Cameron moved back toward Beth, now holding a whole packet of cheese rings.

'I'm Mr. Smart,' the teacher announced, looking directly at Cameron, 'and you are Mr. Oliver.'

Cameron stopped in his tracks. 'That's right.'

'Your reputation precedes you.' Mr. Smart pointed to the opposite side of the room. 'Please take your regular seat, Mr. Oliver.'

Cameron put on an effective pout. 'But Sir, I need to sit with Beth. I love her! How can I prepare her for my official proposal if I can't talk to her?'

Beth's embarrassment increased by the second. She saw the twinkle in Mr. Smart's eyes before he gave Cameron a stern look. 'I don't think anything could prepare anyone for a proposal from you, Mr. Oliver, but if you insist on proposing, do it on your own time, not on mine.'

Something told Beth Mr. Smart was trying not to laugh. Cameron shrugged and returned to his usual seat. He pulled a pen from his pencil case, scribbled on a piece of paper, then tore it from his notebook and tossed it in Beth's direction. She ignored it, trying to listen to Mr. Smart. But it sat there beside her on the floor, mocking her curiosity. When Mr. Smart turned to write on the board, she reached down and picked it. She frowned as she attempted to decipher Cameron's messy scrawl.

I KNOW A CHEESE RING IS PROBABLY NOT WHAT YOU ALWAYS DREAMED OF, BUT IF I CAN GET YOU A DIAMOND WILL YOU MARRY ME?

She screwed up the note, trying not to smile.

'What does it say?' Dara didn't miss a thing. Beth couldn't let her read it. On impulse, she threw the paper back at Cameron. He caught it, opened it, and Beth felt bad that he was expecting some kind of answer. But he grinned as he put up his hand.

What was he up to? Cameron never put up his hand. He always called out.

Mr. Smart turned. 'Yes, Cameron?'

'Sir, I think I should advise you of some of the latest happenings in our school.' Cameron put on a formal expression, his eyes exaggeratedly wide and innocent. The whole class stilled to listen.

'Sadly, and much to my disgust, there have been some students who have insisted on throwing projectiles and the Deputy Principal said that if we choose to throw objects, we choose suspension. Well, I think you should know that Beth just threw this at me.'

He held the piece of paper out to Mr. Smart, and Beth gasped. 'What? You threw it at me! That's your writing!' She knew her face was becoming an unattractive shade of red.

'My dear Beth,' Cameron said, 'if I had thrown that piece of paper at you, it would be with you. So how did it happen to be in my possession?'

Mr. Smart shook his head. 'Go and sit with her, Mr. Oliver. I can see that no one is going to get any work done while you two are separated. But the moment you disrupt this class again, you're out.'

With a triumphant grin, Cameron packed up his things and moved beside Beth. 'I missed you,' he whispered and put an arm around her.

Beth tried to hide her discomfort. 'You got me in trouble.'

He nodded. 'Pain for gain. After all, we're together again, now.'

She tentatively shrugged his arm from her shoulder. There was nothing official between her and Andy, but it still felt like a betrayal to let Cameron put his arm around her. She genuinely liked Cameron and enjoyed his banter, but he didn't *get* her like Andy did, and he wasn't a believer.

Andy caught up with her as she pulled her bike from the bike rack near the school gate. 'I heard you received a proposal today.' He looked amused.

'Who told you that?'

He fell into step beside her as she wheeled her bike out the gate. 'Guess.'

'Dara.'

'Got it first go.'

'What else did she say?' Dara never passed on information without a hidden motive.

'Oh, something about you nearly getting suspended.'

Beth laughed. She couldn't help it.

His mouth tilted. 'I figured there was a bit of exaggeration in the story.'

As always. She tried to think of something else to say to keep him talking, but nothing came. It reminded her of the first time she'd met him. It was a youth event. Andy had tried hard to have a conversation and make her feel welcome, but she was so painfully shy she could only nod or give one-word answers. Eventually, his eyes crinkled with amusement as he said, 'Talking to you is a bit like talking to a teapot.'

And that day she decided she would never be a teapot again. She battled to overcome her shyness and fill every silence with something interesting or relevant. Andy seemed to appreciate her efforts. He appeared to understand that she didn't have his natural gift of easy conversation.

Now was not one of her finer moments. Thankfully, Andy's bus pulled into the curb. 'There's your bus.'

He chuckled. 'Trying to get rid of me?'

She climbed onto her bike, keeping one foot on the ground to steady herself. 'No. Just wouldn't want you to miss your bus and have to walk.'

'What, you wouldn't give me a lift on your handlebars?'

She laughed and pointed to his bus. 'It's waiting for you. I'll see you tomorrow.'

He grinned and waved as he jogged off. 'See ya, Beth.'

CHAPTER EIGHT

Beth slipped into the back of church on Sunday morning. She'd already ridden out to the farm to feed Gilbert, then squeezed in a shower as well. After church she'd finish her English essay, then—

She stopped. Everyone was looking in her direction. Her hands went clammy and she glanced around, realising to her relief, that she wasn't the focus of their attention. A tall, thin girl with bleach-blonde hair walked down the aisle of the church, a haunted look in her brown eyes. A revealing top openly advertised the ring through her navel and a rose tattoo across her abdomen. A stud sparkled on her lower lip. She met someone's gaze and her lips widened into a striking smile. Beth had never seen anyone like her.

Shuffling and murmurs built to a crescendo. 'She's the devil's child!' an old lady whispered loud enough for half the church to hear. Beth winced. She had to admit the girl didn't look like she belonged in church, she looked more like a drug addict. However, there was something enchanting about her.

Beth followed the girl's gaze to see who she was smiling at, and her heart sank. Andy had stopped his conversation with Mrs. Holmes and was smiling back at the stranger, clearly captivated. Or maybe he was just friendly and curious? What was a girl like that doing in church, anyway? It was unlikely she'd feel welcome here where way too many people judged by appearance and had certain expectations. Thankfully, being the daughter of Veronica Bateman, Beth met every one of those expectations. This girl was unlikely to have the same success.

Andy found a seat beside the newcomer who had placed herself at the very front of the church.

'Making an exhibition of herself,' Beth heard someone mutter as the girl swayed sensually in time to the music and waved her hands in perfect rhythm. No one had danced like that in this church before. Some raised their hands in worship, but nothing like this. Beth wondered if the girl felt everyone's eyes on her.

As soon as the service ended, Andy approached the girl, then led her down the back of the church, his eyes shining. 'Beth, meet Anique. She's in our year at school and she's keen to help out on the Cairns' farm.'

Ah. That made sense. She was a ward of the state joining the program. Clare hadn't mentioned Rod was bringing people in already.

'I've told her all about you,' Andy said.

Beth couldn't help smiling. At least this beautiful, exotic-looking girl would know where she and Andy stood. Anique clearly couldn't be a Christian and Andy never looked twice at a girl unless she had a heart for God.

She was stunned when Anique threw her arms around her. 'I'm so excited to meet you. I was, like, so nervous about coming here, but everyone I've met is so welcoming.'

Beth stepped back, but she didn't know what to think. Was Anique on something? No one could be that naturally bubbly and confident, could they? Or that oblivious to the condescending looks they were receiving. Beth would shrivel under the look Mrs. Holmes threw Anique's way.

'Anique is my new neighbour,' Andy said.

She wasn't part of the program?

'The Kemps are fostering me.' Anique's eyes shone, but there was pain lurking in their depths. 'I prayed for like a Christian foster family and instead I got like a Christian next-door neighbour. God is so, so cool.'

'So you're a Christian?' Beth was missing something here.

'Yep. Have been for like a year, now.' Anique beamed, bouncing on her toes. 'I love how God extends His grace to those who don't deserve it. Like, I put my faith in Christ and my new life is so different to the old. My old life was a bit rough, like …' She shrugged.

Beth tried not to be distracted by the way Anique added *like* into every sentence. She was a paradox. She might look and act like a drug addict, but she spoke like a seasoned Christian. 'Anique is a lovely name,' she said. 'I've never heard it before.'

Anique looked pleased. 'I like it. It isn't my real name—I like changed it when I put my old life behind me. So much better than my birth name. It, like, carries a lot of bad memories for me.'

Compassion filled Beth. Did Anique have a story similar to Phil's friend, Gus? 'Where did the name *Anique* come from?'

'I found it on the internet. It means like grace or favour. And God has sure shown me a lot of grace and has made me one of His chosen favourites.'

Favourites? Beth didn't think God had favourites but she wasn't going to burst Anique's bubble.

'So I'll be in trouble if call you Edwina?' Andy grinned at Anique.

The haunted look returned to her eyes and Beth was surprised by Andy's thoughtless comment. He normally read people so well, but he'd not only revealed Anique's birth name, he'd totally misread her sensitivity about it.

'It's my grandmother's name so I don't want to like disrespect it, but it's not me. I'm Anique. Like I feel like Anique.'

Yes, she was so unique that Anique fit. She was clearly a complex person with a painful past, but Beth was drawn to her. Dale and Maria Cairn approached, and Beth could see by their faces that they would accept Anique just the way she was.

Anique's thin frame was swallowed up in Maria's welcoming hug and Andy spoke quietly to Beth. 'So what do you think?'

'She's different. I like her.'

Andy's eyes shone. 'I knew you would. Perhaps she can be a real friend to you.'

'A *real* friend?'

'Anique's not like Dara. She's someone you can trust, pour your heart out to, and connect with on a spiritual level.'

It was nice that he cared, but didn't Andy realise she'd much prefer to pour her heart out to *him*? And wouldn't Anique be the one needing to pour her heart out? She obviously had some deep wounds, and Beth intended to be there for her.

Andy and Anique headed home together, and Clare came to Beth's side. 'A bit mysterious or something, isn't she?'

'She is.' Anique had made an impression Beth only dreamed of making.

'Andy seems a bit captivated by her.'

So Clare noticed it, too. But, if Beth understood God, she didn't need to worry. He was the God who made dreams come true. Wasn't He?

But what if Anique also dreamed of Andy? She was also a believer, so who would God favour? Anique thought she was God's favourite. It was a disturbing thought that Beth pushed to the back of her mind. She didn't want to compete with Anique. She could do without another standard to try to live up to.

She watched as Phil came to Clare and took her hand, his eyes shining with love. Peace returned. *You can't tell me dreams don't come true. Clare and Phil are living proof that they do.*

BETH'S IMPRESSION that Phil and Clare had a dream marriage came crashing down that very afternoon. Clare barged into the house, muttering about Phil, eyes shooting sparks. The way she gasped for breath told Beth she'd run all the way from the farm.

'Complete idiot, he is. Got to prove how macho he is. It's going to kill him.'

'Is everything okay?' It was a stupid question, but Beth didn't know what else to say.

'No! Phil and Rod are testing out Brave Man's Run.' Clare paced the room, seething.

'They're what?' Beth frowned in confusion.

'It's a steep hill that can be used as a vehicle jump ... if you're an idiot,' Clare said. 'Apparently Scott Cairn's the only one ever stupid enough to try it. But Rod challenged Phil and he couldn't resist, could he? I tried to talk him out of it, but no, Phil had to be a daredevil, didn't he?'

Clare sank into the lounge with a defeated sigh. 'The more I tried to talk him out of it, the more determined he was to do it. And then he and Rod went off in the ute as though he hadn't heard a word I said. Now he's either lying at the bottom of the hill half dead, or he's laughing at me with Rod and boasting about his achievements.'

Beth's heart pounded. She couldn't stand the thought of anything happening to Phil, either. She recalled her fear for Grandpa when he was loaded into the ambulance, then for Andy when he faced the flames in the woolshed.

Clare groaned, dropping her head into her hands. 'Why do guys do these risky, thoughtless things?'

Not just guys. Hadn't Beth done exactly the same thing? Feeling like a hypocrite, she shrugged. 'I don't know. Maybe it's a testosterone thing—they think they have to be heroes. Maybe they want to impress girls.'

Clare gave a disgusted grunt. 'Obviously not Phil. He couldn't care less about what I think. I guess guys want to prove something to each other.'

Or maybe they just didn't think it through. The immediate thing became the priority, no matter the danger. That's the only way she could justify her own actions that day on the busy freeway when Grandpa lost his life. She joined Clare on the lounge. Maybe Phil really did know what he was doing. She couldn't imagine him deliberately provoking Clare—he loved her too much, and he didn't have a death wish. So, was the vehicle jump really that dangerous?

Darkness set in, and Clare still sat on the leather lounge, chewing her nails and glaring at the television screen. A vehicle pulled into the driveway and Beth glanced out the window, relieved to see Phil getting out of the farm ute. She'd considered calling Mum but she'd been trying to catch up at the office and wasn't likely to be much help anyway. Now Phil was here, and he'd sort this out.

Clare ignored Phil's voice at the door, so Beth went. He stood on the pristine multi-weave doormat, shuffling his feet, looking worried. 'Is Clare here?'

Beth stepped aside so he could see his wife sitting on the lounge. His face lit into a relieved smile, but although Clare had the courtesy to turn off the television, she kept her eyes on the blank screen.

He moved around the lounge to face her. 'I was worried about you.'

She let out an unladylike snort. Beth didn't blame her. Yes, maybe he'd been worried because he didn't know where Clare was, but she'd been worried for his life.

'I told you I would be okay.' He reached for her hand. 'I'm still here.'

Clare snatched her hand away. 'Only by the grace of God!'

'Clare—'

'Don't! Don't even talk to me.'

Colour rose in Phil's face. 'We need to talk this out, Clare, but not here. Come home.'

Beth winced. She knew Clare. Phil's tone was gentle, but it still sounded like a command. She tried to melt into the background, but Clare shot her a look. 'Stay there, Beth. Phil's just going.'

'Come on, Clare, it's not fair to bring Beth into this.' Phil shot her an apologetic look.

'Why? Scared Beth will see our marriage isn't perfect?'

Beth's face heated. Right now would be the perfect time to disappear.

Phil stood his ground. 'Let's go home, Clare.'

'No. You can spend a night alone and get a taste of what I'd be experiencing if you'd died today.'

He chuckled, a cautious sound. 'That's a bit dramatic.'

'I'm your wife. I actually care what happens to you.'

'But nothing happened.'

Clare jumped up, her eyes blazing fire. 'You are so totally selfish, Philip Cairn! You didn't even care how I felt.'

'Of course I care. Is it selfish to go and have a bit of fun with Rod?'

'I don't believe God saved you from that virus in the Madorean Islands just so you could throw your life away for some stunt.' She drew in a shuddery breath. 'So much for your spiritual maturity.'

Hurt flashed through his eyes. 'That's not fair.'

Clare's chin quivered and he moved toward her. She backed away. 'Go home, Phil. I mean it.'

Anguish shone in Phil's eyes as he gave a helpless shrug and left. Beth wanted to call after him and tell him not to give up, but Clare was clearly too distressed to understand his point of view right now.

Clare sat like stone until the ute turned the corner of the street. Then she bursts into tears. Beth watched helplessly. She'd never seen Clare like this before.

God, what should I do?

BETH WAS EXHAUSTED. She'd tried comforting Clare, tried reasoning with her, tried getting her to eat something, but all to no avail. Clare had been so strong when Phil was lost overseas and thought dead. She couldn't understand this over-the-top reaction.

The garage door slid open and Beth glanced at the clock. 8pm. Mum was home from work. Leaving the washing up, she wiped her hands on the hand towel and called into the living room.

'Mum's home.'

No answer. She peeked over the top of the lounge chair to find Clare fast asleep. She gently shook her awake. 'Clare, Mum's home.'

Clare's sleepy eyes grew panicked. 'Don't tell her I'm here. Please.' She raced upstairs to her old room and shut the door.

Mum was re-heating tea in the microwave ten minutes later when the phone rang. Beth grabbed it, knowing exactly who it would be.

'Beth, it's me.'

'Hi Phil. She's just gone up to bed. I'm worried about her. She's really upset.'

There was silence for a moment, then Phil sighed. 'Can you try to convince her to talk to me? Please?'

'I'll try. I'll get her to call you back.'

'Thanks, Beth.' He sounded worried. Beth was worried, too.

She made her way upstairs, her heart quickening at the sound of muffled sobs through Clare's door. She had no idea how to deal with this. What should she say? At another sob, compassion overcame her fear and she gently knocked on the door and went in.

In the shadowed light she saw Clare curled up on her bed, sobbing into her arms. She rested a hand on her shaking shoulder. 'Clare, it's okay.'

'It's not,' Clare wept. 'I always said I'd never do this—that I'd never be this type of oversensitive, demanding wife. But I just got so scared when he wouldn't listen. I thought he didn't love me anymore, and I felt so helpless.'

'He loves you.' Beth knew it was true. 'Phil's right, you just need to talk. Sort it all out.'

'But then he'll think it's okay to do such risky things.'

'What if it was okay?' Beth dared suggest.

Clare's lips trembled. 'You think I'm being unreasonable?'

'I just think that after losing Grandpa we're a bit more cautious. We know how fragile life is because we already lost Dad when we were little. And I think you're extra fearful about Phil because he nearly died once already. But Phil wouldn't have died unless it was God's time.'

If only she could believe her own words. Was it really Grandpa's time or had God allowed her stupid mistake to steal his time on earth?

A tear trickled down Clare's cheek. Beth's chest ached at the sight. 'But Beth, do you really think God protects us from our own silly mistakes? I mean, we have to reap what we sow, and cars are so dangerous.'

Understanding dawned. Clare was afraid of losing Phil the same way they'd lost Dad. 'I know what Phil and Rod are doing is risky, but I can't imagine Rod condoning anything suicidal. Dangerous, maybe, but even stepping out onto the street is dangerous.' She smiled. 'Andy showed me a Proverb about a man who wouldn't leave his house because there could be a lion on the street. We don't want to be afraid to live because of what *could* happen.'

Clare shook her head. 'Sometimes I forget how old you are, Beth. I always think of you as my little sister, but you're more mature than I am.'

Beth chuckled and gently pushed wisps of hair back from Clare's face. 'I'm glad you think so, but it's much easier to see clearly when it's someone else going through it. I have no idea how I'd have reacted if I was scared for my husband's life.'

Clare flushed and another tear tracked down her cheek. 'How can he respect me again after this? I've hurt him all because of my own stupid fears. I was horrible to him.' Her face crumpled. 'I can't face him now. I'm too embarrassed.'

Beth stepped out of the room, pulled out her phone and called Phil.

'I think you'd better come over.'

He hesitated. 'Does she want me to?'

'I don't know, but she needs you—she's kicking herself for over-reacting and not being the perfect wife.'

'What?'

'I know. She's done a full circle. I reckon she'll listen to you now.'

Phil laughed with relief. 'I'm on my way.'

MUM WAS on the phone when Phil arrived and Beth thanked God for His perfect timing. She snuck Phil inside and he made his way up the stairs two at a time. Beth had complete confidence in him, despite his apparent 'display of spiritual immaturity' this afternoon. She knew he'd do right by her sister.

Still, she followed him upstairs and glanced into Clare's room to see her sobbing into Phil's chest, wrapped firmly in his embrace.

'I'm sorry, Clare,' Phil said in his deep, gentle voice. 'I don't believe what I did was as dangerous as you think it is, but if it worries you that much, I won't do it again.'

Clare cried harder, and Phil tenderly touched her face. 'Clare, it's okay.'

'It's not okay. I can't believe I did that to you. I was so determined our marriage was going to be a happy, harmonious one.'

'It is.'

'But Phil, I—'

'It is. Conflict is inevitable. It doesn't mean we love each other any less. It just gives us a chance to learn what each other wants and needs.'

'But I went about it the wrong way.'

He smiled. 'Maybe. Well, the not-talking thing anyway. I'd prefer you keep yelling at me than stop talking and shut me out.'

Her eyebrows shot up. 'Really?'

'Really.' He kissed her on her trembling lips.

Clare sighed and snuggled into him. 'I've never really learned how a good marriage works. Dad wasn't around, so we never had an example to follow.'

'So let's do it our own way and let's grow stronger through it. Now, are you coming home?'

Clare swiped away tears, nodded and moved in to kiss him again.

Beth headed downstairs. Despite her discomfort at their displays of affection, tonight something warm and happy curled inside her when they eventually came down the stairs, arms around one another.

Clare smiled at Beth. 'Thanks for everything. I'm going home.'

'What?' she teased. 'What happened to our sleepover plans? We could have giggled and talked late into the night.'

Clare snorted. 'Talked about what? I'm married now. I'm not into the guy talk anymore.'

'We could talk about *my* guys.'

'Like I said, I'm going home.'

Phil opened the door for Clare, then turned back to mouth *'thank you'* to Beth before closing it behind them. Beth smiled, amazed at how quickly everything seemed right again. Conflict was something she not only avoided, but feared. Her head said disagreements shouldn't be interpreted as dislike, but her heart had always told her otherwise.

Maybe love changed everything.

'Was that Clare and Phil?' Mum still held her phone and Beth pushed away a twinge of annoyance. Her mother was so busy with work she had no idea what was going on in the hearts and lives of her children in her own home.

'Yes, they've gone home now, though.'

'Without even saying hello?'

Beth didn't answer. She was well and truly ready for bed.

'I'VE ARRANGED a housewarming party for you,' Rod Green announced triumphantly as he wandered into Clare and Phil's house the following afternoon. Beth glanced up from her homework. Rod appeared totally oblivious to the drama his challenge had caused Clare and Phil yesterday afternoon.

Phil raised a brow, looking amused as Rod pulled up a chair and rested his foot against the table leg.

'I've asked these people.' He threw a list at Phil.

Phil glanced down the list. 'Rod, you won't fit all these people in our house.'

Rod obviously hadn't thought of that. He frowned, then swung back in the chair, oblivious to the way his twisting movements added dents to the Lino. 'We could have it in the woolshed, then.'

Phil shook his head, holding back a laugh 'Rod, isn't the point of a housewarming party to have it in the new home? All we have to do is cut a few people off this list.'

'Can't do.'

'Why not?'

'I've already asked 'em all.'

Beth couldn't believe Rod had implemented a plan with no idea how to carry it out, but Phil laughed. 'What about food? Have you arranged that?'

'Of course. I told everyone to bring a plate.'

'With something on it?'

Rod rolled his eyes. 'That's a given.'

'Just checking.'

Rod allowed his chair to fall back to the floor with a thump. 'I thought you might be able to arrange music and games and stuff or whatever you do at a housewarming.'

Phil drew in a breath as though holding back another laugh. 'I think you just mingle and check out the new house—not that we'll be in the house.'

'We'll arrange tours then.'

Clare shared Beth's concerns when she stepped into the room and heard the plans. 'What about drinks and glasses … and I haven't even cleaned the house properly.'

Phil slid his arms around her waist. 'Hey, it's okay. It'll all work out. You don't have to impress anyone but me now, remember?'

Clare's shoulders relaxed and she smiled. But Beth couldn't. She wished she had that same luxury of only needing to please one person. Every day she found herself torn between pleasing herself, Mum, God and everyone else. And visitors, in her experience, meant stress. Preparing for guests was a nightmare. First, Mum would do a major spring clean, working so hard she totally wore herself out. Then anyone who dared to use another glass after the washing up was done, or wear shoes on the carpet after it had been steam-cleaned, was in big trouble.

But clearly, to Philip Cairn, visitors meant a chance to get to know people and develop relationships.

As soon as Rod and Phil left to clean out the woolshed, Beth voiced her concerns to Clare. 'Did he even think about the fact that he's invited people to trespass on your private life? They're going to notice everything about your new house and judge you.'

Clare shrugged, but Beth wasn't finished. 'And the woolshed? What's Mum going to say? It's so filthy.' She shook her head and straightened an offending wrinkle in the lounge cover. 'Some people will refuse to come when they realise where it's being held.'

Clare let out a laugh.

'What's funny?'

'You!'

'Me?'

'Yes, you. You nearly caught me in the same trap you and Mum are in. Does it really matter how tidy our lounge covers are? Only five percent of people in this world are as fussy as you and Mum. I'm living on a farm for goodness' sake, not in a palace.'

'You think I'm like Mum?' It hurt to hear her say it. As much as Beth wanted to impress Mum, she didn't want to be like her.

Clare gave her a quick hug. 'No. You're like royalty. You should have been born a princess.'

'Are you saying I'm a snob?'

'No, I'm just saying you have poise and class that I've never had. It's no good me even trying to be like you.'

Beth screwed up her nose, still pretty sure she should be offended. 'Is that woolshed going to be cleaned at all? I can't see Rod doing it.'

'He won't. Phil will do all the work while Rod tells him what to do.'

'How can Phil stand it?'

Clare straightened the chair Rod left out and took Phil's coffee cup to the kitchen. 'Well they're the perfect team, really. Rod has big plans, and Phil is practical. That's how this whole rehabilitation project is coming together. Rod had the dream and the means to accomplish it while Phil is making sure it all falls into place.'

'Doesn't Rod realise it's not fair on Phil?' Beth moved beside Clare and sorted the pile of dishes in the sink.

'Phil doesn't mind. Rod's always had a bit of trouble with the administration side of things so Phil's just doing the paperwork, filling in the practical details of the plans and searching for the workers we'll need.'

Beth glanced out to the lounge room, at the beautiful clean new carpet. 'You realise everyone is going to be scuffing up your new carpet?'

She caught Clare's expression and frowned. She didn't like being laughed at. 'Aren't you even concerned about it?'

Clare chuckled. 'Why worry when you do enough worrying for the both of us?'

CHAPTER NINE

Beth stood to the side, watching Clare and Phil mingle with guests in the woolshed. She envied them. They were so calm, so natural, so delighted by people. She couldn't be like that no matter how much she wished she was. Cleanliness and punctuality were so ingrained in her nature that she didn't think she could be any other way.

She wandered around, trying not to look as aimless as she felt. The truth was, she was overwhelmed. So many people and so much noise, though she had to admit Clare and Phil had done a spectacular job of transforming the dirty old shed. It almost looked like a reasonably furnished hall. No one needed to worry about stepping in sheep droppings or getting the awful smell on their clothes. But Beth was sure she picked up the faint smell of sheep in the air.

Clare and Phil enthusiastically greeted newcomers, while Rod buzzed around making sure everything was under control—or rather, making sure everyone else was making sure everything was under control. Beth avoided him, hoping he wouldn't ask her to do anything. He'd already given Andy the job of serving drinks —part of the reason she had no one to talk to.

The night was long. Beth didn't want to be part of the games. Some guests seemed to thrive on making an exhibition of themselves. Beth didn't have their confidence.

When guests began to leave, Andy relinquished his job and approached her. 'It's been a great night.' He sat beside her on the corner bench she'd found to quietly watch the proceedings.

She nodded, watching Andy take a sip of his drink. She realised she was staring at his lips and flushed as she lifted her gaze.

A cheeky smile stretched across his face and he held the cup out to her. 'Want to share? I don't have germs or anything.'

The day of the fire. He was teasing. Not wanting to let him get away with it, she took the cup. 'Thank you.'

He raised his brows, daring her to drink. She brought the cup to her mouth, determined to prove she wasn't afraid of his germs. But she couldn't do it. Instead, she swallowed air as dramatically as she could, then blinked at him, eyes wide and innocent. Andy burst out laughing, the contagious sound filling her ears and warming her heart. She couldn't help laughing with him.

Rod appeared in front of them, holding up his phone. 'Gotcha!' He grinned, then squeezed onto the bench between them, showing his phone screen to Andy. 'So you never forget that dreams come true.'

Andy looked puzzled and Rod waved his hand around at the woolshed. 'You know, the Phil and Clare story? They love each other but one nearly dies, then God spares him, they get married and live in the house of their dreams. And to top it off, they have their housewarming in a woolshed organised by the delinquent who used to cause them so much trouble. What more can you want?'

Andy chuckled. 'You better forward me the picture, then.'

Rod pressed a couple of buttons on his phone, and a notification dinged on Andy's. 'Done.' He swaggered off, looking pleased with himself.

Beth reached for Andy's phone. 'Can I see?' Maybe she could convince him to delete it. She'd never been photogenic and she could imagine how bad she looked.

But Andy shot her a teasing grin and put his phone back in his pocket. 'Nup. It's mine.'

'It's safer to share photos than drinks, you know.'

'Yeah, but I like to live dangerously.' Still, he pulled his phone out and showed her. 'Not too bad, hey?'

She had to admit it was a good picture. She didn't see a shy, dowdy girl next to the dream guy she could never have. She saw two young people laughing together, a special connection between them.

'I'll do you a deal,' Andy offered. 'You give me back my drink and I'll send you the picture.'

She didn't want to seem too keen. 'It's okay, you can have both.'

She held out his drink, but Andy shook his head as he swiped his finger across his phone. 'I'll send it to you. You need it to remember me. I won't be around forever, you know.'

She just smiled. Andy had no idea they were destined for each other. He'd be around for a long time to come. How could she love him this way if they weren't meant to be together? She had asked God to take away her feelings if they weren't meant to be, but they'd only intensified. There was one obvious conclusion to draw.

Andy took his cup and stood, smiling down at her. 'Guess I'd better wish the happy couple all the best and head home.'

'Guess you'd better. Otherwise Rod Green might come banging down your door demanding to know why you didn't. Then I'd have to come and visit you in hospital.'

Andy sniggered and tilted his head to the left. Beth turned with a sinking feeling. Rod stood there. He'd heard every word.

'I'm leaving.' Andy gave her an over-enthusiastic wave and walked off, leaving Beth to face Rod. He looked as tough as ever. But slowly that grim mouth widened into a grin.

'You're not scared of me, are you?'

A little. Sometimes.

He lowered himself into the seat Andy had vacated. 'I don't know that I like Clare's little sister being scared of me.' His voice was gruff, but for the first time Beth noticed a gentleness in his eyes, and it gave her courage.

'I'm not scared.' She sat up straighter to blink at him. 'I just prefer to take calculated risks.'

There she went being a hypocrite again. She clearly hadn't calculated the risk well enough that day on the highway. Her life had been saved, but Grandpa's hadn't.

Rod's eyes widened. 'You're a cheeky little thing, aren't you?'

'Not normally.'

He lounged back, and a smile skirted his lips. 'But something about being faced with big fierce bullies gives you a death wish?'

She smiled, surprised at him but more surprised at herself. He wasn't that bad, really. 'Thanks for organising the housewarming for Clare and Phil.'

'No worries. I'm just sorry some of the special people in their lives aren't around anymore.'

His tone held a distinct note of sadness. 'You mean Aunty Joy?'

'Actually, I was thinking of Toni-Lee. I couldn't get in touch with her for the engagement party or even for the wedding.'

Beth remembered Clare's confident friend. She'd noticed the connection between Toni and Rod in the past. Had they been a couple?

'I'm worried about her,' Rod admitted, 'but I'm learning to trust God to look after her. And I pray for her.' His eyes locked on hers. 'Can you pray for her, too?'

'I will.'

He smiled and his eyes held a spark Beth had learned to recognise in Clare's when she spoke of Phil. If she wasn't mistaken, Rod Green was in love with Clare's friend, Toni-Lee. She watched Rod saunter away. *Please God, let Toni be okay. And please bring her and Rod together.*

CHAPTER TEN

Anique arrived for her first day of school without her piercings and with her tattoos covered by the modest school uniform. And yet, she still drew everyone's attention. Beth wasn't surprised, really. She doubted Anique could be inconspicuous if she tried. It didn't take long for rumours to ripple through the school.

'Tenicia Cornford's cousin used to know Anique,' a girl said in a hushed voice during the library study sessions. 'She said Anique got arrested for bashing someone a few years ago,'

'She had to go to rehab,' Abby added.

'Is she an addict?' Dara's eyes were wide, but held their familiar gleam as she soaked up every piece gossip she could.

'Probably. Tina saw her shoplifting on her first day in town.'

One by one, students added to what they had heard, and Beth sat quietly, troubled by the whispered conversations. Didn't they realise Anique was a Christian now?

Dara leaned over and whispered in Beth's ear. 'She has to shoplift so support her drug habit.'

Irritation welled up. 'How do you know?'

'Tina saw her shoplifting.'

'Did Tina tell you that?'

'Abby just told us.' Dara lifted her chin, no longer whispering, and everyone went quiet.

Beth drew in a breath for courage. 'I just don't think we should be passing on second-hand information. Anique deserves a chance, and we don't even know if half of what's being said is true. We should at least confirm it before we say anything.'

'What?' Abby's laugh was scornful. 'I'm not asking Anique if she was shoplifting. I'm not stupid enough to get my head punched in.'

Beth sighed. She couldn't imagine the bubbly Anique assaulting anybody. However, speculation was all too often passed around the school as truth. But not if she could help it. Anique needed support and friendship and she was going to give it.

'You didn't really shoplift, did you?' Beth asked when Anique sat beside her during English, the only class they shared.

Anique laughed. 'So that's the latest.'

'The latest I've heard, anyway.' How could Anique be so blasé about what was being said? 'What should I say to them?'

Anique shrugged. 'With a past like mine, people are always going to say stuff, Beth. It's not worth trying to stop them. God forgives but people don't.'

'But how do people here know about your past?'

'There are some things that like once you've been involved in them, they follow you around forever.'

'Such as?'

Anique searched Beth's eyes as though working out if she could trust her, then her shoulders sagged. 'I was into drugs.'

'But you're not anymore?'

'I'm off the drugs, but it's hard to destroy your links to that lifestyle once you've gotten yourself into it. People, like, think you'll never change and they make it hard.'

'Who makes it hard? Christians? Or everyone?'

'Dealers and anyone connected to the drug scene. They're very good at passing along names and business and trying to draw you back.'

'Even around here?'

Anique avoided her eyes, and Beth knew what she wasn't saying. There were dealers in town. What if that put Anique in danger? Everything within Beth wanted to help, to protect her, but she didn't know how. She was totally out of her depth.

ANDY MADE it his job to ensure Anique fit in at school. Beth tried not to mind that they were so comfortable together, talking and laughing between classes. Her only comfort was that Anique was new, and hadn't been through all that she and Andy had faced together. No one could take away that special connection she shared with him. She would just try to trust God and let things take their course.

Life was definitely more interesting with Anique around. She turned up for her first Youth Group in the high school auditorium wearing so little that Beth's mouth dropped open. If Anique was aware of the stir she was creating, she didn't show it. Her bubbly smile floated around the room, then landed on Beth. Everything about her brightened as she came over.

Despite knowing her mother would be horrified, Beth couldn't help admiring the exquisite butterfly tattoo on her exposed shoulder. 'Wow, that's so beautiful.'

Anique beamed. 'You think so?' She turned so Beth could get a better look.

'The detail is amazing.' Beth studied the sweeping lines and complicated colour blends, committing it to memory to sketch later.

Anique looked around the room. 'So you know like everyone here?'

'Pretty much. Want me to introduce you?' It shouldn't be hard, considering everyone was looking at her anyway.

'Yeah, like that'd be cool.'

Beth did her best to introduce Anique to all the attendees, but they were so awed by her exotic appearance that they became tongue-tied. And so Beth made an effort to speak on their behalf, telling Anique their names, gifts and interesting facts about them.

Anique smiled as they moved toward the back of the room toward a group of year ten boys. 'You are so positive, aren't you? Is there anyone in this world you *don't* like or admire?'

Inadvertently, Beth's eyes shot to Rod.

Anique didn't miss it. 'Is he, like, one of the leaders?'

'Yeah, that's Rod Green.'

'You don't like him?'

'I do, but he can be a bit intimidating sometimes. I don't always know how to take him. He's got a good heart, though. He runs a project to help young people who need support.'

'He looks like he comes from my old world.'

Surprised by her intuition, worry knotted Beth's stomach. If there were dealers in town, would they approach Rod? They would surely know that his dad was a convicted dealer currently serving time. Would Rod be pressured to go the same way?

As though sensing their eyes on him, Rod turned toward them and his eyes locked on Anique. He headed their way, and Beth could tell he was as intrigued by Anique as everyone else.

'Rod Green,' he said in his gruff way, holding out a hand for Anique to shake. 'I've seen you at church, but haven't gotten around to meeting you.'

'Yep. I'm Anique. Beth said you're involved in a project with young people?'

Rod's eyes lit up. 'I am.' He began explaining the project to Anique, and Beth slipped away while she could. She instinctively searched the room for Andy and headed his way. He was chatting with Clare, and moved over to include Beth.

'Thanks so much for making Anique feel welcome.' His smile was warm. 'I'm trying to help her make new friends. Can't have her hanging off me all the time, can I? Wouldn't be good for her reputation.' He grinned and Beth couldn't help grinning back.

Andy clearly considered Anique nothing more than a friend. She glanced back to Rod and Anique who were now in animated discussion. Maybe she shouldn't have prayed Toni would reconnect with Rod. Perhaps Anique was the one God had chosen for him instead. The thought settled her anxious heart.

As the youth left for the evening, the leaders stayed back to talk and pray. Anique lurked in the background, waiting for Andy to walk her home.

'Your talk was great tonight,' Phil said to Andy as they finished praying. 'You come alive whenever you talk about knowing Jesus. I love it.'

Andy rubbed a hand through his hair. 'Yeah, well, I just wish I could get through to them.'

What? Beth had never heard Andy sound so disheartened. What had happened?

Rod looked as surprised as Beth felt. 'You don't think you're getting through?'

'No. They occasionally get moved by what they hear in the moment, but then they keep living the way they always did. Clay and his mates keep saying they're going to live for God, but the things they say and do …' He shook his head. 'Jesus is more of an ideal to them than a friend. They were joking about crucifying a cat tonight …'

Beth drew in a sharp breath and tears blurred her vision. How could someone even talk about such cruelty?

Phil rested a brotherly hand on Andy's shoulder. 'Remember, only God can change them. Only He can make them understand what Jesus went through out of love for them. We just have to tell them about Him, pray, love them ...'

Realisation hit Beth like a stinging slap. She'd reacted more strongly to the idea of a cat being crucified than she did to Jesus. She'd never wept over Jesus' death the way she'd seen Andy do. She'd never danced in triumph over the joy of His resurrection. Something held her back. The other leaders had such passion for God and lived as though He was right there beside them. She believed, but there was something missing. Was she just like Clay and his mates?

Rod stretched. 'Sorry guys, but I have to go. I've got an interview with the project review committee in the morning.'

'That goes for me, too.' Phil rubbed his eyes and Beth noticed the concern in Clare's expression. Phil always looked tired these days.

Rod stood and waved. 'See ya, everyone.' He turned to where Anique lounged in a chair down the back corner of the hall. 'See ya, Eddie. Keep out of trouble, hey?'

Beth cringed. Anique must have told Rod her real name and shared her past. Before she could open her mouth, Anique charged across the room and shoved Rod against the wall with incredible strength for someone so small-boned. Her eyes sparked fire. 'The name's Anique.'

Rod looked down into the angry face challenging his chest. His mouth twitched, but thankfully he didn't laugh. 'Why? You got something against nicknames?'

'That one, yes.'

'So I can call you Snouty and you won't care?'

Anique glared up at him, then shook her head. 'It's stupid, but whatever.'

Rod grinned. 'What about Spitfire? Or Spitty?'

Anique poked him in the chest. 'Just don't call me Eddie. Or Edwina.'

Despite the knot in her stomach, Beth had to admit it was amusing to see Anique's thin frame holding Rod's solid body against the wall. Rod didn't seem to mind and appeared perfectly calm as he tilted his head to the side.

'What about *Antique*?'

Anique screwed up her nose in disgust. 'Now you're just rage baiting me. Call me by my proper name or I won't answer.'

'You told me Edwina is your real name, remember?'

'Not anymore it's not.' Anique spun away from Rod and stalked from the room. Rod's amused eyes met Beth's and he winked. He'd finally met his match and he clearly enjoyed it.

CHAPTER ELEVEN

The doorbell chimed and Beth sighed. After a long day at school and a ride out to the farm to feed Gilbert, she just wanted to relax and get lost in a good romance. Instead, she closed the book and slid it under the lounge cushion. She glanced in the door viewer and held in a groan. Dara stood on the porch. Swinging the door open, Beth made an effort to smile.

'Beth, I'm desperate.' Dara launched herself into her arms and stunned, Beth stepped backward. 'I'm so stressed out,' Dara blubbered. 'I haven't even started our geography assignment. I wanted to do it last night, but my grandmother's in hospital and we don't know how long she's got.'

Compassion filled Beth. She knew what it was like to lose a grandparent. 'Oh, Dara, I'm so sorry.' She moved aside to let her in.

Dara charged into the house and plopped onto the lounge where she poured out her story. 'Mum's not coping. She's started drinking again, and Brett and I had a huge fight and he said he's going to dump me. I'm so stressed out. I have no other choice, I'll have to quit school.'

Dara's life was always full of drama and Beth never knew how much to believe, but right now she seemed genuinely distressed. Beth's heart went out to her. 'You can't drop out now. I'll help you with the assignment.'

Dara's eyes brightened and she sniffled. 'You will?'

'Of course.' Beth got her laptop out. 'Which question have you chosen?'

Dara looked at her blankly. 'I don't know. You choose one for me.'

Beth bit her lip. 'How about if I explain what each one is asking and you choose?'

Dara shook her head. 'Nah, I'll just do whatever you did. Easier that way.'

Beth drew in a breath. Her assignment had taken a lot of research and was a personal interest of hers. She'd looked into the impact of farming on koala habitats. How could she help Dara without doing it all for her and without devaluing the effort she herself had put in? Before she could say anything else, Dara began talking about Brett, launching into the details of how unfairly he'd treated her.

Beth let her talk for a bit, then tried to draw her back to the task at hand. It was exhausting and time consuming, but finally there was some semblance of an essay completed. Beth went into Mum's office to print it off and Dara followed close on her heels.

'Is this one yours?' Dara picked up Beth's completed assignment sitting beside the printer.

'Yeah, I finished it a few days ago.'

'You always find schoolwork so easy.' Dara sounded almost accusing. If only she knew. Beth spent hours labouring over every assignment. Her mother was Veronica Bateman. She had no other choice.

Dara flipped through the paper. 'I'll hand it in for you.'

Beth reached for it, noting Dara had already bent the corner of a page. 'No, it's fine.'

Dara gave a pleading look. 'Beth, let me at least do something for you. You've done so much for me.' Tears filled her eyes. 'Being with you, I even forgot about Grandma lying in hospital with machines beeping all around her.'

Beth's heart welled with compassion again, and she gave Dara a hug.

Dara stepped back and met her eyes. 'Are we really friends, Beth?'

'Of course.'

'Then let me act like one. In a real friendship, helping each other goes both ways.' She slipped Beth's assignment behind her own. 'What is it that Andy said at youth group? Something about us being blessed when we give?'

Beth swallowed hard as guilt niggled. Yes. And Andy had also challenged them not to deny others the blessing of giving. She saw Dara out the door, then sank onto the front steps. Why did she feel so completely drained?

Clare's car pulled in the driveway and Beth looked up. 'Mum's not home.'

'Yeah, she asked me to come over. She's going to be home extra late.'

'She shouldn't have made you come. I'm fine.'

Clare lowered herself down beside Beth on the step. 'You don't look fine.'

'I am. It's just Dara.'

'You let her get to you again?'

There was disapproval in Clare's tone, and Beth needed to make her understand. 'She's hurting and needs support. Her grandmother's really sick.'

'Or so she says. She'd say anything to get attention.'

'I think she was telling the truth this time—there's definitely something going on. I figure that even if she's lying, something is causing her desperate need for attention, and if I can help somehow …'

Clare shook her head. 'Oh, Beth. Sometimes I think your compassion goes too deep.'

'Mine? Clare, you're one of the most compassionate people I know.'

Clare gave a lopsided smile. 'It's true I've had more compassion since I became a Christian, but I was never naturally compassionate like you. It's like you live other people's pain and it tears you apart. Don't you remember the way you used to cry over Golden Books?'

'Only because you and Dan hid them from me.'

'What about *Dumbo*?'

Clare had a point. The story still troubled Beth. Mum had put it away after finding her sobbing over the illustration of Dumbo's mother in chains.

'You're very sensitive,' Clare said, 'but that is a good thing if you use it the right way. God wants to use it for His glory, but Satan wants to use it to destroy you.'

'How do you mean?'

'Well, compassion is a very Christ-like characteristic, but we can't carry people. We're not God. We're supposed to point people to Jesus, not take the place of Jesus.'

Beth frowned. 'I can't tell people about Jesus. I'm not confident like you.'

Clare laughed. 'Confident? You should have seen me at school. I was terrified of anyone even bringing up the topic of God. I thought it was Phil's job to witness because I would just get all embarrassed and tongue-tied.'

Really? Outgoing, popular Clare was scared?

'God can use anyone, Beth. Especially those who know they can't do it on their own. You are free from the despair that weighs down all those who don't know God. Live that freedom!'

Freedom? Beth knew she was free to live forever because of her faith in Jesus, but this earthly body still dragged her down. The concerns of everyday life didn't go away just because she was a

Christian. Regret and shame weighed heavily on her heart. The world was still broken, people were hurting, and there was so much responsibility to live right, to be the best she could be, to not cause others to stumble, and to make their lives easier in any way she could. Brushing a dirty mark off her shoe, she wondered again what made Clare so free.

BETH MADE dinner and insisted Clare bring Phil over to join them. They were dishing up the meal when Mum arrived home. Beth's heart sank, but Phil and Clare greeted her with warmth.

'Join us,' Clare said, throwing some cutlery onto the table while Beth pulled out another plate. She wasn't looking forward to the meal anymore. Everything was less relaxed when Mum was around.

Mum joined them, but she kept her eyes averted from Phil, who rested his elbow casually on the table and shovelled food into his mouth with a fork. Clare handed him a knife. He merely grinned as he placed it back on the table and eyed Mum. 'Clare's worried I'm going to offend you.'

Beth held her breath. Mum put down her knife and fork and finished delicately chewing her small mouthful before looking at Phil. 'Why would I be offended?'

Phil let out a laugh. 'Well, you're just so neat and well-mannered. Clare and I don't even use a tablecloth at home.'

'Phil!' Clare cut him off, pretending to look horrified. 'Don't share our family secrets.'

'That's not a family secret.' Phil quirked a brow at her, eyes sparkling with mischief. 'Now if I told her how you left your dirty—'

'Stop it!' Clare threw a hand across his mouth, knocking over the salt shaker in the process.

Phil chuckled. 'Inside voices, Clare.' He removed her hand from his mouth. 'We're not out in the paddock, remember? Now go and get the cloth and clean up that salt. But make sure it's the table cleaning cloth and not the floor cleaning cloth or the toilet cleaning cloth.'

Beth's breath hitched and she glanced at Mum. To her surprise, one side of Mum's mouth lifted. 'You know, I didn't know you were quite so unrefined when I agreed to let you become my son-in-law.'

'Unrefined?'

Mum sniffed. 'Well, it's clear you use the same cleaning cloth for everything at home.'

'Not quite. We got a new one out the other day.'

There was complete silence, then Clare burst out laughing. Phil grinned and scraped his calloused, work-browned hand across the tablecloth to gather the spilled salt.

Mum jumped up. 'I'll get a cloth.'

'You know what they say?' Clare giggled.

Phil's hand stilled. 'No, what do they say?'

'You're supposed to throw it over your shoulder to avoid bad luck.'

'I wouldn't dare. Not in this house.'

Clare grinned. 'Just the salt, not the table.'

Beth let out a spurt of laughter. The thought of Phil hurling their magnificent cedar table across the room was too much. The more she tried to restrain herself, the more she lost control until she was laughing with abandon. Phil and Clare lost it, too. Clare was still giggling when Mum returned with the cloth. Phil put an arm around her and squeezed affectionately. 'Pull yourself together. If you're out of control it will be the son-in-law who gets the blame.'

'Oh Phil, you're the perfect son-in-law. Mum wouldn't want anyone else. Not really.'

Mum stood patiently behind her, waiting to clean up the salt, but Clare was too busy looking into Phil's eyes.

Phil pulled her into his lap. 'Come here and give your mum some room. It's not like she'd be rude enough to just reach over you.'

'Phil!' Clare jumped away.

'What? We're married. We're allowed.'

'Not in front of my mother!'

Phil just laughed, pulling her back into his lap and holding her there. 'She's allowed to know I love you.' He unashamedly kissed her and Beth didn't know where to look. Mum ignored them as she worked at cleaning up the salt.

Beth wondered if she would ever love someone enough that the rest of the world could fade into insignificance. Could she be that way with Andy?

CHAPTER TWELVE

Beth spotted Dara coming out of class before recess, and raced over, her heart heavy with compassion. 'Dara, how is she?'

'Who?'

'Your grandmother.'

Dara looked confused, then recognition passed over her face. 'Oh, yeah, well, she's not as bad as they thought. She's out of hospital now.'

Beth was stunned into silence. She was a fool. Once again Dara had built up a drama out of nothing. A strange, burning feeling built up from somewhere deep inside, but she pushed it away. Hadn't she told Clare that if Dara lied to get attention, she must need it? 'Did you put in our assignments?'

'I told you I would.'

'Just checking.'

Dara avoided her eyes. 'I have to …' Her voice faded out and she rushed away.

Beth headed to the library, battling unfamiliar anger. She needed to calm down and sketching always helped with that. She settled herself at a study desk and pulled out a pen and sketch pad. Without thought, she outlined a rough sketch of the hat Andy so often wore. Her thoughts circled around him as she worked.

'So, is there anything you're not good at?'

She jumped at Anique's voice behind her, and flipped the sketch book closed. 'Yes. Lots of things.' At Anique's doubtful look, she sighed. 'It's true. It's becoming very clear that I can't make everyone happy and I can't make them appreciate me for who I am instead of what I can do for them.'

Anique laughed. 'Not even God does that.'

She was right. God didn't make everyone love and appreciate Him. He gave them a choice. And that choice determined their happiness.

The bell interrupted and Beth dragged herself to her feet, dredging up a smile for Anique. 'See you 'round.'

Anique nodded and flashed her bright smile, but Beth noticed it didn't quite reach her eyes. Maybe something was troubling Anique, too. But no, she wouldn't ask. She was over trying to rescue people. Her experience with Grandpa had taught her how deadly it could become.

AFTER LUNCH, Miss Doyle handed back the geography assignments. Beth waited eagerly, knowing she'd done well, while Cameron fidgeted beside her.

'Don't worry about giving mine back, Miss,' he called.

Miss Doyle pursed her lips. 'Yours is definitely coming back, Mr. Oliver. There's no way I want to have such rubbish cluttering my desk.'

'But Miss, Beth helped me with it.'

'I doubt that very much.'

'You did, didn't you, Beth.' Cameron shot her a mischievous grin. Beth smiled, refusing to answer.

'I'm telling you, she did,' Cameron insisted, reaching out to catch his assignment as Miss Doyle tossed it to him. 'Wow!' he gasped. 'I got a mark! Twenty-two percent! I like the number twenty-two. It has a nice ring to it, doesn't it? And twos are such noble, dignified looking numbers. With their straight little bottoms and nicely curved tops—a bit like Beth …'

Warmth rushed into Beth's face while Miss Doyle spun back to Cameron. 'That's enough.'

Cameron didn't take the warning. 'It's true. Well, from what I can see while she's covered. I wish—'

Beth sank lower in her chair, face flaming.

'Get out,' Miss Doyle hissed. 'And stay out until you can leave your corrupt little mind outside.'

Beth couldn't look as Cameron meandered out of the room. Miss Doyle continued handing out assignments but, to Beth's surprise, walked straight past her.

She returned to the front of the room. 'Those of you who haven't handed your assignments in will get a fail. If you were having problems I gave you plenty of chances to speak to me about it before now.'

Confusion washed over Beth as Miss Doyle's eyes met hers. She turned to look at Dara, but Dara was looking out the window. Would Dara really do that? On purpose? Cautiously, heart pounding, Beth raised her hand.

'Yes, Beth?'

'Did you get my assignment?'

Miss Doyle shook her head. 'No, and I admit I was surprised. Did you place it on my desk?'

Beth glanced in Dara's direction, then back to Miss Doyle. 'No,' she admitted. 'Someone else said they would hand it in for me.'

Miss Doyle considered her for a moment, then asked. 'Did you type your assignment on the computer?'

She managed a nod.

'Bring me a copy tomorrow, and I'll give you a form your parents can sign to confirm the date you completed the assignment. If they look at the date the file was last modified it will prove it was done before the due date.' She looked around the room. 'Let this be a lesson to everyone. Submit your own assignments.'

Humiliation coupled with red hot anger built up inside, and her throat burned. What should she do? Should she dob Dara in? Or should she first speak with Dara and ask her to confess? After all, in the Bible Jesus said you should speak to the offender first. Surely Miss Doyle didn't think she let Dara put her assignment in because she couldn't be bothered to do it herself? She always took great pride in her work and this was the first time she'd ever been late.

Beth caught Dara as they headed for their next class. 'What did you do with my assignment?' she demanded through clenched teeth.

Dara shrugged carelessly. 'Not sure. Sorry about that.'

'Dara,' Beth hissed. 'What do you mean you're not sure? You handed *your* assignment in.'

'Yeah. I must have accidentally dropped yours or something.' Dara kept walking.

'Accidentally?'

Dara put on an injured look. 'Oh come on, Beth, I was trying to do you a favour.'

Beth snorted. She couldn't help it. 'A favour?'

Dara's injured look disappeared and she let out a sneering laugh. 'Maybe this happened for a reason. You need to learn that school isn't everything. You are such a perfectionist.'

'You need to tell Miss Doyle what you did ... about how you talked me into letting you submit it for me.'

'I don't think so.' Dara pushed ahead and let out a mocking

laugh. 'It's not, how do you say it? —a matter of eternal significance.'

Beth raced to keep up with her. 'It's significant, because it's my life you're messing with.'

Dara's lips slid into an infuriating smile. 'But God is in control, Beth.'

She was throwing her own words back at her. Beth didn't really know what hate felt like, but she figured what she was feeling right now must be pretty close. She threw down her school bag as they arrived at the next class. She wanted to hurt Dara. She wanted to get even for all the times she'd used her, deliberately hurt her and thrown her compassion back in her face.

Her eyes bored into Dara's, needing to wipe the smirk off her face. 'God *is* in control when you let him be, Dara, but if you're honest, you have to admit you've never let him have control of your life. You just keep clinging to your own desires, manipulating everyone, building yourself up to tear others down. You used me because you think I'm weak, but you're wrong. And it's not going to happen again.'

Dara's mouth dropped open. Then her lips trembled. Beth didn't back down. It was something she should have said a long time ago. Maybe not in anger and not in those words, but she refused to be a doormat. Dara had driven Beth Bateman to assert herself and now everyone was in for a surprise.

Dara pushed past students lining up for class and charged down the corridor.

Anique looked at Beth, eyes filled with concern. 'What's up with her?'

'She's having another attention-seeking moment.' Beth knew she sounded heartless and she saw the shocked expressions of her classmates, but even that annoyed her. Why should she always be the one to tolerate Dara's manipulative ways? Who made it her job? Let one of them do it for a change.

'Beth, that's a bit harsh,' Anique ventured.

'No, it's true. I've had enough.'

She bent to get her books and pens out of her bag, refusing to look at anyone. She wasn't going to unload all the details, but neither would she allow herself to feel guilty for standing up for herself. She would not carry Dara any further down this journey of life. She was too weary. Dara needed to find her own faith, her own life, her own friends.

Because Beth was done.

CHAPTER THIRTEEN

Beth bit her lip as she studied the form Miss Doyle and given her. She couldn't get her parents to sign it. Dad was dead and she couldn't bear to think what Mum would say. She couldn't tell Clare and let her know how right she was about Dara; that Beth had been a fool trying to help her.

Instead, she went to Phil. His understanding made her want to cry, but she held it in while he checked the date on her file and signed the form. Then she re-printed her assignment and tucked it in her bag. Nothing would stop her handing it in personally this time.

She handed it to Miss Doyle first thing the next morning, then sat on the bench outside the office. She needed to avoid Dara today—it scared her what might come out of her mouth in anger —and that meant avoiding the rest of the class as well. But when Dara crept into class late after recess, her eyes red-rimmed and her head down, Beth began to feel a niggle of concern. Dara often looked miserable, but this was different. She wasn't drawing attention to herself or asking for comfort. In fact, she looked as though she wanted to run and hide.

When she was nowhere to be seen at lunchtime, Beth went to the office to check the sickbay. It was empty.

'Beth? Can I see you for a moment?' The deputy principal beckoned from her office. Beth nodded and smiled. Mrs. Hendon was a Christian, according to Clare, and a genuinely caring deputy.

'Have a seat.' Mrs. Hendon tapped her pen on the desk, her expression serious. 'I'll get straight to the point. Someone has accused you of copying their assignment.'

Beth's mouth dropped open. Dara.

'I know your integrity has always been of the highest order. I don't believe for a moment that you actually did. You have no need to.' She frowned. 'I'm intending to find out what is going on. I'm sorry, but when an accusation like that is made I have to check it out.'

Beth cleared her throat and managed to speak despite the burn behind her eyes. 'I know it was Dara.' She felt sick to the stomach and tears welled up.

Mrs. Hendon's eyebrows lifted. 'Can you tell me how?'

And so, Beth explained the whole story. 'I don't understand why Dara is out to hurt me and pull me down, but she is.' Beth gave a helpless shrug.

'I'll collect the form you handed in to Miss Doyle and I'll speak to Dara again.' Mrs. Hendon touched Beth's shoulder, her eyes kind. 'Don't let it get to you. You are a high achiever and a genuinely nice person. Those who can't be what they want to be, like to knock down those who can.'

Beth stared at her hands. 'But this isn't what I want to be,' she whispered. 'I don't want to be a tall poppy everyone wants to cut down.'

'Not everyone. I've seen the way most students love and respect you. Don't be discouraged by the one or two who don't.'

Beth nodded, but her heart remained heavy. Mrs. Hendon let her go and she headed straight to the girl's toilets, trying to control the rolling of her stomach. She lost the battle, along with the bite of lunch she'd managed to force down earlier.

By the last class, rumours were spreading that Dara had been suspended. No one seemed to know why and Beth didn't enlighten them, even though a small, bitter part of her wanted them to know. But she refused to lower herself to Dara's standards and spread gossip. She'd already failed to point Dara to Jesus, and adding to that guilt would be too heavy a burden to bear.

BETH RODE to the farm after school, still feeling sick and sad. She fed Gilbert, then headed inside. Phil and Clare were eating afternoon tea at the kitchen table. Their eyes lit up with welcoming smiles.

'Did the situation with the assignment get sorted?' Phil held out a plate of cake, which she declined with a shake of her head.

'Yes, all sorted now, thanks.' She made herself smile. Better to leave it at that.

A heavy rapping noise startled her and she looked up to see Rod through the screen door. He laughed. 'Don't tell me you're still scared of me?'

Beth smiled at the running joke, but it was half-hearted. Rod didn't seem to notice. He pulled the door open and held out a sheet of paper. 'This is a list of names for the project.'

Clare opened the door for him and scanned the list. 'We've been approved?'

Rod nodded and stepped inside. 'Yep. We can go ahead. And these are our first delinquents.'

'Rod!'

He grinned. 'Well, they are.'

Phil frowned as he joined them. 'I haven't found a builder yet.'

Rod shrugged. 'That's okay. There's plenty of other things they can do.'

'But the shearers' accommodation burned—'

'I know. That's why we reduced our starting number. Your parents said they're happy to have the wards stay with them while we build the new accommodation. And we can use the insurance payout from the fire to help with costs. God's worked it out perfectly.'

Phil took the list from Clare and studied it. 'Six? That's a good start.'

'It is.' Rod's eyes lit up. 'They're a great bunch, although I heard that Joel Elliott's a bit of a handful. Not that I can't handle that. I mean, I was a bit of a delinquent myself, wasn't I?'

Phil chuckled. 'I wouldn't say that.'

'No, you're too polite, but admit it, you probably called me something like that once or twice in our high school years.'

'Maybe, but you had names of your own for me—ones that make *delinquent* sound tame.'

Rod didn't deny it. 'Keep the list,' he said when Phil held it out to him. 'Pray for them.' He headed to the door, then whirled back around and roared in Beth's face. She jerked back, hand flying to her pounding chest. He laughed. 'You can't kid me you're not scared of me now, Little Clare.'

Adrenaline still surged and she glared at him. 'The only thing that scares me is your bad breath. Please keep it out of my face in future.'

Phil burst out laughing, while Rod blinked a couple of times as though he'd never seen her before. Then his mouth slowly tipped up and he sauntered out the door without another word.

Beth saw the look that Clare was giving Phil. 'What?'

Clare grinned. 'You're going to end up marrying that guy, Beth.'

She choked on a laugh. 'Not a chance.'

'Yeah, not a chance.' Phil put Rod's list on the table. 'Your mother would never let her daughter marry a delinquent.'

'Phil!'

'What? Those are his own words, remember? And admit it, you know it's true.'

'It used to be true,' Beth corrected. 'He's definitely changed for the better.' Even if he still liked provoking people.

Clare studied her with a knowing smile. 'I find it very interesting that you're defending him.'

'And on that note, it's time for me to leave.' Beth made a beeline for the door.

Phil's brows rose. 'But we haven't finished our discussion about you marrying Rod Green.'

'Discuss it with each other. I'm not interested.'

'Yeah, we should have known.' Clare gave her husband a sideways glance. 'Beth will only marry someone extremely rich, extraordinarily intelligent and incredibly handsome, and Rod Green is none of those.'

'True. Very true.' Phil winked at Beth as she escaped out the door. She couldn't help smiling as she rode home. Clare and Phil always left her feeling seen and appreciated.

CHAPTER FOURTEEN

The wards are arriving at the Cairn's farm soon. I don't know what to think. I'm curious but a bit nervous too. What will they be like? How much will life change with them around?

Beth looked up from her journal. Clare and Phil were only part way through their social work course and while Rod oversaw the project. A government inspector had already been out to the farm to assess the program and plans Rod and the Cairns had prepared.

'The inspector says it's a perfect location and that we have what it takes,' Phil told Beth, his tired eyes lighting up with enthusiasm. 'Now we just need to continue praying for those we're caring for; that God will reach in and touch their troubled hearts.'

Guiltily, Beth acknowledged she hadn't been praying.

'Rod wants me to organise a prayer meeting,' Phil said. 'We need to be praying for a builder, a counsellor and for each of the teenagers.'

Beth nodded, but couldn't help feeling annoyed with Rod. No doubt he'd expect Phil to have the meeting in his own home, too. Couldn't he see how tired and unwell Phil looked?

BETH WAS RELIEVED to find the prayer meeting was in the Cairns' lounge room at the main farmhouse. Dale and Maria welcomed everyone in with warm smiles. The room was messy but had a homey feel, and Beth wondered how it would feel to live there, to feel comfortable and accepted every day of her life.

Anique and Andy turned up together and the group began to pray. Beth's heart was stirred by the way they brought each of the new wards to the Lord by name, asking His blessing on them and the project. Their passion and enthusiasm were contagious.

Andy approached her when the meeting came to a close. 'I feel like God's doing something special with this project,' he said, eyes shining.

She nodded. 'Me too. It's made me think about becoming a counsellor so I can work here in a couple of years.'

Andy looked out the window, his brow furrowed. 'Maybe I could apply for an apprenticeship as a builder or something so I can work here, too. They haven't found a builder yet.'

And suddenly Beth saw it. This was God's plan. The two of them working here as husband and wife. It made perfect sense.

Andy turned to Anique on his other side. 'What about you?'

'I'm going to be a teacher.'

'I'm sure they could use a teacher to tutor any wards who haven't finished school.'

'Nah, like I want to work with young kids, not teenagers. The kids coming here, are, like, too old.'

Beth smiled in relief. Anique understood this wasn't a game.

Rod poked his head between them, his shoulder pressing

against Beth's. 'Too old for what?' Beth moved over. With a grin, he stepped closer and nudged her into Andy. 'Too old for what?'

Anique flashed him a stunning but cold smile. 'If we were talking to you, you'd know, Rodney.'

He raised his brows. 'Call me Rodney and you're giving me permission to call you Edwina.'

Her smile disappeared and she took a menacing step toward him. 'I told you …'

He gave a satisfied smirk at her reaction. 'So what were you talking about?'

Anique's eyes narrowed and sensing more conflict, Beth jumped in. 'Andy and I were just talking about working here.'

'Anique thinks she doesn't want to, but she just hasn't realised how much she could teach them.' Andy gave Anique a playful poke. 'I mean, her dress sense is pretty special and I'm sure the wards would love to learn from her.'

'Not funny.' Anique glared, and Beth wondered once again at Andy's insensitivity. He knew the trouble Anique's *dress sense* was causing at church and school. Why would he say something like that?

He slid his arm around Anique's waist in a manner that looked far too comfortable. 'Of course it's not funny. Our church members need to learn tolerance and they might as well start with you. I'm learning to tolerate you very well.'

Anique spun away from him and charged out the door. The grin slid off Andy's face, and Rod shook his head. 'I think you pushed too far, mate.'

Beth couldn't agree more. 'I'll go and see if she's okay.'

'No, I'll go.' Andy bolted after her.

Beth glanced at Rod. 'Not sure he's the best one to comfort her right now.'

Rod raised his eyebrows with a skeptical look that annoyed her. Didn't he think she was capable of helping? She raced out the door and scanned the yard. All was quiet, but shadows moved near the water tank. She recognised Andy's form and then Anique's smaller one. She watched as Andy placed a gentle arm around Anique's shoulders, then pulled her into his embrace. Anique leaned into him, all anger seemingly gone. Then Anique lifted her face to Andy's and then they were kissing. Even from where she stood, Beth could sense the slow, tender desperation in the kiss. Something deep inside her broke, and she swallowed hard. It was as though she were watching a movie and couldn't tear her eyes away.

'Those two are always fighting.' Rod's voice came in her ear. 'But they say conflict is part of every relationship. If they learn how to deal with it now, it will be better for them in the long run.'

Beth couldn't answer. Her gaze was locked on Anique and Andy.

Rod touched her shoulder. 'Sorry, that was insensitive of me.'

She pulled her eyes from the scene and looked at him.

He cleared his throat, looking uncomfortable. 'I'm not blind, Beth. I know how you feel about Andy. But don't give up. I don't think those two will last. Every guy likes a challenge and Anique is certainly that. Andy will realise it's steady, spiritual maturity he really wants in a girl.'

Rod thought she was spiritually mature? Did Andy think that? If so, why was he kissing Anique? He had always seemed to value spiritual maturity over appearance. Clearly she'd been wrong. He obviously wanted someone stunning. Someone extroverted. And someone thinner. Weight was the only one of those things she had control over. It was time to start an exercise program. She'd ride more, run every chance she had. She'd cut down on bread and biscuits and get herself into shape. It was the only hope she had.

Having a plan of action eased the pain somehow, but if she and Andy were meant to be together, she'd have to find a way to forgive him for kissing someone else.

CHAPTER FIFTEEN

Beth sat in the youth group planning session, her heart and mind in turmoil. Friday would be Clare and Phil's last Youth Group before handing over to Mr. and Mrs. Holmes. And Andy thought he loved Anique. Nothing would ever be the same again.

She half-heartedly listened as Rod threw ideas around the Cairns' table at a rapid rate while Phil added a measure of practicality and direction to them. Andy leaned back in his chair as though enjoying the whole show.

Rod twisted his own chair into the lino as he swung back on it. 'Let's do abseiling.'

Andy grinned in Beth's direction at Rod's outrageous idea. 'Where would we abseil? Down the side of the shearing shed?'

Beth winced. Knowing Rod, he'd accept the tongue-in-cheek challenge.

Mrs. Holmes cut in. 'Abseiling is too dangerous.'

Beth pictured the staid Mrs. Holmes with abseiling equipment tucked in around her skirt, making her way down the side of the woolshed, and smothered a giggle.

Rod looked disappointed. 'Well, maybe we can have a barbeque at the Cairns' place so everyone can meet the delinquents.'

Clare frowned. 'Rod, I think you should stop calling them that, especially now they've arrived.'

'Why's that?' He looked amused.

'Because it's not politically correct.'

Mrs. Holmes leaned forward. 'Too right. Yes, it would be more acceptable to call them something kinder.'

'Like what?' Rod sounded irritated, and Beth tensed. She'd heard him refer to Mrs. Holmes as *unnecessary noise* and she desperately hoped he wouldn't say it to her face.

Phil looked thoughtful. 'What about something that reminds them they are leaving their past behind?'

Andy gave a merry laugh. 'What about *Reformed Crims …*?' His voice faded out at Clare's disapproving look.

'Come on guys, let's be serious. They need our respect and support. We need to see their potential and help them to live up to it.'

The mood toned down and Rod looked around the group. He stopped at Beth as though only just realising she was there. 'Little Clare. What do you think we should call them?'

She blushed as all attention turned to her. 'I don't know.'

'You do. You're just too scared of me to say.'

'You know I'm not scared of you.'

'Then tell me.'

She pictured the way Maria Cairn had set up each of the spare rooms in her home with towels and little soaps on the bed, along with a welcoming chocolate. 'Guests, maybe?'

Rod slapped his hand on the table. 'That's it! We have it. From now on, we have *Guests*, guys. Our special *Guests*.' Everyone grinned, apart from Rod. 'I'm serious. It's a good name, and that's what I'm going to call them.'

Phil reclaimed control of the meeting, and Beth dreaded to

think what it would be like once he and Clare left. Chaos, most likely.

'We'll need to have the barbeque here at Mum and Dad's—they have more room,' Phil said, looking at Mr. and Mrs. Holmes, 'That way we can start with some games as usual—'

'Of course. Of course you would.' Mrs. Holmes nodded emphatically. 'Yes. That makes sense.'

'We might leave the singing—'

'Yes. Of course. There's no need for singing, is there?'

'... until the end.'

'At the end. Okay. Yes, at the end is the most sensible way.'

'We think Beth and Andy should keep their positions as assistant leaders and work with you.' Phil was looking at Mr. Holmes but Mrs. Holmes continued her commentary.

'Certainly. It's lovely to have the young ones involved in leading.'

Andy rolled his eyes toward Beth and she tried to hold back a smile. Mrs. Holmes really was over the top.

Phil continued. 'Clare and I would still like to keep our contact with the group.'

'Of course. Yes, you must have your contact. Contact is so important.'

Andy jumped up from his chair and disappeared outside. Knowing he was out there cracking up was enough to cause Beth to lose control too. With a mumbled 'excuse me', she raced out after him. He stood by the water tank, wiping tears of laughter from his red face. Just seeing him set Beth off into giggles.

'Yes, yes, and why wouldn't you giggle?' He asked in a voice just like Mrs. Holmes'. 'Of course, of course. That's the best thing for everyone to giggle. I used to do it myself when I was a young one ...'

'Stop it.' Beth drew in some deep breaths.

'Of course. Of course I'll stop it. I've no reason not to, have I?' Andy's voice cracked on the last word, setting Beth off again.

She had just managed to gain control when she made the mistake of looking at Andy. His mouth twitched and it was enough to set them both off again. Beth held her sides, tears streaming down her face.

Finally, they both drew in some deep breaths, looking anywhere but at each other.

'You know, I've never seen you laugh so hard before,' Andy said.

She looked up, surprised to see a soft, thoughtful expression on his face—a tenderness that told her that in this moment he was appreciating her—not Anique. He was enjoying being here with her, enjoying their connection. Maybe if she'd been more expressive, maybe if she'd let Andy know how she felt about him before Anique did …

Clare's voice called from the back door. 'What are you two doing out there?'

Andy looked up at Clare and grinned, the moment broken. 'Just regaining control of ourselves.'

Clare walked across the grass to join them. 'She *is* funny, isn't she?'

'She's ridiculous.' Andy shook his head. 'Half the time she doesn't even know what she's agreeing to.'

Clare's smile disappeared. 'I know. It worries me a bit that she's going to be in charge of the group. She's so busy trying to be agreeable that she doesn't think for herself.' Clare looked between them. 'That's why we so badly need you two involved. Rod's great, but he needs, well—'

'Toning down?'

'I guess you could put it that way.'

Beth knew what she meant. 'You mean balancing out. Moderating. Regulating.'

'That's it exactly. He has great ideas but doesn't think about the practical side of them. Enthusiasm is great, but it needs common sense as well.'

Andy nodded. 'Don't worry, Clare. Beth and I will do our best. And we'll try to control our mirth.'

'Mirth?'

'It means amusement,' Beth said and Clare shook her head.

'You two make a great pair. You're walking dictionaries.'

'Thank you.'

'It wasn't a compliment, Andy,' Clare threw back over her shoulder as she headed inside.

Beth's grin faded. She wasn't a pair with Andy. Not the way she wanted to be. Despite her continued connection with him, he had kissed Anique and nothing would ever be the same again.

THE CHANCE TO meet the *Guests* arrived with the Youth Group barbeque. Beth observed from the sidelines, taking it all in, while Andy and Anique held hands and mingled with the guests. Dara and Brett were there, but Dara avoided eye contact with Beth, instead draping herself all over Brett. The guests surrounded Clare and Phil, drawn to them the way most people were. Beth wished she had their ability to be so warm, friendly and entertaining.

Phil's green eyes sparkled with life as he wrestled the youngest Guest for first place in the food line. From her place on the sidelines, Beth observed that Braydon appeared to be the most troubled of the new Guests. He was abrupt, reactive and constantly scowling—until Phil challenged him to a thumb wrestle for his place in line. As soon as Brayden agreed, Phil disappeared, then came back with a fork strapped to his wrist, the sharp tines resting just above his thumb tip. He then cheated in every way possible, leaving Brayden laughing helplessly at his antics.

Clare called for order and threatened to send them both to the back of the line. Braydon hesitated before recognising the teasing in Clare's open, friendly expression.

Phil crossed his arms. 'You wouldn't dare.'

'You know me better than to suggest I wouldn't.'

'I just did.'

It was on. Clare snatched the hamburger buns out of Phil's reach while he tried everything within his power to get to them, from diving under the tables to jumping over them. Finally, Clare had him backed into a corner, tongs in one hand, a tin of beetroot in the other.

'You have three choices,' she said. 'The tongs, the beetroot juice or the end of the line.'

Phil tapped his chin. 'Hmm, I'll drink the juice.'

'Not drink, Phil, *wear*.'

He grinned, and took a step toward her. She eyed him warily, snapping the tongs at his chest. All those around stopped and gathered to enjoy the entertainment. With a roar, Phil sprang at Clare, threw the tin of juice to the ground and captured her tong-wielding hand, holding it high above her head. 'You forgot choice four.'

She struggled before relenting. 'And what's choice four?'

'Embarrass you by kissing you in front of all these people.'

She relaxed, smiling into his teasing eyes, seeming to forget the group watching their every move. 'I dare you.'

When their lips met, the crowd let out a cheer and Beth looked down with embarrassment. They were so expressive and passionate. So in love. But as much as it made her uncomfortable, she dreamed of having what they had.

One of the Guests sped past on his skateboard. Joel Elliott. Didn't Rod mention something about him in one of the meetings? About him being trouble? She tried not to make it obvious she was watching him. He had no family and that was enough to stir compassion for him.

He leapt off his board and met Beth's eyes before giving her a brief nod of recognition and jumping back on. There was something perceptive in his look that made Beth suspect there was more to him than met the eye. He was tall and lean, and she studied his lithe, skilled movements as he manoeuvred his board. He came to a stop beside her.

'Not eating?' He glanced at the line in front of the food table. It had all but disappeared. Everyone else was either eating or going back for seconds.

Beth shrugged, a little flattered that he'd noticed her. 'I don't really like any of the food here.'

He nodded. 'Me either. No pizza.'

She smiled shyly. 'You must need to eat something, though. When you use energy like you do ...' She trailed off, hoping he didn't think she was flirting with him.

'You're right.' He grabbed two plates and handed her one. 'Better eat.'

She looked down at the plate, then watched as he raced his way along the table, grabbed randomly at the food, then paused, waiting for her to do the same.

She put her plate down. 'I'll eat later.' There was no way she could eat with his attention on her.

He studied her before sitting so close his arm brushed against hers. 'Good food,' he said between mouthfuls, 'and good company.'

She gave him a hesitant smile, baffled by the way her heart fluttered in her chest. She felt compassion for all the guests—that would explain it. They'd had a tough life and they didn't know God's love or what it meant to have a home.

'So tell me about yourself,' Joel said, his gaze intense though he couldn't seem to keep his legs still. Beth tried not to be distracted by his restless jiggling, and managed to mumble something about being Clare's sister and not being involved in the program. Joel asked a few more questions, but soon gave up. He downed a few cups of water then raced back to his skateboard. Beth tried not to watch but found it hard to keep her eyes off him.

'He's on drugs.'

She jarred at Rod's gruff comment in her ear. 'What?'

'That kid. He's on drugs.' He squinted as he watched Joel swing around on his skateboard and flip it up into his hand.

Irritation welled up, but she managed to speak nicely. 'He's not a kid, Rod. He's not much younger than you are.'

Rod grinned. 'Okay. That *Guest* is on drugs.'

'How do you know?'

'You can see it in his eyes.'

'You can?'

'Yep.' Rod wandered over to where Clare and Phil stood not far away. 'Watch that Joel Elliott. He's on something.'

Phil nodded. 'I thought so. What do you think it is?'

'Probably just MDMA. His pupils are dilated and he can't sit still.'

Trust Rod to know all the drugs and their effects. *Just* MDMA? Any drug was a big issue. She tried to block out what they were saying, surprised by her depth of disappointment. It was clear she couldn't afford to become attached to any of the Guests.

CHAPTER SIXTEEN

Despite wanting to keep her distance from the Guests, Beth began jogging the farm tracks in her quest to lose weight. When she was stuck inside, negative thoughts and memories of Grandpa's last moments swarmed her mind. Studying helped, but she didn't want to live and breathe school.

She loved the wildlife she spotted on the less-used tracks. Just this week she'd surprised a wombat and two echidnas. If only poor Gilbert would heal and be able to fly free again. There was something exhilarating about being out here in the sunshine amongst the trees.

She jogged past the Cairns' farmhouse, slowing down when she spotted Brayden trying to stop the Cairns' cow from eating the flowers he'd obviously just planted. Amused, Beth slowed down. When Brayden spotted her, he put on a show, using his whole body to shove the cow through the back gate. The cow didn't budge, and he collapsed onto the ground, breathing hard. Beth couldn't help laughing, and encouraged, he got back up and started again. Peggy was a large cow and not easy to push around.

She made her way back to Clare and Phil's, still smiling. Their cottage was a mess, so she pulled out the vacuum cleaner. Clare was so busy with the Guests she didn't have time to keep up with housework.

The door banged and Beth turned. Clare stood there. 'Don't worry about cleaning, Beth. I was hoping you'd spend time with me and the girls.'

'I think I can help better here. You and Phil have been pretty busy since they all arrived.' Besides, the three girls appeared very cliquey and Beth didn't like to intrude.

Clare glanced around the messy lounge room. 'We have been busy, and I appreciate your help. It's just I think the girls could use some ... well, genuine friendship.'

Beth smiled. 'And that's exactly what you've been giving them. You have a gift with people. I'm better at doing background things like cleaning. So leave this to me and go and spend time with them.'

Clare didn't look convinced, but she left to go back to *her girls* as she called them. It wasn't that Beth didn't care about the guests. She just wasn't confident she could make any difference. She'd failed Dara and she didn't want to fail again.

She prayed as she vacuumed, and deep down she knew it was selfish to not at least try to connect. She put the vacuum cleaner away and headed down the road to find them. She stopped at the sound of metal scraping on metal. Andy was helping Phil load building materials into the back of the farm ute. Good on him. Phil was clearly exhausted, his shoulders appearing to slump a bit more each day. A builder hadn't been found and if Andy was going to work here one day, this was good experience for him. Admittedly, it was also refreshing to see him without Anique at his side.

'Look what I found.'

She turned to find Joel behind her. He grasped a tiny duckling in his long fingers. It squirmed and his hand tightened.

Beth's heart lurched. He was too rough and the duckling looked terrified. 'Joel, it needs to be in the pond with its mother.'

'Can't be. I killed the mother. Ran over it with my skateboard.'

Beth clenched her fists as she looked into his calculating eyes. He was lying.

'I did.' He lifted his chin. 'And all the other ducklings, too. It was more fun than bowling. Should have seen them go down.'

Anger burned, but knowing that was his intent, she refused to let it show. Instead, she gave him a level look. 'Then if this one survived, it needs a fighting chance. Put it back in the pond.'

He shook his head. 'Nah, I'll go one better. I'll see how it goes at skydiving into the creek.'

'What's that supposed to mean?' She felt sick.

'I dunno. I'll decide when I get there.'

He jogged down to the creek, and Beth's fury rose. How she wanted to slap his face right now. She charged after him and held out her hand. 'Give it to me!'

'I can't. Didn't Phil tell you I've got Oppositional Defiance Disorder?' One side of his mouth turned up, but Beth was not amused. The duckling had stopped struggling and lay still between his fingers.

'Let me give it back to its mother.'

'I told you, the mother's dead.' He put his face against the duckling's beak. 'Now, little one, let's see how you like extreme sport.'

Beth clutched his arm. 'Let it go!'

He blinked slowly. 'It's not wildlife, Beth. It's an introduced species. Don't tell me you love *all* creatures and would risk your life again?'

His knowing look threw her. There was no way he could know what happened with Grandpa. She'd never told another person.

'Joel, please!' Her pleading made no impact. He seemed to enjoy her distress. 'Don't you dare hurt it,' she hissed, through gritted teeth. 'This is no game, Joel!'

'Oh, it's a game,' he said, 'and I make the rules.'

What could she do? She was desperate now.

His eyes narrowed. 'Tell you what, you do anything that I want for a day—'

Something in his eyes scared her. 'No.'

He shrugged and to her horror, lifted his arm and hurled the duckling into the creek's rushing water. Instinctively, she leapt in after it. Cold water bit her skin, and gasping, she came to the surface. She glanced around wildly. The duckling was nowhere in sight. The water flowed faster and stronger than she'd expected and she struggled to gain a foothold. The force of the water pulled her head under and her throat burned as water gushed in. What had she done? She struggled blindly against the current, waving her arms around, searching for something to hold on to.

A strong arm grasped hers and she found herself dragged to the edge. Joel's wide eyes met hers. 'What the …?'

'Where is it?' She scanned the water for a glimpse of yellow feathers.

A shout came from the bank further upstream, and Andy raced toward them. Beth clambered up the bank, dripping wet.

'What's going on?' Andy demanded, breathless.

Something inside Beth snapped. 'I was trying to rescue a duckling,' she said, every carefully suppressed moment of rage seething out in a voice she didn't recognise. 'Because some people have no respect for life itself.'

Andy stepped back, eyes wide. Beth didn't blame him. She was scaring herself right now. She was shivering, but hot with anger.

'I wouldn't have done it if I knew you'd react like that,' Joel said, his eyes accusing.

She turned on him. 'What it means to me is not the issue. The whole issue here is that killing a duckling for the sheer fun of it is twisted and cruel. You make me sick, Joel Elliott!'

Joel's face fell. 'Maybe I am,' his tone was subdued, 'but I haven't known any other way of life.'

Beth gave him a blistering stare, letting him know his excuses didn't wash with her. Still, the way he switched from cold and heartless to repentant confused her. The cold seeped in till her bones ached and she couldn't stop shaking.

Joel moved toward her. 'You'd better get into something warm.'

She jerked away. 'Don't touch me!'

'I wasn't going to.'

He was lying again. He cast her a hurt look, but she felt no remorse. He turned and walked away and slowly, she lifted her eyes to Andy. His intense gaze set her heart beating faster.

'Let's get you into the warm.'

She didn't object when he put his arm around her and led her back to the house. 'He killed that duckling just to hurt me,' she said, her voice shaking. 'I'm the reason it died.'

Andy just looked at her, then pushed a strand of wet hair back from her face.

'How can people be so cruel?' She finally let the tears flow.

Andy gave a sad smile. 'It might sound warped, Beth, but I think he was actually trying to ... well, I think he wants your attention.'

'No, he just likes seeing me react.'

'Because he wants you to notice him.'

She lifted trembling hands and rubbed her eyes. She knew when someone was antagonising her just because they could— she'd learned how to recognise it in her brother, Dan. 'You're imagining it, Andy.'

He laughed softly and his arm tightened around her. 'It's hard not to lo ... like you, Beth.' His eyes searched hers as though looking into her soul. Overwhelmed, she looked away.

And saw it. A small, motionless bundle of soggy feathers lay on the creek's bank a few metres ahead. She broke free, unable to get there fast enough. Gently, she took the tiny creature in her hands and as its head lolled back she broke into sobs, falling to her knees and holding it to her heart. She despised the power water had to take life.

'Beth, Beth, give it to me.' Andy pleaded, his voice catching. She held it out, and he carefully took it from her hands. 'It's not dead!'

'What?' Hope surged. 'Are you sure?'

Andy smiled as, with great effort, the duckling lifted its weary head. It hadn't drowned. It was merely exhausted. 'I'm sure. Come on, let's get you dry and then I'll get this little one back to its mother in the pond.'

Beth was moved by the gentle way Andy handled the fragile creature. He walked with her to the door, then held the duckling out to give her one last look. 'It's alive and well,' he said as it gave a little peck at his hand, 'Go and get changed into some of Clare's dry clothes.'

He headed to the pond while Beth watched him go. What would it take for Andy to recognise his feelings for her and do something about them?

CHAPTER SEVENTEEN

Joel acted genuinely sorry but Beth knew she'd never be able to look at him the same way.

'What more can I do?' he demanded in frustration. 'You Christians are supposed to be forgiving, aren't you?'

Guilt consumed her. 'You're right. I'm sorry.'

'I don't want you to apologise. I want you to accept *my* apology.'

'But Joel, what you did was just—'

'Beth, stop it! I know what I did was thoughtless and I don't know why I did it. Can't you just let it be in the past and stop looking at me as though I'm a murderer?'

Was he? Who knew why he'd been sent to the program. Beth knew she wasn't being fair. She sighed, and to her surprise, felt the warmth of his fingers as he lifted her chin til her eyes met his. 'Can you try? Please?'

Uncomfortable with his touch, she stepped back and attempted a smile. 'I'll try. Because I know Jesus loves you.'

He breathed a sigh of relief. 'Thank you. Now will you go out with me?'

She let out a disgusted laugh. 'No.'

'Why not?'

Because I still don't trust you. You're a creep. Because someone else claims my heart.

She avoided his eyes.

'Because I'm not a Christian?'

Yes, and so much more than that. Did he seriously think she'd consider it after what he'd proved himself to be?

His eyes held hers. 'What if I was?'

'You're not. There's no *what if.*'

'There is. Come on, what is it? Is it because I was caught with drugs?'

'Were you?'

'Come on, everyone knows.'

'I didn't.' Not for sure, anyway.

'You suspected, though. Admit it.'

Okay, she would. 'You were high at Youth Group, weren't you?'

He smiled. 'Ah, now we're getting somewhere. Yes, I was, but Rod confronted me about it. I'm clean now. That's all that matters.'

'Clean?'

He looked at her like she was stupid. 'Clean means I'm not using.'

She managed a smile. 'Ah, okay. I've had a sheltered upbringing.'

'That's an understatement, but don't worry, now I'm here I can bring you out from under your ultra-clean rock and introduce you to my world.'

At her horrified look, he quickly amended his words. 'I mean, my past world. I'm totally out of it now, and there's no way I'd want you involved in it. I just mean I can help you understand it so you can rescue those who are trapped there.'

People like Anique. Beth nodded, unsure how to react to his

sudden sincerity. But there was no way she could consider going out with him.

BETH RODE out to the farm after school the following day. Her heart sank as Joel approached. She slowed, not wanting to be rude but wishing he'd leave her alone. Her skin prickled as he came up alongside her. She forced herself to be polite but kept her eyes straight ahead and her voice monotone. 'Good afternoon, Joel. Aren't you supposed to be working?'

'Nup. Finished for the day.'

She doubted that.

He waved his hand at the dirt road in front of them. 'You do this every day?'

'Ride? Yes.'

'So you know all the corners of this farm?'

She looked at him. 'No. The Cairns' farm covers a lot of land.'

He was studying her intently as though trying to work something out. 'You been to the conservation land Dale Cairn's got going?'

That sparked her interest. She hadn't even been aware there was any conservation land. 'Where is it?'

'I wouldn't go there. It's not safe.'

'Why?'

'Snakes and wild dingoes. You being a wildlife expert and all, you should know to keep away.'

She shrugged. She would ask Phil about the land later.

He drew her attention back with a sudden change of subject. 'So, have you been thinking about me?'

'What? No. You … you …'

'I what?' He grinned. 'I impress you? Miss Intelligent Dux has met someone smarter than her and she doesn't know how to deal with it?'

How did he know she competed with Andy for Dux each year? He knew too much about her. She shifted uneasily. 'That's not it.'

'Then what is it, hey?' He nudged her playfully with his elbow. 'I'm too good looking for you, too athletic, what?'

She knew she was blushing, and it seemed to encourage him.

'You've got a crush on me, haven't you?'

She shook her head emphatically. She'd never had something as mild and fickle as a crush in her life.

'Come on, admit it.' He smiled, reaching a hand to her face.

She backed the bike away. What would it take for him to get the message? She used her last resort. 'I'm interested in someone else.'

His eyes darkened. 'You know what your problem is, Beth? You're used to getting whatever you want. You've got the intelligence and talent to achieve whatever you want. But love doesn't work like that. Love is about raw emotion and nothing you do can earn or predict feelings. That's why you're so discontent, and why you're always worrying about what people think of you. It's because you can't control them.'

Shock and hurt rippled through her at the way he'd turned on her, but she refused to let him see it. It would be dangerous to show any vulnerability. She kept her voice even. 'Where did this come from?'

His eyes penetrated hers. 'Intelligence comes in useful sometimes. It can be used to discern the way people think. And I've got you and Andy Saunders all figured out. You need to forget about him. It's never going to happen.'

'I'm sorry, but you don't know what you're talking about.' She casually pedalled away, desperate to escape, but needing to appear calm.

'Don't underestimate me, Beth,' he called after her. She pretended she didn't hear.

Once out of sight, she rode furiously along one of the farm tracks, trying to clear her head of the too-perceptive Joel. Tiredness overwhelmed her and her calves ached, but she refused to stop. She really needed to get fit, but for some reason, the more exercise she did, the more tired she felt.

As the wind blew through her hair, her mind and body relaxed. She had missed this, living in Sydney. A kangaroo bounded across the track in front of her and she smiled. This was her happy place. Spotting a wombat, she came to a stop and watched it lumber over a fallen log. One day she would find its burrow, but she'd gathered enough special memories for today. Maybe tomorrow she'd search for the conservation land Joel mentioned.

She was almost back at the cottage when someone called her name. Slowing the bike to a stop, she looked back to see Rod jogging across from the sheds to meet her. He was puffing by the time he reached her. 'I've had an idea.'

Another impulsive idea that made more work for Phil? She hoped not.

'I'm going to arrange a bus to take youth group to a Christian concert in Sydney this weekend. We'll invited the Guests as well.'

'Okay.' Why was he telling her this?

'I'd like you to come as a leader.'

'What about Phil or Andy?'

'Phil's exhausted and needs to rest, and Andy's got some major assignment due.'

'Sorry, Rod, but I have, too.' She'd begun but hadn't finished.

He scowled. 'Come on, Beth, it's just an assignment. What's more important—building the Kingdom of God or getting good marks in school?'

She drew in a sharp breath. Why was everyone attacking her today?

'Sorry, Beth.' His tone softened. 'I shouldn't be taking my frustration out on you. You do what you have to do.'

God, what do I do? School was important and Mum probably wouldn't let her go to a concert anyway. She bit her lip. 'It's just that the concert is only one night, but doing well in school could help me into a job where I can make a difference for a lifetime.'

Rod looked thoughtful. 'I never thought of it like that.'

'You could ask Dale and Maria to go.'

He brightened. 'True. Thanks.' He set off at a jog toward the Cairns' farmhouse and Beth watched him, still not sure if she'd made the right choice.

'Thought you'd like to know I made a commitment to God at the concert,' Dara said as she walked into school Monday morning.

Beth tried to read her expression. 'That's great.'

'Joel Elliott did, too.'

'Really?' That was a surprise.

'We went down the front together.' Dara's smile was smug. 'He looked kind of lost—like he wanted to respond but wasn't brave enough, so I asked if he wanted me to go down with him.'

That didn't sound like Joel. 'And he went down the front?'

'Yep.'

So, the unbelievable could still happen. She needed to stop being such a cynic.

'Did you get your assignment done?' Dara asked.

Beth hesitated. 'Yeah. Why?'

'Well, I couldn't get it done because I thought I should go to the concert. Can you help me throw something together at lunchtime?'

Beth's heart sank at Dara's brazen request. She wanted to say no, but she needed to forgive. Dara was reaching out, and it would be wrong to reject her just because she'd made the choice to stay home when Dara hadn't. It appeared that Dara was meant to be at the concert so she could encourage Joel to make a commitment. If anyone needed God, it was Joel Elliott.

So, she spent her lunch hour helping Dara, constantly drawing her attention back to the task at hand while she regaled her with stories of the concert. Beth wished more than ever that she had gone and witnessed God at work. If only she'd let her assignment go, and allowed herself some encouragement at an uplifting concert.

Did I make the wrong choice, God? If only she'd asked Him before she'd made the decision to stay home.

CHAPTER EIGHTEEN

Beth rode up the dusty road to Clare and Phil's. Joel stood out the front, leaning against a vehicle she didn't recognise. He lifted his hand in a casual wave. She waved back but avoided him. He'd probably tell her he'd become a Christian and she couldn't risk him thinking that would change anything between them.

Phil wandered out of the machinery shed, covered in grease. 'Beth. How's it going?'

She tried to ignore the dirty streak on his face. 'Good. Who owns the ute?'

He glanced at it and his face lit into a wide, triumphant smile. 'That belongs to our new builder-carpenter. We've found our man.'

'That's amazing. Where'd you find him?'

'He's a mate from my school days. He's going to live on site and mentor the Guests as well.'

'Well, he's going to have his work cut out for him.' She nodded her head toward Joel. 'Do you think he could inspire Joel to actually work?'

Phil grinned. 'If anyone can do it, Gus can. He's the hardest worker I've ever known.'

Beth laughed. 'Phil, no one works harder than you.'

His face flushed slightly and he focused on wiping his greasy hands onto a dirty rag. 'I think you've got me on a pedestal, Beth. Wait 'til you meet Gus.'

'Where is he?'

'At the building site with Braydon and Courtney. They're levelling the ground and Gus is preparing some framework.'

'Why isn't Joel helping?'

'Because Joel's supposed to be mowing the grass, but he can't get the mower started. He's waiting for me to fix it.'

Beth rolled her eyes. 'I bet I could get it going.'

'Go for it.'

They exchanged grins and she headed over to Joel. He watched her with a cat-like stare that made her uncomfortable, but she refused to be intimidated. 'Having trouble with the mower?'

He nodded.

'Want me to show you how to start it?'

He made a scoffing noise. 'Bit hard to start a broken mower.'

'How do you know it's broken?'

'It won't work.'

Trying to make her feel stupid wasn't going to stop her calling his bluff. 'Where is it?'

Joel led her to the grass-stained mower sitting beside the house. He gave it a kick. 'It's so old I'm surprised it's still in one piece.'

Beth reached for the starter cord. She'd become an experienced lawn mower since her brothers had left home. To her amusement, Joel darted in front of her.

'I'll just try fiddling with the carby first.' He poked around the engine, and Beth tried not to laugh at his performance. He gave the cord a sharp tug and the mower started first go.

'I'll leave you to it, then,' she shouted above the noise, and wandered back to the shed, shaking her head. Joel might have become a Christian, but his aversion to work hadn't changed.

'Mission accomplished,' Phil grinned at her.

She grinned back. 'Anyone else you need me to motivate?'

'No one I can think of at the moment, but come and I'll introduce you to Gus.'

She followed him to to the building site. She might as well meet everybody's answer to prayer.

THE STARK DIFFERENCE between Joel Elliott and the new builder made Beth want to laugh. Joel was always dressed in jeans and a black, tight-fitting t-shirt that showed off his lithe figure, but the new builder wore a ragged old hat and loose dirty grey overalls. He was bent over a section of framework, pounding in nails with power and precision. He might dress like an old man, but his strength and stamina made it clear he was anything but.

'Hey mate, how's it going?'

At Phil's cheerful voice, the builder looked up, took off his hat and wiped the sheen of sweat covering his brow. Something about him stirred Beth's memory. His wide brown eyes were almost familiar, but everything else about him was … well, average. He was of medium build with medium brown hair and finely chiselled features that gave him a steady, serious look. The dark shadow on his chin suggested he hadn't bothered to shave that morning.

'I'm getting there,' he said without even acknowledging Beth. He returned to hammering.

Phil nudged Beth forward. 'Gus, I want to introduce you to my sister-in-law, Beth Bateman. Beth, meet Gus Richards.'

Gus Richards? The hammering stopped again and he gave her a brief nod of acknowledgment. 'Hello, Beth.'

She met his gaze and it all fell into place. Gus was the abused boy in the photo at Aunty Joy's—the one Aunty Joy had taken in as her foster son. But there was nothing about him that suggested he'd suffered trauma as a child—nothing to capture anyone's attention. He didn't even seem to care about making a good impression.

When it was clear Gus was not wanting to interact, Phil touched Beth's shoulder. 'Want to come with me to check on Brayden and Courtney?'

She might as well. Gus didn't appear to be interested in anything but his work.

'Where are you guys headed?' Rod walked toward them. He stopped in his tracks and stared at Gus. 'That's not him, is it?'

Phil grinned. 'Yep, that's Gus.'

'It can't be.' Rod's brow furrowed. 'How can someone change that much?'

'Knowing God loves you makes a huge difference. And changed circumstances help, too.'

Rod frowned. 'Yeah, I know he used to have to put up with his father's drunken rages and—' he winced, 'idiots who bullied him, but he's totally unrecognisable. He used to be such a skinny little runt.'

'It's been years. Eating well, and solid hard work builds up muscles.' Phil smiled. 'He's a man now.'

Rod's brow furrowed. 'I see that, but I hope he's a man with a bad memory.'

'Gus isn't the type to hold a grudge.'

'I hope you're right. Come with me. I'm going to say g'day, but I might need backup.'

Phil chuckled. 'You won't.'

'Well, at least come for moral support.' He beckoned to Beth. 'You too. He's not likely to beat me to a pulp with a girl there.'

With a chuckle, she fell into step beside them, but tensed when

Gus looked up. How would he react now that he was face to face with one of his childhood bullies?

To her surprise, he didn't react at all. He gave a brief dip of his chin, his expression neutral. 'Rod. I hear you've changed.'

'I have.' Rod's hands went to his hips. 'I guess I'll have to prove it to you, though.'

'You've got nothing to prove to me. It's God you need to show.'

Rod looked taken aback, and Beth felt for him. Gus was calm, but he wasn't being gracious. It was obvious Rod felt bad and needed reassurance. Surely it couldn't hurt to offer it to him?

Rod cleared his throat. 'I know I gave you a hard time …'

Gus didn't even look at him. He went back to his work.

Rod glanced helplessly at Phil and Beth, then cleared his throat again. 'I guess—'

'That was in the past.' Gus bent down to scrabble in his toolbox, still not looking up. 'It doesn't help to dwell on the past. Let's move on.' He took out a box of nails then went back to hammering.

Rod raised his eyebrows at Phil, gave a helpless shrug and walked away. Phil and Beth raced to catch up to him.

Rod kicked a stone on the road. 'I can't figure him out,' he growled.

Beth gave him a bemused smile. 'You and me both.'

Phil didn't appear worried. 'That's just Gus. What you see is what you get.'

'Well, it wasn't a very friendly "get".'

Beth chuckled. She didn't know how to feel now that little boy in the photo who'd made her heart ache with compassion, had become a capable man who clearly didn't need or want it. She just hoped that he would forgive whatever Rod had said or done in the past. But then, had she forgiven Dan—? She pushed the thought aside. She couldn't afford to go there.

Joel was sitting on the grass by the lawn mower as Beth wandered back with Phil. He put out a hand to stop her. 'I want to talk to you.'

She nodded and left Phil to continue on his own. Joel patted the grass beside him. 'Have a seat.'

Reluctantly, she sat cross-legged beside him and waited.

'I suppose you heard about my decision the other night?'

'Dara told me.'

He pulled a face. 'Dara? How did she know?'

'Didn't she …? Never mind.' Dara probably had nothing to do with Joel's commitment. She'd embellished the story again.

Joel picked a blade of grass and played with it. 'So, every-thing's cool between us?'

'Yeah, I guess so.'

He smiled wide, and there was something different about his eyes. There was more colour to them. Did coming off drugs do that?

He stood. 'Well, I'd better get back to work. And you'd better go and spend some time with that rescue bird of yours.'

Was there a threat in his words? Surely he wouldn't hurt Gilbert? He was smiling, but there was still something sinister about him.

Beth was helping Clare prepare tea when Phil arrived home. He drew Clare into his arms and kissed her, then pulled back. 'I'm just going to take another bottle of water to Gus. He's been out there hammering all day.'

Beth saw the way Clare's face fell in disappointment. 'I'll do it.'

'Thank you, Beth.' Clare smiled as she leaned against Phil's chest, seemingly oblivious to the dirt and grease smeared there. 'I'm glad you've met Gus. There's something very natural and likeable about him, isn't there?'

There was? How could someone be likeable if they didn't bother to connect with anyone? Maybe he actually talked to Clare.

Gus was still hammering when Beth arrived with the water. She placed it on a beam of wood in front of him. 'Phil asked me to bring you a drink.'

He paused, his brown eyes acknowledging her this time. She couldn't help thinking they were average like the rest of him. Nothing noteworthy or special. Not even the smallest sign of the hurt little boy in there.

'Thanks.' He set the hammer down, glancing around with one hand still holding together the timber he was in the process of nailing. Beth reached to hold it for him, and watched as he opened the bottle of water and gulped it down in one go.

'Want me to get you another one?'

'No thanks. I'll keep going.'

She jogged back to the house, wondering if Gus would ever try to connect with her, or if he was content to stay in his own private world.

CHAPTER NINETEEN

Beth was walking to class beside Dara when she heard Andy and Anique arguing up ahead. They often clashed, and Beth had mixed feelings about it. She didn't like them hurting, but neither did she like the fact that they were together.

'If you think it's that easy, you can tell them yourself.' Anique's beautiful eyes flashed at Andy.

Andy shook his head. 'That won't work. It's you they're dealing with. They need to know you're serious about not wanting them around.'

Anique stopped in her tracks, eyes now blazing fire. 'You think, like, I want them to keep coming around, don't you. You think I encourage them.'

Andy shuffled his bag from one shoulder to the other. 'I don't know, Anique. I've never been in your situation.'

'Exactly!' Anique glanced behind and saw Beth. Her lips tipped in a forced smile that was hollow and full of sorrow. The pain there haunted Beth. Why wasn't Andy helping her? Wouldn't a caring boyfriend get more involved?

It was time she stopped viewing Anique as competition. She would go to her and offer the support Andy appeared incapable of offering. But before she could, Anique bolted away while Andy sighed and followed after her.

Lord, what should I do? If I can help her, please give me the chance and show me how.

The school day was half over, and Anique was still nowhere to be seen. Beth heard whispers and the school was unsettled, but not even Dara had any information to share. Cameron threw his bag down in front of Beth's desk and sat beside her but she couldn't focus on whatever crazy thing he was saying because she was too uneasy. Something wasn't right. She could sense it. Like a dark cloud hovering, ready to unleash a storm.

Miss Doyle walked in and kicked Cameron's school bag back under his feet before leaning in to speak quietly to Beth. 'Can you go down to the office please?'

Beth's heart pounded as she got up. What was going on?

'Oh no,' Cameron moaned. 'How can I think properly now? I'll be too busy pining for my lost love.'

Beth gave him a half-hearted smile as she collected her bag, while Dara glowered at him. 'Maybe you'll shut up and the rest of us can concentrate.'

Mrs. Hendon was waiting outside her office. She spotted Beth and waved her in. The door shut, and Beth found herself face to face with a pale-faced Anique. Her eyes were red and blotchy.

Mrs. Hendon took a seat and motioned for Beth to do the same. 'There's been a bit of a drama unfolding, and Anique has asked if you can be here, if that's okay?'

Beth looked at Anique, not missing the unexpected answer to her earlier prayer. 'Of course. What's going on?'

Mrs. Hendon cleared her throat and leaned forward. 'We were tipped off that some drugs would be found in Anique's school bag. Of course we have to check out every tip-off and we found quite a bit of ecstasy, which Anique claims was planted. She needs to go to the police station for mandatory tests, and they also need to take some statements.'

Beth swallowed hard and her throat began to burn. 'How can I help? What do you need me to do?'

'Just be with me. *Please,* Beth.' Anique's eyes threatened to spill with tears and Beth's heart tugged. She'd never seen Anique like this before. Angry and assertive, yes. Never helpless and pleading.

'I'm here.' She reached for Anique's hand to discover it was ice-cold and shaking. Anique grasped her fingers, desperation in her grip.

'Please pray for me,' she whispered as they waited for the police to arrive.

'I have been and I will be.'

THE DETECTIVE SERGEANT knew Anique's background and clearly believed she was still using drugs.

'They let you dress like that at school?' he demanded.

Surprised by the coldness in his tone, Beth spun to look at Anique, surprised to find her deliberately slouching in a way that made her shirt come up, revealing her tattoo and navel ring. She gave a careless shrug and didn't answer. She'd transformed into a nonchalant, arrogant, teenager. The change was startling but it had to be a front. There was no missing the terror behind her eyes.

God, please help her co-operate. Help the detective be sympathetic and find the truth.

Beth rested a hand on Anique's arm, hoping the reminder that she wasn't alone would give her courage. To her relief, she sat up straighter and lowered her gaze.

The detective's look was intimidating. 'Let's get to business. I have your statement, but you haven't given me any names. I need the names of anyone who has approached you about drugs.'

Anique looked stricken. 'You know I can't, sir. If any of them are caught, I'm the first on their hit list.'

The detective looked hard at her and when his expression softened, Beth knew he also sensed her genuine fear. 'Okay, no names at this stage. Just dates and situations so we can get you in the clear.'

Anique nodded and started listing times, dates and locations she had been approached. Beth listened in horror. There was a whole other world out there she hadn't known existed.

Then Anique hesitated and glanced at Beth before swallowing hard. 'I was also approached at the Cairns' farm.'

Beth couldn't contain her gasp. Anique couldn't be serious, could she?

She was. She listed times and dates, that coincided with Youth Group. But surely it had stopped since Joel became a Christian? Surely it was linked to him?

It hadn't stopped. When Anique reported yesterday's date at the farm, Beth wanted to weep. What did this mean for the program? Why hadn't she let herself get to know the Guests better? She may have been able to help Anique, to be aware of what was going on. This was going to break Clare and Phil's hearts.

Anique was taken to the hospital for tests and Beth sat outside, her mind so full of thoughts she could pick out none to think.

Anique returned and blew out a breath. 'Well, those drug tests will come back clear and hopefully they'll leave me alone for a bit.'

'Who? The dealers or the police?'

'Both. The dealers know I'm being watched now, and the police know I wouldn't dare use or deal while they're watching.'

Beth nodded, then threw her arms around Anique, giving her

an impulsive hug. Even if Anique didn't need it, she did. Anique hugged her back, then stepped away, tears glistening in her eyes. 'Thanks for being here for me, Beth. I know I can trust you and talk to you. I need that right now.'

'God's here for you too,' Beth whispered, hoping she didn't sound preachy. 'I've been praying for you all day because He put you on my heart. Whatever happens, you have to believe He loves you.'

Anique swallowed hard and hugged her again.

BETH WASN'T sure how much she was allowed to tell Clare and Phil. She wandered down the dirt road to their cottage, deep in thought. She turned, startled, when Joel appeared at her side. 'I hear Edwina Trent was caught with drugs.' There was no compassion or concern in his tone.

Beth glowered. 'She wasn't, and her name is Anique.'

His eyes widened before he quickly schooled his features. 'Sorry. Anique.'

Beth stared at him. Maybe he genuinely forgot her name. Her new name, not her birth name. How far back was he connected with her? Anique didn't mention any prior knowledge of Joel.

His brow furrowed as though he was concerned. 'Have you seen her? Is she okay?'

Beth remained guarded. 'She will be.'

'Did the police hassle her?'

'I don't think I should say.' How did he know she knew anything about the police?

Joel looked disappointed and hurt. 'You still don't trust me. I was just asking because I care.'

'Well, the best thing you can do is pray for her.'

'I think I can do more. I mean, I was into drugs once. Maybe I can help her.'

'I just told you she's not on drugs.' Beth shook her head and took off at a jog. Thankfully, Joel didn't follow.

MUM WAS ALREADY HOME when Beth arrived later that evening. She looked up from the laundry she was folding, and Beth's heart sank at the pinched expression on her face.

'Of all my children, you're the one I least expected to get involved with drug addicts, Beth. When your deputy principal called to ask if you could go to the police station with your friend …' Mum shook her head, lips pursed.

'I just wanted to be there for her. She was set up.'

Mum picked up a shirt and folded in the sleeves. 'I don't want you connected with criminal activity. No one can be friends with a drug addict. They don't have the capacity to care for anything but their next fix.'

'Anique isn't a drug addict. Not anymore.'

'A leopard can't change its spots.'

Beth held back a sigh. How could she make Mum understand? 'She really was set up—all her drug tests came back negative. The last time Anique saw her grandmother before she died, she promised to put her old life behind her and commit her life to God.'

'Hmph. Easy to say. Did she prove she'd really changed before she made these claims that she's a Christian?'

'Her grandmother said she could only change with God's help, and Anique said she knows He is helping. She told the detective that she's approached by dealers every day, but God has helped her resist. The dealers always offer her the first deal cheap or free because they know that once she's hooked again they're back in business. It would be a miracle to resist that without God's help.'

Mum didn't answer and Beth's conscience stabbed her. Did she really believe God was the one who helped people change? In theory, yes, but that wasn't the way she'd been living. *God, I'm tired of trying to change on my own. Please help me lose weight. Help me get fit. It's not working, no matter how hard I try. I need you.*

She fell into bed early, exhausted. Nausea threatened to overwhelm her again as her mind replayed the day. Poor Anique missed her grandmother. That was something Beth could relate to. She still missed Grandpa so much it hurt. Most days she managed to keep him at the back of her mind, but tonight she couldn't. Envisioning his kind, gentle face she cried herself to sleep, only to find herself in a nightmare.

The creek was dragging Grandpa downstream in its powerful torrent. She stretched out her hand, desperately reaching for him. His fingers touched hers, then slipped from her grasp.

'Grandpa!' she cried out.

But the brown curls now being swept about by the flowing water weren't Grandpa's. They were Andy's. He looked up, his eyes wide with terror. 'Beth, help me, please.'

But she couldn't move. She watched in horror as he was swept out of sight.

Beth jolted awake, sobs shaking her frame. 'No, God, please not Andy!'

And she wept until there were no tears left.

BETH RODE out to the farm early Saturday morning to feed Gilbert and see Clare. A heaviness had settled over her and she wished she could shake last night's dream. Maybe she should tell Clare everything. About Dara, Anique, even the sense of unease she felt around Joel. But no. Clare was busy and didn't need to be burdened with her little sister's problems.

Gus was repairing Phil and Clare's front step and her heart sank. She didn't want to face him, but it would look too obvious if she went all the way around the back.

He glanced up as she approached. 'Good morning, Bethany.'

She smiled. 'It's just Beth. Or Elizabeth, but no one calls me that anymore.' Not even Mum. She picked up a stray piece of wood that had made its way into the garden and set it beside him.

'Too messy am I?' His lips tipped in an almost-smile.

'No, no, I just ...' She shrugged, embarrassed. 'I thought you might need it.'

'A scrappy old piece of wood?'

Why did his look make her feel cornered? 'I don't know about carpentry.' It came out defensive. 'I wouldn't know if it's scrap or meant for your building project.'

He raised a medium-brown brow. 'I wouldn't expect anyone to think it's very usable.'

Irritated that she should feel the need to defend herself over something so ridiculous, she moved around him to go up the steps. He held out a hand to stop her. 'Just give me a minute to finish up.'

She held in a sigh. Might as well try to make conversation. 'So where are you from?'

'Sydney.' He placed a level on the step.

'What part?'

He glanced up. 'North Shore.'

He'd bent his head to work again but she persisted. 'Did you like living there?'

'No.'

'You lived here before that?'

He hesitated. 'Yes.'

His short answers left her with nothing more to say. The silence was heavy.

At last he looked up and met her eyes. 'How about you?' At least he was making an effort now.

'I live in Lydon Estate. It's a pretty upmarket part of town ... a bit like the North Shore.'

'Hardly a comparison.'

Beth held in a sigh. Why had she bothered? He was the most closed person she'd come across in her life. Even Rod was warm compared to Gus. How could Phil have thought he'd be good for the Guests? He definitely didn't have Phil and Andy's natural, friendly ease.

Andy. Her dream flashed and heaviness settled over her again.

'You okay?'

The concern in Gus's deep voice surprised her. She nodded, but he had stopped work and appeared to be looking for something more; something deeper than her automatic response.

She pointed to the house. 'I've got some vacuuming to do. And I know you have work to do, too.' She rushed up the partially finished step and inside without looking back.

She was almost finished vacuuming when she sensed someone had come inside. She glanced up.

Gus.

He sat at the table, drinking a glass of water. He was watching her and it seemed rude to ignore him, so she turned off the vacuum cleaner.

'I had a rough life when I lived here,' he said apologetically. 'I guess I don't find it easy to talk about. I prefer to focus on the present and future.'

Surprised by his admission, Beth studied him, then nodded. 'I understand.'

'I thought you would.' He fiddled with the glass, then with obvious effort, asked, 'So what are your plans for life?'

It was a deep question to spring on her from nowhere, and Beth didn't know him well enough to be willing to share her heart. But then, she realised, wasn't that what she'd been expecting him to do when she asked him about his past? Was he making a point? The serious expression in his brown eyes suggested he wasn't. His question was genuine, and despite it being awkward, she appreciated his attempt to connect. 'Um, I guess I'd like to be in a job where I can help people.'

'What kind of job?'

'Physiotherapist, maybe.'

'Have you always wanted to do that?'

His eyes hadn't moved from her face, as though what she was saying was important to him. 'Only recently.' *When Clare gave up that career path and Mum expressed such disappointment.* 'When I was younger I wanted to be a wildlife rescuer, but I don't think that's what God wants from me, anymore.' Memories tugged at her heart. It was a dream she'd had since she was a little girl, but she couldn't live it out. Not now.

Gus set his glass down on the table. 'You'd be surprised what God wants.'

Beth smiled. Maybe, but sometimes it was as though she knew exactly what God's plans were. Like for her and Andy. And yet, she couldn't shake the ominous feeling in her gut. The dream. She couldn't stand it if something happened to Andy like it did to Grandpa. And if it was her fault—well, she wouldn't be able to live with herself. She picked up a cloth and swiped at the dust over the fireplace, holding back tears.

Gus stood. 'Phil's asked me to look at the building plans on his desk.'

'No worries.' She kept her head down. If it had been Joel she would have watched his every move, but she instinctively trusted Gus despite his abrupt ways.

'What's wrong?'

She turned to see him beside her. He was looking at her hands, and his wide brown eyes held genuine concern. She realised for the first time that they were shaking. 'I'm not sure. Something's just not right.'

'With the world or with you?'

'With me.' She shrugged. 'I had a bad night. Nightmares.'

'About?'

'Things that have happened ... the things I most dread happening.' Why was she telling him this? Tears stung her eyes, and she tried to wipe them without him noticing. Nothing like breaking down in front of a near-stranger. She was usually such a poised, controlled person. 'Sorry.'

His brows shot up. 'What for?'

'I just ... you shouldn't have to put up with me like this.'

'There's nothing to put up with. You're allowed to express your feelings. I asked you, didn't I?'

She shrugged, embarrassed.

'You don't like being human?' Those medium brown eyes rested on her.

She smiled through tears. 'Well, no, I guess not.'

'And you don't like people knowing you're human?'

'No.'

'You like being invincible and impressive.'

Her laugh came out hollow. 'Don't we all?'

He sat back down at the table. 'I don't know. We shouldn't try to hide who we really are. It's deceptive.'

Beth recoiled. He had no idea what she was going through; what it was like to feel ashamed and inadequate all the time. To have so many regrets.

'I've cried before.'

Her eyes darted back to his. She wasn't expecting that. Awkward. How was a girl supposed to respond to a tough guy telling her he'd cried?

He leaned forward and rested on his elbows. 'My father despised tears so I didn't cry for years, though God knows I had reason to.' His steady gaze met hers. 'I cried when I heard Philip Cairn was dying, and when I first understood all God has done for me. I couldn't help it. But tears can be healing.'

Why was he sharing this? He was a paradox. First so closed, and now pouring out personal information like she was a close friend. Strange.

She sat down and faced him, feeling she owed him honesty in return. 'I think I'm too afraid to get too close to God, or love Him too deeply, because I won't be able to handle knowing He died for me. It's too much. Too overwhelming.' She'd never admitted that to anyone before. Not even herself.

'You've never read the account of Christ's death and cried?'

She shifted uncomfortably. 'No.'

'I suggest you do. Read it, I mean. It's more than a story. Let yourself feel it and remember it really happened. You can't change the fact that He loves you and died for you. It's already done. Ignoring Him is not going to do anything except hurt Him and you.'

He sounded abrupt again but his words stirred something in her heart. More than a story. She did believe that, but sometimes it just didn't feel real. God didn't feel real. Maybe she didn't want Him to. But Gus has given her a challenge and she would accept it.

BETH SAT ON HER BED, Bible open. She didn't even know why she was shaking. Maybe because this story—this truth—could be life changing. But as she began to read from John chapter 18, she wasn't reduced to the overwhelming tears she feared. Instead the truth sank deep into her heart—Jesus understood and shared her compassion for people. He loved her despite her poor choices. He went through all that awful torture for her.

She read how Peter denied he knew Jesus, and Jesus turned to look at him. She imagined the expression in Jesus' eyes would have a been a little bit like Gus's—warm, brown, concerned, and a little bit sad. But Jesus' eyes would also be understanding, forgiving, and loving. Jesus loved her with a love richer than she'd ever experienced or felt before. There was something so much more powerful and consuming than romance and emotions. Reality. Sacrificial love. *True* love.

Thank you, Jesus. I do want to get to know you more. Help me overcome my fear and live in the reality of your love.

CHAPTER TWENTY

Beth arrived at the farm cottage after school to find Clare sitting at the table, looking bemused. She held up a piece of paper. 'Rod's arranged a shearing day in our woodshed. He wants our Guests to arrange the food—give them catering experience or something. The only problem is, it's Phil and I who have to supervise—which is harder than doing it all ourselves.'

Beth frowned. Didn't Rod realise how much Clare and Phil were already doing? It annoyed her that he was so oblivious to the extra work he created. 'What's a shearing day?'

Clare gave a half-hearted chuckle. 'I'm not sure exactly, and I'm not sure Rod knows, either. All he's specified is that he wants Phil and his dad to give shearing demonstrations.'

Beth huffed out a laugh. Who wanted to sit and watch Phil and his dad shear?

Clare tilted her head. 'I thought you could invite Dara and Anique?'

Her heart sank. 'Why?'

'Because the Guests need to spend time with others their own age.'

Maybe, but she couldn't imagine Dara and Anique being the best influence on them. 'Dara would only come to flirt with all the guys.'

'You mean she's competition? I've noticed you haven't made any effort to spend time with the girls out here.'

What was she saying? Beth pushed back her hurt. 'They're cliquey. They don't want me around.' She cringed when Clare gave her the older-sister look she so despised. 'I'm not an extrovert like you are, Clare.'

'I'm not saying you should spend all your time with them. I'm just suggesting you invite Dara to the shearing day.'

Beth was confused. She'd though Clare didn't like Dara. Had defending her and not telling Clare what had happened at school backfired? 'She's manipulative and attention-seeking remember?'

'Which is why she needs God. If you're too worried about protecting yourself to invite her, I will.'

Beth's throat stung. 'She comes to Youth Group. That's enough. And the farm is a safe space for me—one where I'm free from her deception and manipulation. I need that.'

Clare's eyes narrowed and she set the list down on the table. 'It's not always about you, Beth. I've seen the way the guys take notice of you out here. I think you secretly enjoy it, and you're worried Dara and Anique will be competition. It's okay to enjoy their attention, but just be careful you don't lead them on. And don't protect yourself at the cost of peoples' spiritual well-being.'

Beth's mouth dropped open. Rod had said something similar when she'd chosen to put her schoolwork before the Christian concert. Holding back tears, she left the house without another word. Clare didn't understand. The farm was her only refuge; the one place she felt she belonged. She couldn't lose that.

DARA ARRIVED at the farm shearing day holding Brett's hand. 'Clare rang and invited me,' she told Anique. 'She needs someone who can connect with the younger girls.' She looked sideways at Beth before moving on. Beth breathed out a heavy sight. Dara was always embellishing facts, making herself the hero of every story.

'What are you looking so worried about?'

Beth managed to smile at Joel. He had a way of sneaking up on her that left her uneasy. 'Do I look worried?'

'Would I ask why if you didn't?' His mouth turned up in a sideways smirk.

'I never know with you.'

He opened his mouth to say something, but Beth noticed Clare watching, and slipped away. No need to prove her theory that Beth enjoyed male attention. She searched for some females to talk to.

Anique and Andy stood beside the dessert table, chatting with Phil. The three girls from the program were talking with Rod and Gus. A group of girls from Youth Group sat together giggling and talking behind their hands. They'd never included her when she'd moved to town a year ago, and she'd given up trying connect with them. Even in Sydney she'd been the quiet, shy girl who moved from group to group, but never quite fit anywhere.

Dara joined the group of girls, and Beth caught her name. Dara let out a high-pitched laugh and nodded at whatever the girl had said. 'Cameron Oliver would get it on with Beth Bateman if she'd stop giving him the red light. It's like she thinks she's too good for him.'

Another girl made a scoffing noise and whispered to the girl next to her.

And that was exactly why Beth didn't want to fit in. Yes, she preferred male company, but only because she couldn't seem to develop genuine, close friendships with girls. They always ended up seeing her as competition. She slipped away to sit on a hay bale away from everyone. Rod came to sit beside her and she looked down, hiding her flaming face behind her hair. Obviously he'd heard Dara's comment, just as anyone within a ten metre radius had.

He ran his hands down his jeans. 'I don't know why you bother with Dara. She knows what's right and wrong. She just chooses to ignore it.'

Beth glanced up to see Dara now at the drinks table. She drew in a deep breath, and Rod followed her gaze. 'Don't worry, she's too far away to hear.'

Beth laughed nervously. 'You don't know Dara.'

'Maybe not as well as you do, but I'm not in any rush to, either. She's toxic. But if you need me, I'm here.' He grinned and put his arm around her. 'Nobody's game to cross the legend that is Rod Green.

She released a tense chuckle. What if Clare was still watching? To her relief, Phil's voice boomed through a speaker, announcing, 'Dessert's ready, guys.'

Rod jumped up to join the mob charging toward the tables. Phil held his arms out to stop the stampede, then lifted two fingers to his mouth. His shrill whistle stopped everyone in their tracks, and Beth smiled. Mum had been horrified the first time she'd heard Phil give that whistle. Maybe it wasn't dignified, but it was effective.

'Righto you lot,' he yelled, 'Anyone with a birthday in January can go first.'

'No way!'

'Not fair.'

'Come on, Phil.'

Anique and Brayden went to the table, while everyone else groaned and complained.

'Anique, grab some for me while you're there,' Andy yelled,

but Anique shook her head and shot him a triumphant smile. 'Get your own, Mr. December.'

Andy looked around and Beth's heart sank as his gaze met hers. He knew her birthday just as she knew his. 'Beth? Aren't you having any?'

Everyone turned to look at her. 'No.' Fire burned her cheeks.

'Can you get some for me, then?'

'And me,' another person called.

To Beth's relief, Phil stepped in. 'Everyone gets their own. February birthdays, your turn.'

Andy moved to her side, eyes twinkling as he leaned over and whispered into her ear. 'You could get some for yourself, take a mouthful, find yourself full and give me the rest.'

Beth bit back a smile. 'Germs, Andy.'

He let out his loud, merry laugh. 'You know I'm not scared of your germs. Never have been, remember?'

'Aren't you scared of *any* germs?' She was ultra-aware of the way his arm brushed against hers.

'No, and especially not yours. You're the cleanest, most particular person I know.'

'Particular? You make me sound fanatical or something.'

'Aren't you?'

'No.'

'Really?' His grin turned sly and Beth jumped up, out of his reach.

His eyes narrowed and the look in them set her heart racing. 'Watch out, Beth Bateman, I'm not finished with you yet.' Before she could escape, he leapt forward and pulled her into a bear hug. Just as quickly, he let go and sauntered away. She looked down at her shirt, expecting to see dirt or at least something there. It appeared perfectly spotless and unwrinkled. He'd had no ulterior motive? He'd hugged her just because he wanted to.

ANIQUE BECKONED for Beth to join her and Andy as the shearing got underway. Andy moved over to give her room, and then made friendly comments in her ear about Phil's shearing. It felt as though he was paying more attention to her than his girlfriend, but Anique didn't seem to mind. Beth was relieved there was none of the usual conflict between them today.

Phil finished shearing the sheep and stepped back as it ran down the slide. 'Anyone want to have a go?'

Silence.

'Come on, it's not that hard.'

Andy pushed Beth forward. 'Beth will.'

She gulped and took a step back. 'No ... no, I don't want to.'

Andy gave a sly smile. 'But Beth, don't you want your chance to prove you're not, how did you put it ... fanatical? Well this is the perfect opportunity. Go and shear that dirty, smelly thing.'

'No.' Her voice was drowned out by the chant Andy began for the crowd. 'Be-eth, Be-eth, Be-eth.'

Cornered. Reluctantly, she moved toward Phil, considering whether it was possible to dive into the middle of the flock of sheep outside and somehow blend in. Nope. Her shirt was red, and she knew it matched her face.

Gus suddenly jumped the wooden rail and landed by her side. 'I'll have a go, too.' Those brown eyes met hers for just a second before he moved toward the large, woolly creature waiting patiently by the pen.

'You hold the handpiece and I'll hold the sheep,' he said. Beth nodded, grateful he would be the one wrestling the sheep. She watched as Gus's muscled arms grabbed the indignant sheep and flipped it onto its back. He'd done this before, she realised. Eyeing the sheep askance, she approached, while the crowd cheered her on.

'Batesy! Batesy!'

She smiled. Rod Green obviously began that chant. He was the only one to ever call her that.

Gus turned the handpiece on, and she gingerly moved it over the sheep. She was so afraid of cutting the poor creature that she hardly clipped any wool. Gus watched silently with his serious expression before finally taking the handpiece from her fingers and shearing the patient sheep properly. Beth stood back, trying not to notice how strong and sturdy Gus was. She refused to be like Dara and all those other teenage girls who were only interested in how good a guy looked.

Gus had the sheep sheared in no time and the crowd let out a cheer.

'Is there anything you can't do, Gus Richards?' Phil asked as Gus handed the handpiece back to him.

'Not much. I'm blessed with being better at most things than other people are.'

And all Beth's admiration came crashing down. She was no longer impressed by the quiet, strong man. He had an ego to match his biceps.

'So did I prove myself?' Beth asked Andy as she slid safely back behind the rail.

He chuckled. 'No! You hardly touched that sheep.'

'Only because I was worried about hurting it—not because it was smelly or anything.'

Andy shook his head, still chuckling and Beth looked across at that moment to meet Clare's eyes. Dismay filled her. Yes, she was with one of the guys again, but Dara had been surprisingly scarce —much to her relief. Shame overcame her. She needed to make an effort. Leaving Andy's side, she approached Dara. 'How's it going?'

Dara turned away.

'Dara?'

Dara spun back to face Beth, tears sparkling in her eyes. 'So I don't know right from wrong, huh?'

Beth's heart sank. 'I didn't say that.'

'But Rod did. I do have ears, Beth.'

That was an understatement. Beth touched Dara's arm. 'I'm sorry for what he said.'

Dara shook her off. 'Yeah, whatever. You didn't defend me because you agree with him. I'm not stupid.'

'I didn't mean to hurt you, Dara.'

'But you did.'

Beth's mind raced. How could she fix this? She knew from experience that every word she spoke would be taken negatively and twisted. She didn't want to lie, but she needed a way to stop the truth from hurting. 'Rod's not an easy person to argue with, Dara. Even if I'd tried to defend you—'

'Real friends stand up for each other, Beth.' Dara stalked off, swiping at tears. She made a beeline for Phil and buried her head in his shoulder. He awkwardly patted her on the back, and Beth hoped Clare would notice.

'You lied to her,' a quiet, deep voice said from behind.

Beth turned to face Gus. 'What?'

'You lied. You agree with Rod, don't you?'

Beth stared at him, defences rising. 'I don't know.'

'What do you mean you don't know? You seemed to know your mind pretty well when you were talking to Rod.'

Beth glared. 'It's all a matter of how you look at it, Gus. You don't know the full story.'

'But you and I both know she's selfish and couldn't care less about anyone but herself.'

How dare he accuse her of lying? She'd done whatever she

could to avoid that, and she was so tired of people thinking they understood her when they had no idea. She rubbed a hand across her forehead where a headache was forming. 'I don't want to talk to you about it. I've got a lot on my mind.'

He opened his mouth to speak again but she darted away. It had been a confusing day and she didn't know what to make of Gus Richards. Sometimes he was attentive and caring, and other times he was cold and abrupt. How was anyone supposed to get close to him? Well, apart from Phil who had a gift that way and seemed able to connect with any person God brought his way.

Maybe Gus's past made him the way he was. Compassion crept in until she remembered his confidence and ego. He didn't need compassion.

CHAPTER TWENTY-ONE

Avoiding Gus wasn't easy. He seemed to be everywhere at once, constantly working and always observing. He was taking such a load off Phil and Clare's shoulders that she couldn't resent his presence. He clearly had a gift for helping others. If he would just work a little on his ability to relate to people, he could go a long way.

'That's a very thoughtful look,' Gus said, looking up at her from the building plans he'd been discussing with Clare. He wore an even raggier pair of overalls than usual with a tear in each knee and frayed sleeves.

Beth swallowed under his gaze. She couldn't tell him she was thinking how socially inept he was.

'She's probably thinking about Andy.' Clare winked.

'Wrong. I'm thinking it's time I dusted your bookshelf again.'

Gus looked up at the shelf with a studied frown. 'What's this business of keeping your books in height order?'

Clare laughed. 'That's Beth for you.'

Beth crossed her arms. 'Why, what's wrong with it?'

'It looks like a book shelf in a display home, that's all.'

Beth frowned. What was wrong with having a bookshelf that looked good? Besides, it wasn't even Gus's house, and Phil and Clare weren't complaining.

'I thought Andy was taken,' Gus suddenly said.

'He is.' Clare shot a teasing smile in Beth's direction. 'But Beth's always enjoyed a bit of competition.'

Beth stiffened. 'I hate competition.'

'That's a bit harsh.' Gus frowned. 'I thought you were friends with Anique.'

'I didn't say I hate Anique. She's nice. I just hate competition.'

'Ah …' Gus almost smiled. 'So, it would be easier if you didn't like her.'

'Exactly!' A blush crept into her cheeks when she realised she'd just confirmed her feelings for Andy.

Gus chuckled, and it was a nice sound. For a man so hard to get to know and like, she was finding it difficult to dislike him. He folded his arms across his chest, and it hit her.

She was attracted to him!

But she couldn't be. She hardly knew him. Clearly it was merely physical attraction; an infatuation; a fickle crush.

And that would prove Clare right. The safest thing would be to get away from him. Talking with Gilbert the galah would be a good idea right about now. She jumped up from the table and rushed out the door, down the backyard, and to the chicken pen.

DALE AND MARIA walked into church that Sunday with Brayden and Joel in tow. Feeling Joel's intense gaze on her, Beth avoided his eyes and searched for any of the girls from the program. They didn't seem to be here. Maybe they weren't coming.

The sound of Phil quietly strumming his guitar and singing

drew her eyes to the front of the church. She loved it when Phil led worship. There was an ethereal quality to his voice.

'Hi Beth.' Andy waved on his way past with Anique to find a seat. She smiled in return, and considered joining them in their seats down the front. But no, she should sit near the back and wait for the girls to arrive.

They finally arrived, looking hesitant as they came in the door, eyes darting in all directions. Beth gave them a wave and smile, hoping Clare noticed the effort she was making, but even the girls didn't appear to see her. They had all turned to look behind.

And Beth saw why. Her heart did a funny little jump and she tried not to stare. It was Gus, but it wasn't. The bristles on his chin were gone, his face smooth and clean-shaven. His brown hair was neatly done rather than poking up in all directions as though he'd run his dirty building hands through it. He'd replaced his overalls with a dress shirt and pants. He looked in her direction and she hoped he didn't realise she'd been staring.

'Good morning, Beth.' He dipped his chin, then slid into a pew beside the girls. Embarrassed, Beth put her head down and tried to still her heart for worship. But Gus kept invading her thoughts. Gus without that raggy old hat covering his face was quite a distraction.

Lord, help me.

He did. Phil's melodious voice filled the church, drawing her mind back to God. Phil's singing was like Andy's praying; it took him closer to heaven and right into the presence of God. Beth was drawn along with him. This must surely be a taste of heaven. She imagined the angels had voices like Phil's. Maybe God would gift her with a spectacular voice in heaven, too.

She looked at Clare, down the front of the church. How blessed she was to be married to Phil. But Clare's eyes were not on her husband. They were closed, a serene, joyful smile on her uplifted face as she worshipped God. What was it that made Clare so able to focus on God and so completely confident Jesus loved her?

The service finished with another song—one that Phil wrote—and Beth didn't move. Everything felt surreal. The emotion of the worship had left her feeling overwhelmed and the sermon about trusting God had challenged her. People around her got up and chatted as though nothing had happened. She needed time to think.

Gus was the first to interrupt her thoughts. 'Good service,' he said, sitting beside her.

'Yes.' She cleared her throat. 'Phil's voice is an amazing gift.'

'It is. I've heard better, though.'

Beth stared at him in shock. He was so ungracious. His critique was not only unnecessary, it felt irreverent. She wished he'd go away. She glanced around. 'Have you met everyone?' Maybe she could palm him off to someone else.

'I think so.' He wasn't going to make it easy.

'What about Dara's mother?'

'Yeah, I used to live next door to them years ago. She caught me on the way in.' His steady gaze and improved appearance weren't so appealing coupled with his abrupt nature. 'I think Dara's mother has plans for me,' he added seriously.

'What do you mean?' Dara's mother had plans for every young man she met, but Beth wasn't going to tell Gus that.

'She made some comment about me looking good in decent clothes, and that I've bulked up since I've been in the building trade, and then she reminded me Dara is single.'

She was? Maybe she'd had another fight with Brett. As much as Gus annoyed her, Beth couldn't help her grin. 'So does she think you'd make a good husband for Dara because you used to live next door, or because you've bulked up?'

'I doubt it's because I used to live next door. That was years ago—back when Dara was in nappies and dribbled all over every-thing. Not exactly the sort of memory that makes you attracted to someone.'

Beth tried to muffle her giggle. Gus Richards didn't seem to realise there were rules about what you should and shouldn't say.

One side of his mouth tilted. 'What's funny? Shouldn't I have said that?'

'You can say what you like.'

'But you wouldn't have said it?'

How did he read her thoughts? She shrugged. 'No, but I'm not you.'

'I say things that are inappropriate?' he pressed until she met his wide brown eyes and relented.

'You do tend to break the rules of social etiquette.'

'Whose rules? Yours or everybody's?'

'Everybody's.'

He pulled a face. 'Rules like that are convoluted, anyway.'

'Convoluted?'

'Twisted. Warped.'

What was this? She was the one who was supposed to be the walking dictionary. Maybe she'd met her match.

His look turned thoughtful. 'Maybe it's my lack of social etiquette that has protected me from marriage.'

Beth stifled her smile. As if he needed to be protected from marriage. 'So I take it you're not interested in marrying Dara?'

'No, I don't plan to ever get married. Life's busy enough without the concern of a wife.'

Beth didn't know whether to laugh or be indignant. He made it sound like having a woman in his life would be a curse. Maybe it was better for the women of the world that he felt that way.

When Phil tapped Gus on the shoulder to ask him a question, Beth seized the opportunity to slip away. And ran straight into Mrs. Holmes.

'Ah, Beth, so good to see you, it is. So good to have the young people here. I really believe youth group leaders need to attend church and be outstanding role models. Makes sense, don't you think?'

'Um…'

'You don't strike me as the type who is blown about by the wind, this way and that way.' Her eyes shot to Anique. 'You need to be of steady character, not making a spectacle of yourself …'

Beth took a deep breath, not quite sure what was going to come out of her mouth. She was cut off by Gus's hand on her shoulder. The warmth took her breath away.

'Beth, sorry to interrupt, but when you're ready, Phil's asked if I can take you home.'

'I'm ready.'

His lips twitched. Maybe she'd sounded too enthusiastic, but she desperately wanted to get out of there.

As they walked past a group of preschool-aged kids, they put out their hands. 'Hey Gus, high five.'

To her surprise, Gus's face became almost expressive as he high-fived each of the grinning kids. She blinked, trying to take it in. Gus Richards was a maze of contradictions. She followed him to his ute. He unlocked it, and she climbed in the passenger side. It was clean. Not what she'd expected.

She made herself look straight ahead, determined not to be caught looking at him again. 'Why did Phil and Clare need you to drop me home?'

'They were invited out to lunch, so I offered.' He indicated and swung out onto the road.

'I appreciate it. Are you taking me to the farm or my house?'

'Whichever you want. Clare said there's sandwiches in the fridge at at the cottage, and there'd be enough for both of us.'

Beth hesitated. Being home alone wasn't fun, but eating with Gus was not an option, especially when he looked as good as he did today. She wouldn't be able to swallow a bite. 'I've got school-work I should be doing at home.'

'Okay. Let's get you home, then.'

She gnawed at her lower lip, trying to think of something to say. She was relieved when he spoke first.

'The minister told me that lots of young people became Christians because of Phil and Clare's witness in their school years.'

'Yeah, they're gifted that way.'

He glanced at her. 'You don't think you are?'

'I can't witness the way Clare can.'

'Perhaps that's because you're not Clare.'

She heard the smile in his voice and looked at him. 'I mean I don't have the ability to have an impact on anyone.'

'We all have the ability to make an impact. We just do it in different ways.'

Not in her experience. Some people were born to make more of an impact than others. She didn't have the right personality for it, and in her opinion, Gus's abrupt, closed manner wouldn't help him change lives either.

He pulled into the driveway.

'Thanks for the lift.' She jumped out and made her escape.

He gave a brief nod and drove off. He was so hard to read, but she was probably better off not knowing what he was thinking. He was so not like Andy.

Andy.

She had homework to do, but the longing to see Andy overwhelmed her. She hadn't talked with him at church or youth group lately in case Clare saw and judged her motives. But she missed him. He was her closest friend and he always made her feel better. Even when he was with Anique, he always made time for her.

AFTER A BITE OF LUNCH, she walked up the steps to Andy's porch and hesitated. Raised voices filtered through the front door.

'I had no say in it.' That sounded like Anique's voice, becoming louder with each word. 'I wish for once you'd trust me,

Andy Saunders. You think you're so strong and that you have it all together, but you've never been through what I've been through. You're so self-righteous and ignorant!'

Beth wanted to run from the conflict, but she caught a glimpse of Andy's face through the screen and hesitated. He looked cut to the heart. How could Anique speak to him this way? And why didn't Andy realise she wasn't good for him? He needed a soul-mate–someone who loved and understood him like she did.

Her heart constricted as Andy turned away, his face bleeding anguish. He struck the wall with his fist then kept moving down the hall. She opened her mouth to call after him when Anique turned. Her face filled with relief.

'Beth!' She flung the door open and raced out. 'I was just about to ring you. Quick! Come over to my place before anyone sees you here.'

The urgency in her tone, and the fear in her eyes set Beth's heart pounding. Anique rushed her across the lawn and into the house next door. What was going on? Were the drug dealers still hassling her?

Anique shut the door behind them. 'Beth, I'm in trouble. I can't tell you what's going on but you need to be careful.'

'What? Why?'

Anique swallowed hard, her eyes wide. 'I can't tell you. Just believe me, and be very careful what you say.'

'About what?'

'About me.' Anique scanned the room as though anyone could be listening. 'For my sake, trust no one, Beth.'

'But—'

'Please!'

What was going on? Beth hated the terror in Anique's eyes. It was infectious.

'You need to get out of here before anyone sees you. Go straight home, and don't let anyone know you saw me. Don't tell anyone about this conversation—and I mean *anyone*.'

This was crazy. Beth felt like she was in some kind of television drama. She wanted to ask questions, to shake Anique and force her to tell her what was going on. Instead, she gave her a quick hug. 'I'll be praying for you.'

Anique didn't respond except to open the door and almost push her out. Once on the street, Beth broke into a run, looking behind every few minutes. If Anique wanted to set her on edge she'd done a good job of it. Her first instinct was to tell someone. Clare. Phil. Andy. But Anique said to tell no one. Apparently, she was in danger and all alone.

Not alone.

She remembered the overwhelming feeling of God's love during the worship service this morning, and as she ran, she prayed.

Help us, God. Help me. I'm scared and I hate it. I've lived my whole life in fear.

She'd never confessed it to anyone before, but it was true. She tried to be poised and controlled because she was so afraid of making mistakes; afraid of letting people down. What would people think if they knew she had caused Grandpa's death? She wouldn't be able to bear it—it was hard enough living under her own self-condemnation.

CHAPTER TWENTY-TWO

Beth's sleep had been filled with nightmares, and ominous thoughts plagued her all day.

What if the danger Anique warned me about is real?

It is real. God sent her to warn you so you don't make a mistake and let someone else die.

Beth warred with the internal voices. If only she knew which were here own and which were God's.

She rode out to the Cairn's farm after school and prayed for Anique. *Give her strength and courage, Lord. Bring her through this, and fill her with Your peace. Let her know You in an even deeper way.*

She realised that in praying these things, she was asking God to make Anique into everything Andy admired. Deep down, resentment bubbled. Anique had told her not to talk to anyone—including Andy. Until now, she'd been able to confide in him about anything. Not only had Anique come between them, she'd amplified the fear Beth already fought on a daily basis. If only she could turn back time and leave Anique out of the picture. Because if Andy married Anique, Beth would have to fight envy every day of her life. She would never marry. It wouldn't be fair on her husband, because anyone other than Andy would always be second best.

The other option is to wait around until Anique dies.

She gasped, horrified by her own thoughts. Slamming on her brakes, she gulped in great mouthfuls of air. *You're a horrible person, Beth Bateman! You're boy-focused, unfit, emotional, messed up, out of control and really, really spiteful. No wonder Andy's chosen Anique.*

She tried to shut out the voice that came whenever she felt tired and discouraged, but the words wouldn't stop. Spinning her bike around, she pedalled back home, intense loneliness and fear chasing her like a wild beast hunting down its prey. Throat burning, she charged inside and slammed the door behind her before falling onto the cold leather lounge. Curling up in a ball, she willed the silence to swallow her up and stop the pain, but instead, broken sobs burst out, stealing her breath.

A knock sounded on the door. She froze. What if it was one of the people Anique warned her about? What if they'd come after her as well?

'Beth? Are you there?'

Andy! But what if she said the wrong thing? What if she increased the lurking danger? She swiped at her tears, shaking, waiting.

'Beth, it's me.' This time he rang the doorbell. What if Clare had told him she hadn't turned up at the farm to feed Gilbert? She'd worry if she thought Beth wasn't at home. With a shaky breath, she forced herself to open the door.

'What took you so long?' His teasing smile faltered. 'What's wrong?'

A rebel tear tracked down her cheek. Anique's words plagued her. *Trust no one.*

If Andy hadn't made the mistake of committing himself to

Anique, they wouldn't be in this mess. But Andy was the most trustworthy person she knew. It was ridiculous to hold back from him.

His brow furrowed. 'Beth? What's going on?'

She couldn't speak. More tears escaped, and his eyes searched hers. 'Is it to do with me?'

In some ways it was.

'Me and Anique?' he pressed.

What was she supposed to say? Her head pounded as thoughts raced around. Andy took her arm and led her inside. He pulled her down onto the lounge beside him, concern crevicing his brow when her tears came faster.

'Beth,' he groaned, pinching the bridge of his nose. 'What have I done to cause you this pain?'

'It's not you,' she managed between sobs. 'It's me. Everything just keeps getting harder. I don't like who I am, but I don't know how to change. I keep hurting people and everything just feels so out of control. I'm scared … of everything.'

Andy said nothing. His shoulders hunched and he leaned forward, his head almost touching his knees. Finally, he reached over and pushed a strand of hair back from her face. 'Beth, its okay. You don't have to be in control. God is.'

'Is He? Then where was He when my dad crashed into that tree, or when I ran out onto the road and made my grandfather have a heart attack? Where was He when Anique was approached by those drug dealers?'

And where was He now that Andy and Anique were a couple and yet seemed so wrong for each other? Why had God let them all fall into danger?

Andy continued studying her. 'Even in this, Beth,' he finally said. 'Even in all these things, God is here. He's in control and He has a plan of redemption.' He said it with such confidence.

'But does His plan always involve crushing our dreams? Or letting us make choices that destroy them?'

Andy searched her eyes, then sighed. 'That's a good question —one I don't have the answer to.' He looked down at his hands. 'Anique and I broke up this morning.'

She heard him but it didn't sink in.

He bit his lip. 'It's permanent. We aren't meant to be.'

'Why?' Her mind swirled, unable to make sense of what he was saying.

'Many reasons.' There was such pain and regret in his voice. 'I care for her deeply, but we see things very differently.'

'I'm sorry.'

'You are? Really?' He looked up and his lips tilted in a knowing, almost amused smile.

'I'm sorry for your pain.'

He chuckled. 'I thought so.'

She rested a hand on his arm. 'Are you okay? Really?'

To her surprise he didn't answer but instead leaned over and pulled her into his arms. 'I am, now,' he said into her hair, his muffled voice tender.

She soaked up the warmth of his embrace, the way it made her feel, and she knew she would remember this forever. No more was said, but a thousand words had been spoken. Andy understood she loved him. That's what mattered. And she was certain he returned her feelings. It was there in his eyes and touch. She'd confessed what she'd done—that it was she who had caused Grandpa's heart attack — and he hadn't rejected her or demanded to know the details.

They walked out to the farm in companionable silence, and Beth treasured his presence beside her. Phil and Clare called times like these *eternal moments*—times when the world seemed to stop still to watch God's amazing plan unfold, and to experience and feel the depth of every breath, every thought, every second of time that passed. This was the closest to happiness she had ever felt, and she couldn't help smiling.

Even in this. Especially in this. God was in control. He loved her and would make all things right.

Andy spoke as they turned in the Cairn's gate. 'There's something special about this place, isn't there?'

'There is, and it's not just the people.'

He lifted his eyes to the hills. 'I always feel closer to God out here.'

The breeze gently tousled his hair and his eyes shone. Beth wondered at how united their thoughts were. What brought him to her house that afternoon when she most needed him? It had to have been God. How else could Andy sense what she felt, and experience it at the same time?

The *eternal moment* was broken when Andy spotted Phil in one of the sheds. He called out, and Phil responded with a cheery wave.

'I'll see how Phil's doing,' Andy said, then gave her a long look she couldn't quite define. 'Catch you later, Beth.'

She smiled as she watched him go, then continued up the dusty track to the cottage. Funny how Andy didn't seem put off by her weakness and fears. If anything, he seemed to appreciate her more. She'd spent so much time and effort trying to hide her true self when she obviously didn't need to. A weight rolled off her shoulders.

The cottage looked beautiful today. The ducks rested peacefully in the pond and she forced Joel's cruelty from her mind, instead focusing on the calm they exuded. She fed Gilbert, then sat watching him, enjoying the silence.

A car engine hummed in the distance, coming closer. Only it wasn't humming. It was roaring. Someone tore down the track, leaving dirt flying up behind them. Thoughtless. Didn't anyone think about how much dusting Clare's house would need if they stirred it up like that?

The car screeched to a stop at the front gate, and uneasiness settled over Beth. She watched closely as a rounded woman with short wavy blond hair got out and opened the back door of the car. She lifted out a baby, relaxed in sleep. That's when Beth caught a glimpse of the woman's face.

Slowly, recognition dawned. Toni-Lee, Clare's high school friend had come home. But she looked so different. Her face had filled out and no longer showed off a bright smile with braces. The once long, shiny hair was short and dull. What had happened? And who owned the baby? Was this why Rod had been worried about her?

She looked up to see him heading their way. *Thank You, Lord.* Rod was obviously trying to look casual, but Beth saw the tension in his jawline.

Toni froze when she spotted him. 'Rod.'

A tense silence followed as they eyed each other. Then Rod pointed his chin at the baby. 'Is it yours?'

'Don't be so rude.' She shuffled the bundle in her arms. 'You haven't even said hello to me.'

'Sorry. I just ... well, how are you?'

'Good.'

'Really?' There was caring in his tone, and for the briefest of moments Toni's mask crumbled. Beth wondered if Rod had seen the flash of heartache and uncertainty.

Toni stood taller, mask back in place. 'Do I look sick or something?'

Rod ignored her question. 'You're married?'

She let out a derisive laugh. 'No, I'm not into that. I have a partner, though.'

Rod shoved his hands in his jeans pockets and Beth knew the answer had hurt him. It was obvious he still had feelings for Toni.

'Is Clare home?' Toni glanced at Beth. 'I need her to look after the kid for me. If anyone can do him some good, she can.' She spun back to Rod, expression fierce. 'So long as she doesn't teach him religion. It only hurts people.'

'Toni, it wasn't religion that hurt you.' Rod's voice was a gentle.

'Whatever.' She spun away from him and carried the baby up the front steps to the cottage.

Clare answered the door and cried out with joy. 'Toni! Oh, it's so good to see you!' She drew her inside and shut the door.

Beth looked at Rod, who shrugged helplessly. 'Well, she's here. I guess that's a start.'

Beth nodded, but she felt for him. How could Toni treat him so heartlessly? Still, everything would turn out right, just as it had with her and Andy.

'Keep praying,' Rod said.

'I will.' Beth smiled with confidence. 'God's in control, Rod. Even in this.'

BETH GAVE Clare and Toni some time before she headed inside. Gus was in the kitchen getting himself something to eat, while Clare sat with the baby in her arms, gazing down at it with such tenderness it brought a lump to Beth's throat.

'He's beautiful, Toni.' Clare reached a reverent hand and touched the baby's cheek, then looked at Toni who sat across from her.

'You're so clucky, Clare. I knew you would be.'

The coldness in Toni's voice surprised Beth. 'You don't think he's beautiful?'

'I think he's a lot of hard work.'

It was then that Beth noticed the dark rings beneath Toni's eyes. The bubbly girl she'd met at Youth Group a few years ago was gone.

Toni didn't even look at her child. 'He's so demanding and I have to give and give, but never get anything back. He doesn't even smile, just cries and eats and sleeps and cries some more.'

Clare's eyes widened, and Toni's eyes flashed. 'That's right, judge me for being so negative. We can't all be perfect like you, you know.'

Clare looked down and Beth wanted to defend her. *There's no reason to speak to her that way.*

'I know I'm not perfect,' Clare said in a quiet voice.

'Yes, you are. Even saying you're not perfect is part of how perfect you are. You'll make a great mother.'

A smile softened Clare's face. 'Someday, I hope.'

'No, not someday. Now.'

Clare frowned in confusion, and Beth moved closer, ready to step in if her sister needed her.

Toni crossed her arms. 'It's your fault I'm in this mess. If you hadn't convinced me to become a Christian, I never would have gone through with the pregnancy. But I couldn't get God out of my head, and now this poor kid is stuck here in this awful world with me as his mother.' She looked Clare in the eyes. 'That's why I'm giving him to you.'

'Pardon?' Clare's nervous laughter filled the room.

'I want you to look after him. Give him a proper home and a family and teach him that God loves him.'

'But Toni—,'

'Please, Clare. He has no life with me. I can't love him. I can't even care for him.' Despite her pleading, Toni's face remained expressionless. 'The nurse said he's not putting on weight or meeting his milestones. I can't keep going.'

Clare shook her head as though trying to process what she'd heard when Gus came to the kitchen door. Toni stood abruptly.

'I have to be going.' She charged out the door before anyone could stop her.

Clare and Beth sat frozen in shock, but Gus appeared unfazed. 'Do you want me to go after her?'

Clare shook her head. 'No. Not if that's how she feels about the baby.'

'She has post-natal depression.' Gus came and looked down at the infant still in Clare's arms. 'Toni has depression,' he said again. 'My mum had it, too. With me. She abandoned me and left me with my dad. Then she felt so guilty about it that she thought she didn't deserve me and that I wouldn't want anything to do with her. I didn't see her again until I was fourteen.'

'But how could Toni do this? How can you abandon your own child?'

Gus brushed a finger across the baby's cheek. 'Don't judge her too harshly, Clare. She loves him. That's why she brought him here to you. She knows she's in no state to love and care for him, and if she let the department take care of him, she might never get him back.'

Clare stared down at the baby in her arms. Beth came closer and, looking dazed, Clare held him out. 'I have to go and get Phil. He'll know what to do.'

Beth took the sleeping child and an ache formed in her chest. He felt thin and fragile and appeared so vulnerable in sleep. She looked helplessly at Gus, trying to work out how best to hold him.

Gus smiled down at the little boy, his expression registering such tenderness that Beth automatically held him out for Gus to take.

He stepped back quickly. 'I don't know how to hold a baby.'

'Neither do I'.

'No, but you're a woman—it comes naturally to you.'

Beth frowned. 'You're so ... such a stereotyper. Feminists would have your head if they heard you say that.'

'Maybe. But now you're teaching me what's acceptable. Soon I'll be so charming and conformist that I'll fade off into society and melt into non-existence.'

Beth looked at him standing there in his dirty overalls and doubted there was any chance of that. The baby stirred, opened his eyes and blinked up at her. Then his face screwed up and he let out a wail.

Beth panicked. 'What do I do?'

Gus took pity on her and reached for the wriggling baby. He rocked him gently and spoke to him in deep, quiet tones until the crying quieted to a small whimper.

'I think you're the natural,' Beth whispered when the baby closed his eyes and fell back asleep. Anique had said trust no one, but in that moment, Beth knew she could trust Gus. Implicitly.

Gus lowered himself to the lounge, the baby sound asleep in his arms. Phil and Clare charged into the house, followed by Rod.

Rod shot questions at Clare. 'Didn't she at least say where she was staying so you can contact her? I mean, she didn't just abandon the baby did she? Does she expect you to adopt or foster, or what? Has she got anything legal in place? How selfish is she to just dump him on you?'

Gus looked up. 'She did the best thing for him.'

Rod came over and peered at the baby. A strange look passed over his face. 'How old do you think he is?'

Clare shrugged. 'I don't know. He's not a newborn but he's not a toddler. Maybe about the age of the Carson baby at church. I think he's 9 months now.'

A look of shock, then wonder filled Rod's eyes. 'That's my son,' he said. 'Toni had my son.'

'How is that possible?' Beth blushed at the obvious answer to her question, but Rod was too busy staring at the sleeping baby to respond. Phil and Clare came to look, too, and Beth joined them. She looked between Rod and the baby. The shape of the little boy's eyes was similar to Rod's, but it was the jawline that convinced her.

'Can it be?' Clare whispered.

Rod gave her a look filled with regret. 'Toni and I went through times in our Christian walk where we went off track. We ignored God, drank too much, and, well, made choices I wish we hadn't. I repented and recommitted my life to God, but I don't think Toni did.'

Clare bit her lip. 'So what do we do now? I don't know anything about caring for a baby. And Toni didn't leave anything for him.'

Phil looked down at the bundle still in Gus's arms. 'We have to notify the police or child services.'

'Don't.' They all looked up at Gus's sharp tone. 'You do that and you take this child away from his parents. They'll never get him back without a major court case. Just care for him until Toni feels better.'

Clare didn't look convinced. 'But Gus, I don't know if it's even legal for us to care for him. And we have our Guests to look after. We don't have time to care for a baby.'

Rod stepped forward. 'I'll do it. I'm his father so there's no problem legally. I doubt Toni expected to run into me here, but I think it's all part of God's plan. He's in this.' He glanced at Beth and smiled, acknowledging her earlier assurance. 'I'll get both Toni and this little boy through all this.'

'You can't.' Gus had reverted to his usual abrupt tone and Beth tensed. Surely Gus wouldn't try to stop Rod caring for his own child? 'Only God can do it. But if you take on this kid and don't treat him right ...' His voice faded out but Beth was shocked by the anguish in his expression. She knew his father had abused him, but he'd never shown any kind of emotion about it until now.

Rod met Gus's gaze without flinching. 'I'll treat him right. But I need you to tell me all about this depression thing. I'm probably the best hope Toni's got—apart from God, of course.'

Gus nodded and in that moment any earlier animosity disappeared. Beth watched in amazement as connection and understanding passed between them—all because of this tiny baby. Only God could have arranged that.

Rod looked around at the gathered group. 'What next? I don't even know what it eats.'

Beth tamped down her irritation that he called his son *it*. 'Maria can probably help. She would know how to look after a baby.'

Her suggestion received a collective sigh of relief. 'Good idea,' Phil agreed with a smile bordering on amusement. Beth understood. Rod Green caring for a baby was like a bull mothering a kitten.

'I'll give her a call.' Rod pulled out his phone, then stopped and looked at Clare. 'Does he have a name?'

'William.'

'William?' His face softened. 'My grandfather. She named him after my grandfather.'

Phil looked dubious. 'Toni knew his name?'

'Yeah, we talked about our grandparents. They were more like parents to us, really.'

Beth couldn't imagine Toni talking to the tough Rod about personal things, but clearly they'd had a more intimate relationship than she'd ever imagined. Baby William was proof of that.

'I'm going to call him Billy.' Rod looked at the baby again, then at Gus. 'I won't let him be hassled for his name.'

Gus nodded his approval and with something close to a smile, Rod focused his attention back on his phone.

A few minutes later, Maria arrived and bundled up both Rod and baby William to take them back home and care for them. Beth smiled. Maria would make an amazing grandmother when Clare had children someday.

BETH DIDN'T SEE Rod again until he wandered into the cottage the following afternoon with dishevelled hair and bags under his eyes. He flopped onto the lounge and groaned. 'I had to get away. That kid doesn't let me sleep more than two hours at a time. I don't know what I'd do without Maria.'

Beth held back her smile. Poor Rod. She stopped dusting the coffee table and sat across from him. 'It's not as easy as you thought?'

He rubbed his eyes. 'You've no idea. He doesn't even acknowledge me. I do all this stuff for him, talk to him, feed him, change him, and all he does is cry when he wants to be fed.'

Beth chuckled. 'Toni said something like that. And she looked even more exhausted than you do.'

'Yeah, I was worried she was on something when I first saw her, but it was just lack of sleep.' He looked out the window and stiffened as a car pulled up outside. 'She's back.'

Beth dropped then dusting cloth. 'Do you want me to leave?'

'No! No, stay there. It's me who needs to leave.' He scrambled up and darted into the kitchen.

Beth opened the door with a smile before Toni had a chance to knock. 'Hello Toni. Clare's not—'

'I forgot to leave his things.' Toni dumped what looked like a bag of nappies on the verandah. 'I've got some more.' She charged back down the steps.

Rod peeked out of the kitchen as Toni dragged a folded pram from her car, then hauled it up the steps. Toni looked up and stopped short, her eyes going wide.

'Hey Toni.' Rod sounded calm, but Beth could tell he was flustered.

'Where is he?' Toni demanded. Rod stepped forward, but she backed away, looking panicked. 'Where is he, Rod?'

'He's safe. Maria's looking after him right now, but I helped all night.'

'Why?' Toni sounded breathless. 'Why isn't Clare ...'

Rod held out his hand, then thought better of it and shoved it in his pocket. 'Because he's my son and I figure he's best in my care ... you know, legally and everything.'

'He's not your son! He's mine.'

'Ours.' His voice was gentle but there was steel in his jaw. 'We could be a family, Toni. If you marry me.'

'Marry you?' She pointed a shaking finger in his face. 'You couldn't even cope with being my boyfriend, remember?'

'That's because I wasn't walking with God. Now I am.'

Toni's shoulders sagged and Beth noticed the hint of a tremble in her lower lip.

'Please Toni.' Rod's voice softened again. 'I love you and I never meant to hurt you.'

Toni stared at him, then, to Beth's horror, laughed in his face—a horrible, mocking sound. 'Rod, what's gotten into you? You sound like a love-sick puppy. But we both know you're not capable of any kind of love.' With that, she bolted back out to the car and dumped two more bags and pieces of a wooden cot onto the ground. 'They're for you. Have a good night's sleep!' She jumped into her car and sped away.

Beth was confused. How could Toni remain unmoved by Rod's obvious love and concern? Her romantic heart broke for him. She drew in a shaky breath. Maybe God could only make dreams come true if both parties shared the same dream.

Rod looked at the pile of items Toni had left. He picked up a tin and gave a rueful laugh, holding it up to show Beth. 'We could have done with this last night. Maria called all her friends trying to find formula for him. She ended up getting it from the hospital.' He laughed again, but it sounded hollow. 'It's weird, isn't it? I can talk baby now. Maria gave me a speed lesson last night when I was going to feed him cow's milk from a cup. Formula is what you feed babies who can't ... well, you know, have their mother's milk.'

A hint of red tinged his cheeks and he looked out the window, absently turning the tin in his hands. Fatherhood had aged him overnight. Or maybe it was his burden for Toni. Or lack of sleep. Probably all of the above.

He put the tin down and poked through the pile before he shrugged. 'Guess I'd better borrow Gus's ute to get all this stuff back to the farmhouse. Maria will know what to do with it.' He smiled, looking up at Beth. 'Even Phil's dad is a bit of an expert on babies. I'm learning from the right people. Who would imagine Dale was such an involved father? He started to tell me how he used to change Phil 'til I called TMI.'

Beth couldn't help laughing at his expression. Too much information, indeed.

CHAPTER TWENTY-THREE

Beth came downstairs to the kitchen and stopped in the doorway. Mum was on the phone, and she didn't sound happy.

'You can't let Rod Green bring up that poor baby. And you're newly married, Clare. You don't want another person living in your house.'

Clare must have told Mum how Gus was moving into their cottage to make room for Rod and the baby in the main farmhouse.

She backed away from the door, but Mum saw her and held up a staying hand. 'Yes, yes, okay, I'll talk with you tomorrow.' She ended the call and sighed. 'Did you know about this? Rod can't be trusted with a baby.'

'He's Billy's father.'

'Maybe so, but that boy is rough and uneducated. He wouldn't know a thing about bringing up a child.'

'That's why Maria's helping him.'

Mum clicked her tongue. 'Clare should have taken him to the police or Department of Families.'

Beth felt her defences rising. 'What, and let him grow up without knowing God?'

'He needs a real family. That's what's important.'

'He has a real family. His parents.'

'And how are two louts like that going to bring him up to have a decent education, to lead a successful life?'

Beth frowned. Mum might be a professional businesswoman with inspiring goals and achievements, but she had her priorities wrong. She considered herself a Christian, even though she'd stopped attending church when Dad died. God wasn't a priority. Cleanliness and social etiquette took precedence. Normally Beth did her best to impress her, but if it meant taking on Mum's values and denying who she really was, it wasn't worth the sacrifice.

Mum got up from the table, looking like Dan had put soap on her toothbrush again, and Beth retreated upstairs. She didn't have the energy to deal with Mum today. She was tired. No, she was exhausted. The heaviness in her body weighed her down more and more with each step up to her room. It was getting harder to keep up with her self-imposed exercise regime. Her mind was foggy, and even schoolwork had become an effort. Nothing seemed to help. Falling onto her bed, she let sleep claim her.

Andy wandered down the dusty farm road. Beth called out to him but he didn't hear.

'I still love you,' she shouted. He didn't so much as turn around. She tried to run after him but her legs wouldn't move. Someone was holding her back, not letting her go. It was Dara.

Dara bounced enthusiastically, her fingers cutting into the flesh of her arms. 'I'm pregnant,' she said with a beaming smile. 'Brett and I are expecting a baby.'

'Does Brett know?'

She looked down. 'No, I can't bring myself to tell him. He doesn't want a baby.'

Beth snapped. 'That's not true,' she screamed at Dara. 'You just want this whole thing to be a drama. Don't you get that this is a person you're messing with? Don't you understand what it means to bring a new life into the world?'

Dara just smiled. 'Of course I do. Clare will look after it for me.'

Ferocious, burning anger raged through Beth and she reached out and struck Dara across the face.

But Dara just kept smiling.

Beth woke to find herself drenched in sweat. Anger still burned within, and her body shook with the intensity of it. 'Help me, God,' she whispered into the darkness. 'Something's wrong with me.'

Maybe she was going insane? She fought back terror. She believed God was in control, didn't she? So why couldn't she live like He was? Why was she so bound up in fear? She forced herself to remember the times she'd felt God's presence, and finally, peace covered her like a blanket. She fell into a dreamless sleep.

CLARE AND PHIL'S washing had piled up, and Beth was pretty sure Clare hadn't ironed in weeks. She set to work. She was pegging out the first load of washing when Joel appeared. She hadn't heard him approach and it put her on edge. He gave a warm smile, looking too clean and well-presented to have been working. He always seemed to find a way out of helping at the building site.

He sat on the fence near the washing line. 'They still got you working?'

'I choose to help.'

If he caught the barb behind her words, he didn't show it. 'I know you do.'

She tried to relax, act natural. 'How's everything going?'

'Good. Especially now I've found better company.' He studied her appraisingly, and warmth rose into her cheeks. He certainly didn't lack confidence. Maybe that came with having good looks and intelligence.

'God is really changing me,' he said, his gaze steady. 'It's nice to be in his favour.'

'That's what Anique says—,' Beth snapped her mouth shut. It wasn't safe to talk about Anique.

'Is that right?' A strange look passed over his face. 'You spend a bit of time with her?'

She looked away. 'Some.'

'I wouldn't have thought you'd be close, her being Andy's girl-friend and all.'

God, help me. How much is safe to say? He was looking at her closely. She'd already said too much.

'Are you okay?' His voice had turned soft and deep.

'Yeah, I'm fine.'

He left the fence and took one of the wet shirts from the basket, then hung it on the line. Beth couldn't help staring.

He laughed. 'What? I do work when I think it's a worthwhile cause.'

'You don't think the program that's helping you is worthwhile?'

He screwed up his nose. 'I do, but maybe I still have some of my old rebel ways. I instinctively want to make trouble for anyone to do with Juvenile Justice.'

The program wasn't Juvenile Justice, but Beth didn't bother correcting him. He reached for another shirt at the same time as she did, then stopped, his face too close for comfort. 'Beth, I've been meaning to talk to you.'

Her heart beat uncomfortably fast, and she forced herself not to look away. His eyes were dark, cold, and ... hungry. His breathing changed, and panic set it. Surely he wasn't planning to kiss her? She stepped back.

His look turned pleading. 'Beth, I know you don't know me that well and I've had a rough past, but I really have changed since I became a Christian. I've admired you from the day I met you, and to be honest, I'm attracted to you. But more than that, I think you're good for me.' He moved closer and ran a finger down the side of her face. 'Will you consider going out with me?'

She felt sick. Taking another step back, she swallowed hard. Saying no was the only option, but he was speaking again, eyes filled with hope. 'Won't you at least give it a try? I know you have feelings for Andy, but he's spoken for, and I think if you just give me a chance you'll see that we're good together. Don't you Christians say that love is a choice, not a feeling?'

She nodded. Love *was* a choice, but she didn't miss the way he said *you Christians* as though he wasn't part of that.

His eyes lit up, and in that awful moment she realised he thought she'd nodded yes to being his girlfriend. 'Joel …'

Her words died as he pulled her into his arms and wrapped her in a firm embrace. 'I knew the moment I saw you that you were the one for me.'

'No, Joel, I didn't mean …' His eyes were focused on her lips, his head lowering as though he hadn't heard her. *Help me, please God.*

A throat cleared nearby, and Joel sprang back. Gus stood on the back step, his steady gaze challenging Joel.

Joel grinned up at him. 'Okay, okay, boss, I'm going back to work.' Gus raised his brows and Joel turned to Beth with a dark possessive look. 'We'll finish this later.'

'Wait!' She had to explain; to set things straight, but he'd disappeared just as quickly as he'd appeared. She ran to the gate and looked up and down the road, but he was gone. Breathing hard, she ran back to Gus. 'Do you have his phone number?'

'They're not allowed to have phones.'

'Do you know where he'd be?'

'No. He has free time.'

'So why did he say he was going back to work?'

Gus frowned. 'Some mind game he's playing, probably.'

Beth groaned. She didn't have the energy to run around the farm trying to find him. Her fingers shook and her breath was unsteady as she hung the last of the washing.

Gus sat down on the step. 'Was he inappropriate with you?'

Was he? She wasn't sure, and she didn't want him kicked out of the program. He obviously needed to be here. 'No, he just misunderstood.' She collected the empty washing basket, her legs still shaky.

'Can I get you some afternoon tea?' Gus's eyes held concern.

'No thanks.'

'Not hungry?'

'I just don't want to eat.'

'Why?' Now that he was making an effort to connect, she wished he wouldn't. She placed her foot on the first step. He didn't move. 'You'd be healthier if you put on a bit of weight.'

He was so rude. Why couldn't he keep his opinions to himself? She stepped around him.

'Be careful with Joel,' he said.

She stopped, irritation bubbling over. 'Why?'

'I just don't think you should trust him.'

She agreed, but she wasn't going to tell Gus that. She wasn't in the program and she didn't need his help. He seemed to think he was better than everyone else. 'Doesn't he meet your standards?'

'I think you'd be better off single.'

She barked out a laugh. 'You've got this thing against relationships, haven't you? When you've got a girlfriend I might take your advice seriously.'

'Sometimes an observer sees things others don't. As a man with the gift of being single, I have more wisdom to offer than you realise.'

She lowered her hand from the doorknob. 'You seriously think being single is a gift?'

'Marriage would be a hindrance.' He stood and brushed down his overalls. 'Jesus didn't have a wife, the Apostle Paul makes it very clear he's better off without one, Solomon lost his wisdom when he got involved with too many women, and think of poor old Samson—a woman caused his demise.'

Beth glared, opened the door and moved up the step so she could meet him eye to eye. 'You talk as though women are the curse of the world, but I don't think you can claim to be perfect, Gus Richards.'

He grinned. 'I didn't eat the apple ...'

'If you knew your Bible you'd know it wasn't even an apple— and I don't see Adam trying to stop his wife.'

His grin widened. 'You think it was Adam's job to stop her?'

'Yes. He was the one put in charge of the garden. He was supposed to protect her, not blame her for his own choices.'

He let out a warm laugh. 'Exactly. He was meant to protect her, but instead, he got her into trouble. Better off being single, like I said. You need to be careful—those boys you're associating with might just get you into trouble.'

'Boys?' She couldn't believe this guy. 'They're not much younger than you, Gus Richards. If they're boys, then so are you.' With that, she charged into the house, hearing his chuckle behind her. It was a pleasant sound but she was too annoyed to like it. She hung the laundry basket with more force than necessary and huffed out a breath. No one got under her skin like Gus did. What was it about him that brought all her negative thoughts and feelings to the surface? She didn't like it.

The back door banged and she knew he'd followed her inside. No silent, unexpected arrival like Joel. Then to her relief, she heard Phil and Clare's voices coming up the front path. She raced out to meet them. 'Do you know where Joel is?'

'No, sorry.' Clare caught her by the arm. 'But we've got some news if you have a second ...' Her eyes were wide with excitement.

'What is it?' Were they expecting a baby? Already?

'My husband is going to be famous.' Clare bubbled with excitement.

'I wouldn't say that …' Phil's cheeks had a red tinge, but his green eyes sparked with renewed life and energy.

'Scott shared one of Phil's songs at Bible College, and there's a guy there who's into recording and promoting Christian music. He wants to help Phil get his songs out there.'

'That's great.' Beth was genuinely excited for him. 'But what about the work here? Now that Rod's looking after his baby, he doesn't have as much time for the Guests …'

Phil's eyes lost some of their sparkle, and he looked old and tired again. 'I haven't been doing much apart from administration anyway, and I can do the music in my spare time. I've got quite a few other songs already written.'

He did? It shouldn't surprise her. He had such a gift. He was unlike any other man she'd ever known. Apart from Andy. Her mind went back to Joel and what she needed to do. 'Congratulations,' she said to Phil, 'I've got to go and find Joel.'

She rode her bike around the farm, until she could pedal no more. Joel was nowhere to be found. No one seemed to know where he was. Finally, Beth asked Phil to drop her home. She'd have to write Joel a letter. Not the best option, but if he was going to be this hard to find, she had no choice. She'd write it tonight and get it to him tomorrow, somehow.

BETH ENTERED the cottage after another full day of school. She'd fed Gilbert and gone looking for Joel, but he was still making himself scarce. She stared down at the envelope holding her letter, then, with a shrug, placed it letter carefully on the table. Phil or Clare would get it to him.

Someone knocked on the door. Hopefully Joel. She'd told enough people she was looking for him.

It was Anique. Beth opened the door and invited her in. 'Is everything okay? You weren't at school today.'

Anique's eyes turned stormy. 'Things aren't good, Beth. I've come to say goodbye.'

'You're leaving?'

'I'm being moved to another foster home. It's getting too dangerous here.'

'You'll be safe there?'

'Yes, but they can't take me in 'til next week. I can't go to school—I'd be putting my life on the line.'

Why did people have to be so dramatic? And why did she attract all the people with issues? She'd had enough of it. Maybe having Anique out of the way would be a good thing. For everyone.

Anique stiffened and Beth followed her gaze. Her eyes were on the envelope on the table, Joel's name boldly printed on the front. 'What's that?'

'Just a letter.' Not that it was any of her business.

Anique's eyes widened into panic. 'It's true then? You're involved with him?'

Beth wanted to groan. How many people had Joel told that she was his girlfriend? What a mess. 'It's all been a big misunderstanding …' Her voice faded out when Anique spun around and charged out of the house, the door banging behind her.

What had just happened? Should she run after her? She was tired of searching for people. Joel was proof this farm had too many places to disappear. She collapsed onto the lounge with a sigh. She was so tired of drama, tired of trying to work out what was going on, and tired of running after people. It was easier to just let everything go and stop caring.

'Beth?' Andy stood at the door. *What now?* 'Did she go off at you, too?' He looked apologetic.

'No, she just took off. I upset her somehow.'

He gave a rueful laugh. 'Join the club.' He came inside and sat down, his brow furrowed. He fiddled with the wrinkles in the lounge cover, looking troubled.

'Andy,' she said softly, wearily. 'It's going to be okay. God's in control, remember? I have perfect confidence he causes happy endings. Remember Phil and Clare? God works everything out.'

Slowly, he smiled. 'You're right as usual, Beth my friend, but as for happy endings on earth, I'm not sure. Heaven is the only happy ending I'm counting on. And it will be better than we could ever have imagined.'

His eyes were sparkling again and Beth wondered at how easy it was to encourage him and return his joy. All she had to do was mention God or heaven. God was Andy's ultimate joy and heaven his ultimate goal.

CHAPTER TWENTY-FOUR

Beth's letter was still sitting on the table after school the next day. Why hadn't Phil or Gus passed it on to Joel? The last thing she wanted to do was search the farm for him again, but this was crazy. Was she his girlfriend or not? Well, she wasn't, but he supposedly didn't know that. Why would he declare his feelings for her, then disappear? All she wanted to do was close her eyes and rest her weary body, but she had to set this straight once and for all.

Her bike had a flat tyre, so she set off at a jog. There were so many places to look. Gus had been working on the new accommodation building with the Guests, Dale had been teaching them how to shear and do farm work, Phil was teaching some of them guitar, and Rod had been counselling them in-between looking after baby Billy. So where to start?

Andy often helped out in the sheds, which was added incentive to head that way. She stopped outside the shed door. Raised voices came from inside, and one of them was Anique's. Why was she here? Hadn't she indicated she needed to lay low? The sooner she left for good and took all her drama with her, the better.

Anique's voice came again, and this time Beth detected desperation in her tone. Andy's voice responded, followed by a deeper one that Beth didn't recognise. She'd ask if they'd seen Joel, and hopefully the distraction would be enough to extinguish their argument.

She stepped inside the door and stopped. Anique stood in the middle of the shed, tears streaming down her face. Beth had never seen her cry before. She was facing a man who had his back to Beth, and to the side, was Andy.

'Andy, get out of here while you can. Please. This is not the time to be brave. I don't need you to protect me.' Despite speaking to Andy, Anique's eyes were fixed on the stranger, her body coiled like a spring, ready for action.

'Don't send him away.' The stranger's menacing tone sent shivers down Beth's spine. 'It'll be more satisfying to take both of you out.'

'No! Andy, you don't know who you're dealing with. I'll be okay. Just leave. Go. Now!'

Everything within Beth wanted to grab Andy's arm and drag him out of there. She crept forward until she saw the unknown man. And that's when she saw the glint of metal in his hand.

A knife.

Andy moved into view, and his face was flushed and angry, his dark hair drenched with sweat. 'I'm not leaving here without Anique, so put the knife down.'

Beth had never seen Andy so fierce, but the stranger laughed and moved closer to Anique, knife poised. Beth watched in horror as he grabbed her around the neck in a headlock. Where was her phone? She'd left it at the cottage. *Lord, help!*

Andy bent low, and with a roar, charged at the man. The man staggered back, and lost his grip on Anique, who scrambled across the shed floor, away from him. The man regained his balance and hunched forward as he moved menacingly toward Andy. There was something dark and evil in his yes. He lifted his knife.

'Run!' Andy commanded, and this time Anique obeyed. She charged past Beth and into the paddock while Beth stood frozen, unable to look away. The man lunged forward, and Beth screamed as the knife sank deep into Andy's chest. His hand flew up and he gasped, eyes wide. The man yanked the knife from Andy's chest and bolted, while Beth stared aghast at the flow of red spreading across his shirt.

'Andy!' Her voice broke. He still held his chest, fighting for breath. His eyes were wide, his face pale, and he fell heavily to the ground. He struggled to get back up, while Beth screamed his name in-between panicked sobs.

'Andy? Andy, what do I do?' Desperation clawed at her heart. Andy was the one who always took charge, but now he looked as terrified and helpless as she felt.

He collapsed back to the ground and turned slowly to look at her. 'Get help, Beth,' he whispered and his voice gurgled in the back of his throat, every syllable an effort. Then he closed his eyes. Beth darted a look around. What could she do? She didn't have her phone and she couldn't leave him here alone.

'God,' she sobbed. 'Oh God, help us.'

First, she needed something to hold against his bleeding chest. She ripped off his shirt, his silence and stillness more frightening than his gurgling breaths. She knelt beside him and held his shirt to his chest to stem the flow of blood. Between desperate sobs, she begged God to save him.

A ute tore down the road and Dale charged in the door.

Beth spoke between strangled sobs. 'Andy's been killed!' She didn't know why she chose those words, except that somewhere deep inside she believed them. Dale skidded to her side and grabbed the shirt from her blood-soaked hands, returning firm pressure to Andy's chest.

'The ambulance is on its way,' he said. 'Anique's at the gate waiting for them.' He patted Andy's pale face. 'Andy. Andy, can you hear me? Hold on mate, we're here.' He glanced up at Beth, returning pressure to Andy's chest. 'Can you check if he's breathing?'

Beth placed shaking fingers against Andy's neck and moved her cheek to his mouth to feel for breath. 'Help him God. Please!' She couldn't look at his chest. She focused on his face. She longed to smooth back his wayward curls—to move him from the ground and onto something soft and comfortable. 'I can't feel his breath or his pulse,' she cried, her voice strangled by tears.

'Do you know CPR?'

She nodded, trying not to look at the pool of blood in the dust. It was so wrong that Andy's blood should be mixed with dirt. Something so precious and full of life … and yet, to dust he would return.

Stop it. Think positive.

Dale nodded to Beth, and she began chest compressions, while he continued to press down on the blood-soaked shirt. Beth counted to thirty, hating that she must be hurting him even more, but desperate to get his heart beating again. Then she moved to his mouth, now more grey than red. She bent and placed her lips on his, wondering at the irony of it all. His lips were soft and lifeless, not warm and alive like she'd always imagined. She was giving him the kiss of life, but he would never know it.

No, she couldn't think that way! She would share her own life, her own breath with Andy and she wouldn't give up until those blue eyes fluttered open and looked into hers with that merry sparkle she loved. And he would know she saved her first kiss for him—for a moment more important than either of them could ever have imagined. That's how it was supposed to be. Andy would regain consciousness and the first thing he would see was her, her tears of joy and eyes of love looking down into his. Then she would unashamedly run her fingers through his thick black curls and know that he was hers–that she finally deserved him.

What am I thinking?

There was nothing romantic about the methodical counting

and breathing as they worked in the dust, sweat dripping down their foreheads and into their eyes, the blood on the ground turning into mud in the dust.

Sirens screamed up the road, but neither of them stopped.

Paramedics raced in. They bent over Andy, taking the blood-soaked shirt from Dale. Beth ignored the way Dale stepped back. She ignored the gentle hand laid on her shoulder.

'Keep going,' she rasped.

They moved in with a defibrillator and pulled her back. She watched as they shocked him several times. Blocking out the reason they all shook their heads and stopped, she raced in to continue her own compressions. She was aware of voices around her, of Dale speaking her name, but nothing was more important than saving Andy's life.

'Beth.' This time the paramedic knelt down beside her as he said her name. Quietly, sorrowfully. Still, Beth kept breathing, counting. Breathing, counting.

'Beth.' It was more urgent, insistent this time. He touched her shoulder and bent to look into her eyes. 'There's nothing we can do now.'

And she saw the truth there. In the pity, the sorrow, the compassion. 'Are you sure?' Her whisper was a desperate plea for hope.

'I'm sure.'

It felt as though the breath of life had left her soul. She couldn't look at Andy's body anymore, couldn't watch as he was taken away. She buried her face in Dale's shirt, and as his strong arms surrounded her, she felt the refuge of her Heavenly Father's arms, giving her strength for one more breath. And one more breath. Dale wept and Beth knew her Heavenly Father was weeping too. Not for Andy, but for the pain, the loss, the awful reality of death that was so overwhelming it couldn't be expressed let alone fully felt in one moment of time—perhaps not in a lifetime. And so, unable to fit inside her heart, it broke it in two and flowed free.

'BETH, the police are here. Are you okay to speak with them?'

Beth stepped back from Dale, and blinked. Then she gazed around at a world she'd never seen before. This grey, broken, muddy, desperate place. Andy's body was gone. The ambulance was gone. And in their place were uniformed police holding curious onlookers at bay and partitioning off the shed with blue and white tape.

She averted her eyes from the blood and nodded as the police approached. With great effort, she managed to force words past the barrier of pain swirling upward in waves and blocking her throat. She wasn't sure what they were asking or what she was answering, but she must be making sense because they nodded and took notes. Dale stood by her side and she thought he must be holding her because she knew she didn't have the strength to stand. He was the one source of comfort–the one symbol of God's love remaining in an empty, shattered world.

When the police finally left, Beth turned to find Clare and Phil surveying the scene with wide, disbelieving eyes. Clare let out a strangled cry, then ran to Beth, clinging to her as though her life depended on it.

Phil put his arms around them both, his eyes glistening. 'Let me take you home.'

On shaky legs, Beth moved toward the door. Phil came to one side, Clare the other, and together they walked back home without a word. Beth hated the eerie silence, but she doubted she'd ever speak, let alone eat again. Why did she have to suffer the agony of breathing when she didn't want to take another breath? Something inside her had died, and this time it was more than a dream.

IN THE LOUNGE ROOM, Clare broke down into anguished sobs and was drawn into her husband's comforting embrace. A dazed feeling came over Beth as the couple wept together. She and Andy were supposed to be supporting one another in a tragedy like this. But he couldn't be there for her anymore. She no longer had a dream. Or hope. The world would never hold excitement for her again. The only spark of happiness she had ever felt had been completely extinguished and she felt cold and nauseated.

Clare came to sit beside her. 'Oh Beth,' she bit her trembling lip. 'What can I say? You were the one to comfort and support me when Phil was lost on the mission field. You reminded me love is not in vain. You dreamed my dreams for me when I was too weary to dream anymore. I don't know how, but I'm going to do that for you.'

Yes, ironically Beth had been right to believe and dream for Clare. God preserved Phil's life and here they were together. As for her, there was no dream left for Clare to dream for her. It was over. Shattered, crushed, obliterated.

FUNERAL PLANS WERE UNDERWAY. Beth was weary of the anguish. If only Andy's life had been spared and she could be the one in heaven, free from this world. Right now, every breath brought pain in her heart too physically real to be purely emotional. At other times there was a complete void; an absence of feeling that scared her.

'Pete asked Phil to sing at the funeral,' Clare said as she walked by Beth's side along the dusty road of the farm in the twilight. Beth was too weak to run, but had finally agreed to join Clare for a walk.

'How is Pete?' Beth felt for him. Losing a brother was something she couldn't begin to imagine. She couldn't bear to think of losing Tim or Dan, no matter how much Dan had picked on her though childhood.

'He was struggling when Phil went to see him this afternoon. He asked Phil all sorts of questions about life after death. He can't make sense of what happened.'

Beth couldn't, either. She looked up into the sky, feeling that emptiness again. In the past, the stars in the quiet evening were exciting. They promised life would fulfil her dreams. Now they were insignificant pinpricks of light in an all-consuming darkness.

Clare stopped. 'Beth, there is someone for you.' Her voice was quiet, almost a whisper. 'I know you can't bear to think of it now, but there is. And you will love him more than you ever knew you could love anyone.'

Tears stung her eyes. 'I can't believe that, and I don't want to.'

'I know, but someday you will. For now, just hold onto hope. Cling to the knowledge that God is good and that He can redeem anything. Even this. Think of Andy in heaven and know he didn't die a day sooner than God always planned.'

How could redeeming this be possible? Marriage to someone else could never fix this. Humans were fragile, their lives so easily snuffed out. God was the only One who would never die. Was He the only connection she still had with Andy? Was He the only One who could give her the sense of safety and belonging she was searching for? Because right now, life didn't feel safe—God didn't feel safe. She'd thought He made dreams come true, but how wrong she'd been.

God …? She didn't even know what to pray. *Jesus, help me.*

Gus cooked tea that night. No one else could focus. He shuffled around the kitchen as though he was perfectly at home there. Was there anything he wasn't good at? Beth didn't want to be impressed by him, especially when he was so aware of how capable he was. She resented that he was here and Andy wasn't.

He set a plate of food in front of each of them. The last thing Beth felt like was food, but she didn't want to offend him. It took a long time to swallow the one mouthful of stir-fry she'd forced into her mouth. Why should she eat when Andy would never eat again? It was strange that he no longer needed food. But she didn't feel like she needed food, either.

'How is it?' Gus asked, looking around the table as Clare and Phil lifted forkfuls of stir-fry into their mouths.

'Delicious!' Clare said, and Phil nodded his agreement.

It sounded so inappropriate.

'What do you think?' Gus looked directly at Beth.

She managed to swallow and mumble, 'You're a good cook.'

'It doesn't look like you've even had any.'

Helpless anger overwhelmed her. Who cared about his stupid food? Andy was dead! She struggled against tears. Even the concern in his eyes annoyed her. He had no idea what she was going through. He didn't know or love Andy.

'You need to eat,' he said. 'To keep up your strength.'

She'd had enough. She slammed her fork on the table and cast him an angry glare. Then she stomped out without another word. She didn't have to answer to Gus Richards. She deliberately let the front door slam behind her, something she'd never done before. Mum would be ashamed, but she didn't care. She stormed along the dust road, anger fuelling each step. She needed answers. There could never be closure until she reached heaven herself, but understanding what happened and why, would help.

No one could tell her why Andy was killed or who was behind the attack. Anique refused to say for fear of her own life, and the police weren't making any headway. Fury filled Beth every time she remembered Anique running from the scene. How could she have left him? How could she have let him become involved in her drug dramas? And how could she now refuse to bring justice for Andy? She wanted to shake her until she spat out the truth.

Beth wasn't sure where she was going. She'd never walked some of the farm tracks she was following, but she just needed to get away. Away from Gus, where she could sort out the thoughts swirling around in her head. She wondered if Andy felt any pain as he died. Not as the knife went in—that was a given—but in those moments he breathed his last. Could she have saved him? Did he know he was dying? Was he frightened? Did he wish someone was there other than her?

She remembered the day that felt so long ago when the flames raced toward the woolshed. He feared for his life that day, but God spared him that time. He was absolutely confident it must not be God's time for him to die. Why tease him like that?

And why was now his time to die? And why in such a way? How could God be in this?

She stopped mid-thought. A vehicle's engine hummed somewhere nearby. They might be looking for her, and she didn't want them to worry. They'd been through enough, so she followed the sound, not knowing which paddock she was in, nor which direction she was headed. She could be on the Cairn's conservation land but she wasn't sure.

The sound stopped, but she caught a flash of light on a metal structure through the bushes ahead. Making her way through, she found herself standing in front of a shed she hadn't known existed. It was different from all the other work sheds on the farm.

Was she still on the Cairn's land? Confused, she glanced around, stopping when she heard voices. One of them filled her with terror—the voice of the man who'd killed Andy. He was in a heated exchange with another man. Beth needed to run, but the pounding of her heart left her dizzy and unable to think or move.

A truck backed up to the shed, and one of the men piled sacks and containers into the back. Trembling, Beth managed to duck behind a tree, out of sight. Then she caught sight of another figure in the shadows. The way he stood so casually, just watching, was familiar.

'Joel!' She didn't mean to scream his name, but terror had overtaken goods sense. Thankfully, the men jumped into the truck and it screeched away, leaving Beth in a cloud of dust. She needed help, and God had sent Joel to rescue her.

'Joel, where have you been?' She stumbled forward and threw her arms around him, clinging to his safe, solid form. 'Joel, you need to call the police. That man who just left—he stabbed Andy. He killed him!'

Joel pushed her back. 'Get out of here, you idiot!' he hissed.

Stunned, she stared at him, a feeling of dread seeping into her bones. 'Joel you aren't involved in this are you?'

Joel laughed, a cold, mocking sound. 'Involved? I run this thing. Well, I did until you just messed it up. Now I've got to get out of here.'

'Joel!' She couldn't believe it; didn't want to. She clung to her last hope. 'Don't do this. Remember your commitment to God?'

The feral glint in his eyes was frightening. And confusing. He'd said he had feelings for her. Surely he would never cause her harm?

'Beth, I never believed. My commitment kept everyone off my back, that's all.'

His words broke over her, dumping a bucket of freezing reality. She turned to run, but he grabbed her arm. She struggled, lashing out at him, but he quickly had her restrained, and she knew in that moment that he knew exactly what he was doing. He dragged her to the shed where he picked up a rope.

'Let me go!'

His face contorted into a sneer. 'Oh, sorry, what could I be thinking? Of course, I'll let you go.'

His fingers dug into her skin and she winced as he pulled her over to a tree. Petrified, she used every bit of strength she had to struggle, but he was stronger than he looked. He shoved her against the tree, and she cried out in pain as her head connected with wood. He pinned her there, his gaze darkening as he looked into her eyes, then down at her lips. She let out a terrified squeak, wanting to beg God not to let him touch her, but unable to form the words.

'Don't worry, I won't humiliate you any more.' He leaned in, his breath on her neck sending shivers down her spine. 'You've done a good enough job of that yourself. I never fancied you anyway.'

'So why did you say you did?'

'I had to keep an eye on you. Keep you away from this place. I know all about your love of wildlife, your crazy rescue mentality, your grandfather … I know all about you.'

'How?'

'I have friends in high places. Friends who know your stupidity got your grandfather killed.'

No one knew what happened with Grandpa. Except Andy. Beth's throat burned, but she refused to cry and let Joel see how hurt and scared she was. She grasped at straws. 'God loves you too much to let you get away with this. You'll be caught.'

He didn't answer. She looked around wildly. He flung the rope around the tree one more time before securing the end. 'Ask God to send someone along. If He loves you, He will.' Then he moved his face menacingly close. Beth was desperate to back away, but she couldn't move. 'If you tell anyone anything I've told you, it will be more than Andy who needs a funeral.' The low, threatening, voice didn't even sound like his.

Beth watched in horror as he went into the sheds then came back out a few minutes later, with an armful of items she couldn't identify. He took off into the bushes.

She glanced around. It was just on dark. Dread descended upon her. How would anybody find her? She shivered with fear rather than cold, longing for a reprieve from the awful ache in her heart. How could it feel like it was breaking when it was already shattered?

If she screamed, Joel or the man who murdered Andy might return. She'd never felt so alone. Her head and legs were heavy, but the ropes cut in every time she moved. She couldn't stand the silence or the pain of her own thoughts. Darkness crept in like a smothering blanket and panic rose in her chest.

'Please help me. Someone …' Her whimpers were swallowed up by the darkness.

OVER THE NEXT FEW HOURS, Beth was as much tortured by her own thoughts as by the cold darkness and the ropes binding her. Her skin scraped and scratched against the rough bark of the tree, and the ropes cut into her, but her heart was cut deeper.

I thought God made dreams come true. If Andy was still alive he'd sense something is wrong. He would come and find me.

'Who are you, God?' Her hoarse voice quaked into the darkness. 'I thought I knew You. I thought I knew how You work, but I was so wrong.'

She'd been betrayed. By God. By Joel. By those who had not come to find her. She just wanted to see Andy. How she missed him. She wouldn't see him again for a long, long time … unless she died here tonight.

I want to die.

Her thoughts became crystal clear.

Andy and I are meant to have a joint funeral, not a wedding. Even in this. God is even in this. This is how He planned it all along.

Even so, her survival instincts cut in. She'd fought for so long to be in control that she couldn't let go, even when she wanted to. She stiffened at another noise. Was it a wild animal? Joel? A criminal come to find drugs, or finish her off? A rustling sound came from the ground and another in the tree above. It was too dark to distinguish the shapes.

Just rats and birds rustling the leaves, she told herself, but she was too on edge to believe it. Something moved closer. Too big to be a rat or possum.

Dingoes.

Were there really dingoes out here? A scream caught in her throat at the low, rumbling growl. With terror, she realised that whatever it was, there was more than one. She strained to see through the darkness, but the night was completely black. Ferocious growls now surrounded her and she knew this was it.

With a whimper, she shut her eyes, wishing she could black out. 'God, please help me!'

An image flashed through her mind. Daniel in the lion's den thousands of years ago.

Do you believe it's more than just a story? Really? Do you believe God can also protect you from wild animals?

Why would He? He didn't protect Andy from that knife. He didn't protect Grandpa from the heart attack. How could she know God's voice from her own tortured, human thoughts?

'God what are you saying?' she whispered.

And then she saw a vision of Andy. He stood surrounded by a bright light, smiling at her, his blue eyes full of understanding. 'God's in control,' he said, 'even in this.'

And Beth wept.

What happened to those dingoes she would never know, but the next thing she heard was voices in the distance. She opened her eyes to see small slivers of light flashing through the trees. She strained to hear, too afraid to call out in case it was someone who meant her harm. Her heart pounded so hard she was sure they'd be able to hear it.

The group of lights broke up and feet crunched through the brush. Beth held her breath as one of the lights came closer.

'Beth?' It was a kind, familiar voice.

Gus.

But who could she trust? Really?

She tensed, wondering if she'd be able to make a run for it if he untied her. She couldn't feel her body, apart from a tingling in her fingers. A light shone in her face, causing her to blink, and someone took a sharp intake of breath.

'Beth, it's me, Gus.'

CHAPTER TWENTY-FIVE

Gus set down his light to shine on both of them, then pulled out a knife. It glinted wickedly in the light and Beth couldn't breathe. He moved toward her, the light shining off the deadly metal blade. Terror rose in a ball inside her until it reached her throat and burst out in a piercing scream. This was it.

Gus stopped, eyes wide as the sound echoed through the night. 'Beth, I'm only going to cut the ropes.'

It took a moment for his words to register. He looked shaken and she realised he was speaking the truth. He set off a flare, and helpless sobs overcame her. He took a cautious step toward her. 'Can I cut the ropes?'

She nodded and watched as each one fell away. Suddenly she was falling; she couldn't feel her legs. Gus's strong arms caught her, holding her firm. She wanted to cling to him, but her arms wouldn't work. 'Don't let me go,' she begged.

'I won't.' His arms tightened and he held her head against his chest in a fierce, protective way. He smoothed her tangled hair and wiped her tear-streaked face.

'There were dingoes,' she said through strangled sobs. 'Joel tied me, I wanted to die and be with Andy, but God didn't let me.'

He nodded. 'I want to hear it all, but first we have to get you somewhere warm and safe.'

Footsteps crashed through the bush, voices called out, and blinding lights surrounded them. Arms reached out to embrace her, and Clare's voice came in her ear.

'Oh Beth, what happened to you? I was so scared we'd lost you, too.' And then she was crying, holding Beth so tight it hurt. Gus still held her up and her skin was beginning to feel bruised and cold. Feeling was returning.

'She can't walk,' Gus said.

'We can get the SES to bring in a stretcher.'

She didn't know that voice. She clung to Gus. He held her closer. 'I've got her. I'll carry her up to the roadway. It'll be quicker.'

THE NEXT FEW hours were a blur. Beth was vaguely aware of an ambulance, of Clare by her side, of doctors, Mum panicking and pacing the hospital floors, police questioning her. And Gus. He sat in the hospital room, a steady, calm figure of stability in all the chaos.

She didn't want to go home. It was too quiet there, too lonely. Despite being worried someone might be lurking, Mum agreed to let her stay with Phil and Clare so long as they locked all the doors and windows and kept phones by their side. Police were still keeping a vigil on the farm.

Gus insisted on taking the lounge so Beth could have the spare room. Despite everything that had happened, she felt safer here with Phil, Clare and Gus. Mum tucked her into bed and left to go home. Clare sat looking at her, holding her hand as though she'd never let her go again.

Beth whispered through the ache in her throat. 'Clare, do you really think dreams come true?'

Clare hesitated, then swallowed hard. 'Not often. I believe God has a better plan for us than we can ever imagine. But Beth, even if our dreams do come true, they're usually so different in reality to what we expect. I dreamed of marrying Phil, but I really had no idea what it would be like to be married to him.'

Beth closed her eyes. After a while, a small choking sound came from Clare and something wet dropped onto her hand. *Don't cry for me, Clare. I'm not worth it.*

Clare moved out of the room and Beth opened her eyes, staring into the darkness. Silent tears flowed down her cheeks, but she controlled the sobs threatening to shake her body. Phil and Clare were in the next room, and she didn't want to add to the grief and worry they already bore.

Feeling totally alone, Beth went over the trauma of the last twenty-four hours until it was all so clear in her mind she knew she'd never forget one detail.

THE POLICE WERE DELIGHTED with the concise information Beth provided the following morning. Mum sat beside her as the detective in charge reported the men who'd raced away in the truck had already been caught, but that they were yet to apprehend Joel.

'We knew there was a leader around somewhere, but Joel is extremely clever and hid behind the program and his newfound religion. We're not sure how he managed to get himself into the program except that he uses a few different aliases. He's actually 22 years old.'

Beth gasped. 'He doesn't look that old.'

'No, which he uses to his advantage. There have been suspicions about him for a while, but no solid evidence until now.'

Beth was confused. 'So why did he admit to me that he was the ringleader? He must have known I'd tell someone.'

The detective looked grim. 'Every criminal makes their mistakes. Perhaps he thought he would never be caught or that you wouldn't survive the night, but more likely in his panic he didn't really think about what he was saying.'

The thought that Joel might really want her dead didn't sit well. To think she'd thought males were more trustworthy and didn't have hidden agendas like Dara. How wrong and judgmental she'd been.

The police questioned Rod, too. He was devastated that Joel used the program that way.

'There's no way you could have known,' an officer reassured him. 'We're investigating, but there is no obvious neglect on your part. You were never expected to know where everyone was at every moment of every day. This is not Juvenile Justice.'

Still, Rod looked troubled as he led the police to the Cairns' home so they could go through Joel's room. A whole section of the farm was to be cordoned off until investigations finished.

Beth selected a book from Clare's bookshelf and tried to read, but ended up gazing out the window at the pond in the front yard. The ducks were the only ones calm and oblivious to the chaos going on around them.

'Been resting well?'

She looked up. Gus leaned against the back door frame but she couldn't meet his eyes. What must he think of her after the way she'd clung to him last night?

'Yeah. Sorry I took your room last night.'

He moved toward her and she looked up to see he was smiling. He had something in his arms. 'I brought you some pet therapy. Are you up to it?'

She tried to see. 'What is it?'

He gently lowered a warm, feathered creature into her lap. 'I'm told it owes you it's life.'

She looked at the defenceless creature, remembering Joel's cruel streak. She should have known. But she was confused. This mass of feathers no longer looked like a duckling. It was much bigger and its neck had grown long and curved.

She gasped. 'It's a swan?'

'A goose. I noticed it in the pond the day I got here, and realised the mother duck had rejected it. It was bigger than all the others, so I Googled it and discovered it's a gosling. I made a box for it, and it lives in the Cairns' laundry for now.'

Beth stroked the gosling's soft feathers and it snuggled in under her elbow. 'So how did a gosling end up with the ducks?'

'Either a goose egg was put under the mother duck, or Joel found it somewhere else and everyone just presumed it was one of the ducklings.'

She sighed, her heart heavy. 'Joel. He must have known it was a gosling when he threw it in the water. No wonder it survived.' She looked down and stroked its feathers. 'Why do I attract the wrong people?'

Gus moved to sit on the lounge beside her. 'Not because you're like them.'

She rubbed the sores around her wrists where the ropes had cut in, and studied Gus. He had a strong, calming presence. 'Gus, can I tell you something?'

He nodded, his steady gaze never leaving hers.

'I thought Andy was the only one on earth who knew I killed my grandfather. But Joel knew. I am the reason my grandpa died.'

She waited, but Gus didn't blink. When he spoke, his voice was level. 'Are you telling me this to test me?'

'No. I just want someone else on earth to know. Someone I can trust.'

He didn't move a muscle, but his face softened, and in that moment, Beth knew. She did trust him. He was a steady, safe place in a world of chaos and pain. When she'd called out to God for help, He'd sent Gus to save her.

She swallowed. 'It's the only thing I didn't tell the police about Joel, and maybe I should have, but I needed to tell someone I trust first.'

He sat on the lounge across from her and leaned forward, elbows on his knees. 'So tell me.'

And so she told him, reliving every moment, the memories as vivid as the day it happened.

'Grandpa! Stop the car!'

Grandpa slammed on the brakes. 'What is it?'

'A galah. It's injured.' She snapped off her seatbelt, threw open her door and raced across the three lanes of the city motorway to where the pink and grey feathered creature lay with its wings out, crumpled on the roadway.

'Beth!'

She turned at Grandpa's cry to see a truck bearing down on her. Without thought, she snatched up the bird and threw herself back against the guard rail just in time. The truck let out a long, loud honk, but Beth's eyes were on the galah. It didn't look good. Her eyes darted both ways before she dashed back across the road to where Grandpa sat in the car. She opened the door and slumped into the seat.

'I'm okay, Grandpa, but this galah needs help. Can we stop off at Belinda's?'

He didn't answer.

'She's the wildlife carer down the road.' Grandpa surely remembered Belinda, didn't he? Beth was constantly on Belinda's doorstep, helping with injured wildlife.

It was then that she noticed. Grandpa wasn't breathing right and his face was pale. He looked kind of dazed.

'Grandpa?' Still he didn't speak. Didn't move. Then his hand went to his chest and she noticed the look in his eyes. Fear. She reached a hand to his arm. Clammy.

'Grandpa?' She fumbled in her bag for her phone. Something was

very wrong. It must be his heart. He'd been seeing a specialist the last few years.

With shaking fingers, she managed to call an ambulance.

By the time they arrived, Grandpa was in a bad way. Beth stood over the ambulance stretcher and took his hand.

'I'm so sorry, Grandpa. I should never have made you stop. I didn't mean to scare you so badly!'

He smiled, squeezing her hand, every breath a struggle. 'Never lose your beautiful, compassionate heart my Beth.'

And they were the last words she ever heard from him. Grandpa's heart failed him that day. Despite Belinda's best efforts, the galah didn't make it either.

'Everyone presumed Grandpa pulled over to the side of the road because he wasn't feeling well,' Beth told Gus. 'I couldn't bring myself to tell them the truth.'

'But someone must have known.'

Beth bit her lip and nodded. 'Yes.'

'I'm sure there were witnesses.'

'But how did Joel know?'

'I don't know, but I intend to talk to the police and see what we can find out.'

He went to get the cordless phone from the kitchen and Beth heard his deep voice rumble from the next room. Slowly she leaned back on the lounge, and the gosling shuffled up to snuggle in under her neck and close its eyes. And Beth felt safe for the first time in years. She drifted off to sleep.

BETH WOKE to a knock at the door. She glanced around, unable to see Gus or the gosling. Instead, Dara stood at the door, her face tear-streaked as she sniffed back tears.

'Come in.' Beth was too tired to get up. Out the window, she could see Gus cleaning the duck pond. Indignant ducks quacked around him, and the gosling followed his every step. He glanced up, meeting her gaze through the window, and she knew he was keeping an eye on her.

Dara flopped onto the lounge beside Beth and let out a wail. 'Oh Beth, I feel like I'm falling apart. I can't believe we've lost Andy. What can we do?'

Her sobs increased, but Beth wasn't moved. 'Believe and trust God.' It was an automated response, but she was drained, with nothing left to give.

'But I want to do something—something to make sure we never forget him. We can't just let him die!'

'He did. He has.'

Dara's jaw dropped and the tears disappeared. 'Beth! What's up with you?'

You just keep trying to take from me but I'm empty. There's nothing left.

Dara crossed her arms, her lip quivering. 'Can't you even cry for him? I thought you were friends.'

'No.' Friends was such a shallow word. 'We were more than that. We had a spiritual connection beyond what anyone else will ever understand. He made my life worth living, and now he's gone I feel nothing.'

Dara stared at her, uncharacteristically silent, and Beth watched her expression as the words registered. 'You were in love with Andy,' she breathed in wonder. 'All this time and it was Andy Saunders. I thought you couldn't love anyone—you seemed so detached from any feelings.'

Beth remained silent.

'You know, Andy and I had a good talk about you,' Dara said tantalisingly. 'He said some things that really helped me understand you more.'

Beth knew she was being expertly reeled in, but she couldn't help asking. 'When?'

'That night you won the award for your artwork and didn't tell any of us about it.'

'I told Andy.' Why did she say that?

'Yes, and he went to the dinner with you. He told me all about it.'

Beth refused to ask her what Andy said. Dara would embellish it. Yet it was torture not knowing. Dara had her dangling in her web. Again.

'Do you want to know?'

She forced herself to shake her head. 'It was between you and Andy.'

'Fine. But he thought more of you than you think, Beth.'

Beth turned from Dara without another word, went into her room and shut the door. She couldn't deal with this right now.

DESPITE NOT CARING whether she lived or died, Beth was relieved when a police officer arrived at the farm with Mum to let her know Joel had been caught.

'We will need you to testify,' he told Beth apologetically. 'Joel has requested a committal hearing to speed up the court process.'

A grunt of disapproval came from Gus.

'She should be safe now, though,' the officer said, looking at Gus.

And once again Beth wondered if someone had appointment Gus as her bodyguard.

Mum agreed to let her testify. 'I'm proud of you for having the courage,' she said. To Beth's surprise, she didn't care. All her life she'd wanted Mum to be proud of her, and now that she'd achieved that, she found it made no difference.

'Can I sit with you?' Dara asked as Beth and her mother walked into the church for Andy's funeral a few days later.

Beth couldn't give today. It was too much to ask. It would cost her the very air she breathed. 'Sorry, but I'm sitting with my family.'

To her relief, Dara just gave a little huff and went to sit beside Brett.

Sitting with Mum, Clare and Phil, Beth stared at the coffin down the front of the church. Her blue-eyed hero was in there. It was so wrong. Here she was, feeling such devastation—living in such pain—when the source of her grief wouldn't smile or cry ever again. Not on earth, anyway. Andy had had so much to offer. She was the one who belonged in that box.

'Isn't it wonderful for him?' Mrs. Holmes turned to whisper. 'In heaven so young, free from the pain of this world.'

Beth gave the smallest hint of a nod but she wanted to spit in her face. How could Andy's joy at being in heaven outweigh the grief in this room; the heavy, overwhelming weight in her own heart? Mrs. Holmes could keep her spiritual platitudes to herself.

Clare reached over to hold Beth's hand, and she grasped it tight in return. She couldn't let go of the tears burning her throat because if she did, they might never stop.

Phil went forward to sing, and Beth heard Clare's quiet cries of anguish beside her. Clare would never say it was all wonderful because Andy was now in heaven. This was a broken, messed up world, and they were stuck in it without Andy.

As they stood around the grave, Beth was confused by the way people greeted one another like it was a normal Sunday morning. Smiles felt so fake, words so hollow. She glanced around. Toni stood beside Rod, and baby William—or Billy—was in Rod's arms. He looked bigger, healthier and brighter. It was good to see life and hope in this place of death.

She watched as Andy's coffin was lowered into the ground. His brother Pete stood on the other side of the grave, his head bowed, so heavy with sorrow that Beth feared he would collapse beneath it.

'Go to him,' Clare whispered.

Beth's eyes shot to Clare. Why her? Phil and Clare were Pete's friends, and so much better at reaching out to people. And yet, she was so moved by compassion she found herself ignoring what anyone else thought, and went to Pete's side. He looked up, and the sight of his tears set off her own. She was deeply moved when he put his arm around her. His sorrow was intense, yet he still gave. For the first time she wasn't intimidated by the handsome Pete; they now shared a common experience, a common sorrow.

'He knew this would happen,' Pete whispered brokenly. 'He always knew it.'

'What do you mean?'

'He used to talk about when he was going to die.' Pete's lips lifted in a sorrowful smile. 'He so badly wanted to see Jesus face to face.'

Pete was right. Beth remembered Andy's expression whenever he prayed. She'd never doubted he would go straight to heaven when he died, but now his body lay lifeless in that box, his lively blue eyes closed forever, it was harder to swallow. Every part of her yearned to open the lid, to hold him tight, demand he breathe again, but she was scared of what she'd see in there.

'He once said he'd be willing to die if that's what it took for me to believe.' Pete's voice caught. 'I guess it happened.'

Beth drew in a sharp breath. If Pete came to believe, it would bring some comfort, but it would never make up for Andy's life.

God, Pete and I both know nothing can ever make up for this.

My son's death has. It will be okay.

Beth's eyes stung. It hurt to breathe. How could God the Father have willingly given up the life of His son? Let Him die? How could He have thought that her coming to believe in Him would make up for it?

How much God must value her. Love her.

She wept.

CHAPTER TWENTY-SIX

Beth didn't like being back home—Mum had never been good with emotion, and holding every feeling in check for her sake, was hard work. Clare said Mum had hardly cried even when Dad died, and Beth remembered how awkward it was when Grandpa died and Mum wore sunglasses for a week. No one could tell what she was feeling, and her tight-lipped expression gave nothing away.

The doorbell chimed and Beth's heart jumped.

Andy?

Then she realised it would never be Andy again and her heart broke all over again.

'Beth, it's Anique Trent,' Mum said, leading Anique into the living room. *Anique.* Beth hadn't thought of her for several days. She hadn't been at the funeral.

Ashamed of all the feelings rushing through her as she came face to face with Anique, she reminded herself the competition was over. Andy was gone. 'How are you?'

'I'm struggling.' Anique's brown eyes were cesspools of pain and regret.

'What happened that day?' Beth whispered.

Anique stiffened. 'Like, I had the situation under control. I was recording Cain, getting evidence against Joel. I didn't need Andy to protect me, but he always had to be like the hero, didn't he? Like he had to be the strong, invincible one. Do you know how humiliating it is to have everyone think he had to save me?'

Beth was shocked speechless. Anique bursts into tears. 'Sorry. Sorry. I sound like a horrible, heartless person. He died trying to save my life and all I can do is feel angry with him.'

'It's a lot, I know. Grief is a rollercoaster of emotions.'

Anique shook her head 'I don't like the fact that he died thinking he was saving me.' She wrung her hands. 'Everyone thinks it's so romantic or something, but I don't want to feel indebted to him. He made a choice that I have to live with.'

'You wish he hadn't saved your life?'

'He didn't save my life. Everyone just thinks he did. Seriously, like, I would have gotten out of there safely. I've like dealt with situations like that before, and I knew how to handle Cain, but Andy messed it up. I just wish the whole thing had never happened. I was ready to move on—forget about Andy. But now people expect me to always be thinking of him, grateful he gave me a second chance at life, or whatever. But I didn't ask him to get involved. And I don't want to be *the girl that Andy Saunders saved*. Our relationship was full of drama and conflict. I want to forget him, forget the hurt, and move on.'

Beth tried to understand, but everything in her wanted to defend Andy. 'I guess it's a bit like Jesus dying for us, isn't it? We didn't ask Him to, but once we're confronted with it, we have to either accept gratefully or totally turn our backs and say we never needed it or wanted it.'

Anique was quiet for a long moment, and Beth placed a hand on her bone thin arm. 'Sorry, I know your situation is different. Andy wasn't God, he didn't actually save you, and you have no obligation to remember him.'

'But I do! And everyone knows it.'

'Maybe not where you're going. You're still moving aren't you?' To Beth's relief, Anique nodded. 'So you don't have to remember Andy. Others will carry on his memory. You just think of God. He's the one who really saved you, when Jesus gave His life for you.'

'But Beth, why am I still here? Everyone knows Andy was the gifted one—he had so much to offer. And me ... I've hurt so many people and made a complete mess of my life.'

You and me both, Anique. 'I don't know, but I believe Andy completed all that God wanted him to do. Perhaps he was given such outstanding gifts because he had so much to accomplish in such a short time. You and I have a lifetime. We should feel privileged that God still has more for us to do.'

The light returned to Anique's eyes, but Beth knew it would be a long time before she could live out her own words of wisdom. There was still a part of her clinging to Andy with every breath, every heartbeat. She would keep him alive, even at the cost of her own survival. Anique wouldn't do it, so she must.

As Beth hugged Anique goodbye, she marvelled at how right her first impressions were. Anique made an impact wherever she went. More than Beth had imagined possible.

THE EMPTINESS that came after the weeks of intense emotion drove Beth crazy. There was nothing to look forward to in a day. No future to dream about. Nothing to hope for.

She forced herself to think through the upcoming committal hearing for Joel. She'd re-lived the experience a thousand times but having to do it in front of people was a different matter.

'It's rare for a witness to be called at the first hearing, but Joel has insisted on a defended committal hearing to speed up the process,' the police officer told Beth. 'He's hoping to get off, but don't worry, he won't. We'll make sure of that.'

It was rumoured that Joel had charmed other Guests on the farm, too—especially the girls. None of them had suspected he was running a drug lab in the bush, and it made Beth feel a bit less foolish.

Rod said more Guests would arrive once the accommodation was finished and the investigation into how Joel infiltrated the system was complete. The Guests would include three wards of the state from Sydney who wanted to learn how to run a farm.

'They're all young men in their late teens,' Rod told Beth, as though that would interest her. 'One of them is already a believer.'

It made no difference to Beth. She'd made a conscious decision to avoid the opposite sex. It was too hard to know who to trust, and she clearly had poor judgement, so why bother? She wasn't going to marry now that Andy was gone, and she didn't want to give anyone the wrong impression. Phil and Gus were the only ones who weren't a threat to her decision to remain single. Phil was married and Gus was against marriage.

'Where are the girls?' she asked Gus when she found him working alone at the construction site.

He stood and stretched. 'What girls?'

'Courtney and ... the Guests.'

'Don't you even know their names?'

He looked so disapproving she wasn't game to admit she didn't. 'Where are they?'

He sat on one of the sawhorses. 'I sent them off to have a break. They shouldn't be long.'

She turned to leave, but Gus spoke again, waving his hand around at the building now well under way. 'What do you think?'

She made an effort to look. 'It's big.'

'It is.' He took a drink from his water bottle, then held it out to her. She declined with a shake of her head. 'Are you doing okay?'

She didn't know if she wanted to answer. He always listened

and tried to understand, but he could also be insensitive and abrupt. Safest to be honest but vague. 'I'm surviving.'

'Missing Andy.'

She looked down. 'Yeah. I'm looking forward to heaven.'

'I hope you're going to let God take you in His own good time.'

Her head jerked up. 'Of course.' Offended, she glared at him. 'I'd never consider suicide.' How could she like and dislike him so intensely at the same time?

'Good.' He set his water bottle down, giving her his full attention. His voice softened. 'So you've been thinking a bit about heaven?'

'Yes, and it leaves me with so many questions.'

'Like?'

'Like, will our bodies all be the same age in heaven? Or will they stay at the age we died? Will Andy always look 17, and will Grandpa always look 79?'

He nodded. 'I admit I've wondered about that, too.'

'I want to know if we will recognise each other.'

'I suspect so. The disciples recognised Moses and Elijah at the transfiguration. Maybe we'll look a bit like we did on earth.'

'But what about those with defects—those who are obese or are born with only one arm?'

He shrugged. 'I don't know. Will we even consider them defects in heaven, or will we realise God formed each of us exactly as he always planned?'

Beth frowned at him. 'It's not God who causes defects. It's the Fall. God sometimes intervenes with miracles, and other times He allows the impacts of free will and human sin to play out.'

'I disagree.' His gaze steadily held hers. 'David says in Psalm 139 that we were knit together in our mother's womb. God formed every single part of us. He's God—He doesn't miss a stitch.'

'I don't know … Why does it all have to be so confusing?'

'Isn't it enough to know God knows? Can't you just trust?'

She crossed her arms. 'I do trust Him, but it's not wrong to have questions.'

'No,' he conceded, his tone more gentle. 'So, what other questions do you have?'

'I want to know where Andy is.' Her throat burned, her eyes stinging as she tried to hold back her tears. 'Not his body, but his soul—everything that made him Andy.'

'In heaven.'

'But where is heaven? Can he see me? Does he remember me? Will I recognise him in heaven? Or is everything I loved about him gone forever?'

She spilled out her heart, knowing the only answer this side of heaven could be, *I don't know.* No one could know. But could she have the faith to trust anyway? To accept God loved Andy more than she ever could, and leave him in Jesus' loving arms?

You won't be able to live until you let him go.

Was that God's voice or her own mind? How could she know when God was speaking to her when so many other voices filled her heart and mind?

Gus stood abruptly. 'Aren't you happy for him?'

He didn't understand. He might be a good listener, but he was pretty thick sometimes.

'Isn't it good he's in heaven?' he pressed.

Beth gritted her teeth. 'You are so insensitive.'

His eyes widened. 'What have I said this time?'

She didn't bother to answer as she turned on her heel and stalked away.

BETH FOUND the three girls down by the creek eating morning tea. They watched her with suspicion as she joined them on the grass.

She didn't blame them, really. She'd never made an effort to talk to them before.

'I'm Beth. I wanted to say hello, but I'm ashamed to say I don't even know your names.'

'Why should you know our names?'

She supposed she deserved that, but she ploughed on. 'Because I should have at least made an effort to connect with you. A lot has happened, and, well, we need each other if we're going to get through this.'

The one she had a feeling was Courtney gave a careless shrug. 'Don't worry about us, Beth. We're okay.'

Tears stung her eyes. 'But I'm not.'

They shuffled uncomfortably, looking anywhere but at her. She should have stayed home. Now they'd talk about her, gossip about her, probably make fun of her. She felt sick at the thought. Actually, the nausea had been building all day, and she was losing control. She jumped up and moved to a nearby bush where she retched. Over and over. While they watched. Drawing in a deep breath, she bolted back to the cottage without looking back. After washing her face, she fell onto the lounge chair and let the tears flow.

'Anyone home?' Gus knocked and Beth sat up, desperately trying to dry her eyes and straighten her hair. Then she brushed at a dirty mark on her jeans. What was she doing? As if Gus cared how she looked. She probably got the mark from dirt Gus left on the lounge anyway.

He walked in, full of life and energy. How could he work so hard but never look tired? These days all she had to do was get up in the morning and her energy was drained for the day.

'I need a drill,' Gus said. 'Mine stopped.'

'Well I don't think you'll find one in here.'

He wandered over to the cupboard. 'Phil said he keeps a spare here somewhere.'

He scuffled around in the cupboard, then held up the drill. She expected him to go, but he kept looking at her. Then he lowered himself onto the lounge, his expression thoughtful. 'So you can't get through grief just by knowing the other person's happy?'

Was he challenging her to a debate? She opened her mouth to tell him to forget the whole conversation they'd had earlier, but the kindness in his expression stopped her. Despite his tone, his brown eyes said he was desperately trying to understand, and she realised he must have been thinking over what she'd said all morning. 'No, you can't. Grief has a mind of its own.'

'And you really loved Andy.'

'Yes.'

He didn't seem bothered by her short answers and just sat, not seeming in a hurry to leave.

'My dream has been shattered,' she finally said. 'The world can't ever feel whole for me again. I can't be happy Andy died, because I can't expect to ever feel excitement or joy again.'

'Not even at what God's done for you?'

She knew he wasn't meaning to hurt her. He was genuinely surprised. 'I'm talking about my dreams for love and romance. I can't marry because I can't expect any man to be second best and I will never love anyone else like I love Andy. He made the world an exciting place for me. I dreamed of marrying him for a long time. My dreams have been shattered.'

Gus said nothing until she looked up to meet his eyes. 'I've never been impressed by all that romance stuff.' He pulled a cushion out from behind his back. 'It's unrealistic and deceptive.'

Cold seeped into her chest. 'What?'

He knocked the unwanted cushion onto the floor. 'It can't last. A guy gets romantic for a time purely to get the girl, but it's not sustainable. It's too much to expect him to live up to a girl's romantic expectations. He'll inevitably let her down.'

Her teeth clenched. 'Some people are naturally romantic. Andy wasn't being fake.'

'I wasn't talking about him in particular, but I do think he was a bit too liberal with his hugs. It wasn't appropriate the way he gave them out freely to all the girls in the youth group. It's not fair to make girls think you're romantically interested when you're not.'

No other living person had ever made Beth so angry. She snatched the cushion up off the floor and shoved it down beside her on the lounge, out of the way of his dirty hands. He was so opinionated and self-absorbed that he drove her crazy. She found herself pursing her lips the way Mum often did.

He quirked a brow. 'You disagree?'

There was so much she could say. Instead, she forced herself to shrug.

He let out a sigh. 'I wish you'd be honest with me Beth. Stop putting on your show of poise and control and let people get to know the real you. Are you scared you're not likeable or something?'

The poise and control he accused her of came undone. 'You have no idea what you're talking about,' she hissed. 'It's common decency to try to make some kind of impression and make someone feel special. I never took Andy's hugs as romantic. They were the way he cared; the way he showed people he understood. I reckon even Jesus hugged people. You should try it sometime. But you're so selfish you just do and say whatever you want to without thinking about how it might come across. There's no way you could ever love anyone—'

'I know that. That's why I'm not getting married.'

'But your selfishness is the only reason! I wish you'd look outside of yourself and your achievements for a moment and try to understand the way other people think, instead of expecting them to always bow to your ignorant opinions.'

He shoved at another cushion and before she could stop herself, Beth leapt forward and grabbed it. 'See, you can't even let someone else have a cushion in their own home if you don't want it there!'

'It's still in their home. I didn't chuck it out the door.'

'There you go again. Listen to my meaning, Gus, not my words. Stop being so literal. You know I meant you couldn't leave it on the lounge. Why can't you make an effort to be normal?'

Gus's brows shot up. 'It's a cushion—it just takes up space. They're totally useless things.'

He was too much. She hurled the cushion at his head. It flew past and knocked a picture off the wall. She gasped and her hands flew to her mouth. Gus's eyes were wide and she knew she'd shocked him, too.

She fell back against the lounge with a groan, burying her head in her hands. 'Look what you made me do ... No, sorry, it's not your fault. I didn't mean all that. Well, yes I did, but I didn't intend to say it ... I mean ... I'm just digging myself in deeper with everything I say. I'll be quiet now.'

She heard his chuckle and dared peek at him through her fingers. His expression had softened and he appeared pleased rather than offended.

'You did it,' he said triumphantly.

'I did what?'

'You were honest with me, and expressed how you really feel, and now you're kicking yourself for doing exactly what I challenged you to do.'

She shook her head, stood and stomped out of the house. Gus Richards was too much. Her whole world was falling apart and all he wanted was to challenge her to be who he thought she should be. Well, she wasn't going to do what he wanted. She was tired of living up to other people's expectations.

CHAPTER TWENTY-SEVEN

Beth didn't know where to go. She stormed out the back to where Gilbert clung to the side of his cage. He flapped his wings. Then to her surprise, flew from one side of the chicken pen to the other.

She remembered Belinda talking about this once. One of her rescue birds had fallen off a perch and the jolt had caused his dislocated wing to slip back into place. Had Gilbert's wing been merely dislocated? Was it possible he could be released?

'Gilbert,' she whispered. 'You might be able to fly free soon. You really might!'

A car pulled up outside the cottage, and Beth tensed. When would she feel safe again? The car looked like her brother Dan's, but he lived hours away in the small town of Caldon.

Yet, there was something familiar about the young man now walking toward the cottage. His height, his build, his wayward brown hair. Only, the arrogant, sauntering gait was missing, and his shoulders were slumped. He looked up and their eyes caught. It was him.

'Beth.' He moved steadily toward her and she tried to read his expression. Something was different. He reached her and stopped, just looking at her. Then she heard the words she thought she'd never hear from him.

'Beth, I came to tell you I'm sorry. For so many things.'

She took a step back, confused. And then saw Gus come out the back door. Looking out for her. She was still annoyed with him, but she didn't need to be rude. 'Gus, meet my brother, Dan.'

'Daniel.'

Her eyes shot back to Dan's. 'Pardon?'

'I want to be called Daniel.'

'Like Grandpa?'

He nodded and Beth's lip quivered. She gestured to the house, unable to speak, and he nodded back, following her up the path. Gus held the door open for them, his gaze not missing a thing. When they sat, he sat beside them.

'I owe you so many apologies, Beth.' Dan's eyes, usually so teasing, were dark and sorrowful.

Beth shook her head. 'Don't, Dan—Daniel. It's okay.'

'It's not. I'm sorry for the times I stole your books. I'm sorry for the way I laughed when the magpie swooped in and ate your pet butterfly as soon as it came out of its cocoon. I'm sorry for killing ants to upset you. I'm sorry for the time I laughed because you wanted to give your arm to that little boy who had lost his in an accident, and for telling you yours was too ugly and he wouldn't want it anyway.'

Her lip quivered. 'Dan, don't.'

He ploughed ahead. 'I'm sorry for taking your journals and stomping on your heart so many times. I didn't understand what a gift you were. I'm sorry for hurting that lost little girl who just wanted to be loved.'

That's when Beth lost it. Great, rasping sobs came from deep within as hurt she didn't even know she was still there gushed forth like a fountain released from the depths of the desert.

And Dan just sat there, sorrow so deep it overshadowed him,

enveloping his whole being. Beth pulled herself together for his sake, drawing in deep breaths.

Finally, he spoke. 'Can you forgive me?'

She swiped at her tears and drew in another shaky breath. 'You came all this way to say sorry?'

He nodded. 'Lots has happened, Beth. So much. I can't explain it all right now—there's ongoing police investigations—but you have to know I'm sorry. I just need to know you're okay.'

Tears welled again. 'Oh Dan, I'm sorry too. I've made so many mistakes …'

'If you're talking about Grandpa, you know you didn't kill him, right?'

She spun to look at Gus. 'You told him?'

'He didn't tell me anything.' Dan drew her attention back. 'A truck driver called the police about a girl on the highway rescuing a galah. Said she was nearly run over. There's a statement on the police records.'

Beth was astounded. 'But, but then how do you know?'

'Not all police are trustworthy. One of them was feeding information to Joel. And using me, too. But justice is being done. And you're safe now.'

Beth shook her head, trying to take it in.

'I'm so sorry, Beth,' he said again. And she knew he was.

'You're forgiven, Dan.'

'Daniel. Dan is gone. I don't want to be that insensitive person I was, ever again.'

Beth remembered being tied to the tree. Daniel in the lion's den. She smiled at him. *Daniel.* The man of God. Then she noticed Gus looking between them. 'What?'

He shrugged. 'I just think you two need to hug.'

Beth glared at him. Gus didn't know their family. Didn't understand the unspoken rule. No affection. It wasn't going to happen.

But Dan stood, his expression uncertain, and for the first time she felt compassion for him, rather than fear of his scorn and teasing. She stood and threw her arms around him, amused by the way he awkwardly patted her on the back.

Then she shot Gus a meaningful look over Dan's shoulder. 'Who are you to suggest we hug? It's not like you offer them freely.'

'No, but he's your brother. No one could say it's inappropriate.'

Beth bit her lip to stop her smile, unable to be annoyed with him, even though it felt like he'd won.

Dan moved away, still looking awkward. 'Never lose your compassionate heart, Beth,' he said, echoing the last words Grandpa had said to her.

She swallowed hard. Miracles could happen. Maybe she would fly someday. She and Gilbert, both.

BETH KICKED the dust along the road, working through the last few days. Dan had gone home after spending the night on Clare and Phil's lounge. He'd even visited Mum. He was different. So different. It was hard to take in.

She looked up to see the girls from the program heading her way. She tensed as they approached.

'We want to ask you something,' said the one with dark, curly hair.

She waited, nervous.

'We need help with our geography homework for school and Phil said you're good at it.'

She hadn't been expecting that. Especially after they'd watched her inelegantly retch into a bush last time they'd talked.

'So, will you?' the taller one asked.

'I ... I think Phil would be able to help you better.'

'He's always tired or busy.'

It was true. Beth's heart felt lighter, but she was cautious. 'Okay. I'll help. When?'

'Now?'

She'd given up, thinking she'd blown her chance of ever being friends with them, but they'd come to *her*. They sat at the table in the main farmhouse and the girls introduced themselves. Courtney, Emily and Tarryn. Then Beth explained longitude and latitude. She sensed them studying her as she pointed to the maps in their text books. Were they even listening?

'Were you and Joel going out?' the strawberry blonde named Emily asked. Nope, not listening.

'Definitely not.'

'I thought he asked you.' That was Tarryn.

She drew a steadying breath. 'He did, but he just wanted to use me.'

They looked confused. *Truth.* Gus had challenged her to be open and honest. *Help me, God.*

'I haven't told anyone about this except the police ...' She bit her lip and they leaned closer, hanging on her every word. 'Joel just wanted a Christian girlfriend so it looked as though he was living the Christian life. All he really wanted was money. He told me that, then tied me to a tree and left me to be eaten by dingoes.'

Their eyes widened and Taryn shook her head. 'I knew it. You can't trust Christians.'

'He wasn't a Christian. He was just pretending.'

'All Christians are hypocrites.'

Beth smiled at the way Courtney and Emily tried to shush Tarryn. 'Genuine Christians are trustworthy.'

'Like who?'

'Phil. Clare. Rod and Gus.'

Tarryn screwed up her nose. 'They're just naturally nice people.'

'Nope.' Beth shook her head. 'You don't know what Clare used to be like. Or Rod.'

Their eyes widened. 'What were they like?'

'Um, you'd better ask them. I don't know if they would want me telling you.'

'But we won't tell!'

Beth wondered if she'd said too much already. Was it her business to talk about their past? But it was her past, too … 'Clare and my brother Dan were pretty horrible to me when I was little … well, actually, until Clare became a Christian. And she was a rebel. She and my brother stole my mum's favourite casserole dish and buried it. I remember her burning down Dad's rose bush just because I was scared of fire. Mum was so upset because Dad died when I was about two …'

The girl's stunned looks silenced her. She didn't like remembering the Clare of her childhood, and Clare wouldn't, either.

'What about Rod?' Emily asked.

Beth chuckled. 'He used to go to Youth Group just to hassle everyone. He would stand there and smoke even though it was against the rules. I've heard it rumoured that he …' she stopped. 'Look, I really shouldn't be telling you. The fact is, he became a Christian and his whole life changed.'

'What about you?' Emily wanted to know. 'What did you used to do?'

'I … I don't know.'

'You've always been good?'

'I tried.' Beth swallowed hard. 'But I made my grandpa stop in the middle of the road to rescue an injured bird and he had a heart attack.'

'In the middle of the road?'

'No. In the car while I ran to get the bird.'

'So you didn't kill him. He was driving, and it was his choice to stop.'

She was right. But there was so much more. How could she

explain all her anger, her jealousy, her futile efforts to control the world? 'I think not having majorly obvious sins can make it harder to be a Christian.'

They looked confused.

'It's when people are pretty good that they think they're fine on their own. They think they don't need God. That's the most dangerous thing of all, because if you don't think you need God, then you never put your trust in Jesus to save you.'

Each of them studied her with open interest.

'Did you think you didn't need God?' Tarryn pushed the text book aside.

Did she? The truth was, even though she'd prayed and asked Jesus to forgive her sin at Youth Group a few years back, she'd gone back to trying to survive on her own, without God. She'd been trying to prove she was good enough to deserve the sacrifice Jesus has made on her behalf. Not consciously, but that's what her actions had been saying.

And what a mess she'd made of it.

'Maybe that's why I didn't try to make friends with all of you when I should have. I was too busy trying to do everything myself instead of listening to God and trusting Him.'

'But you're different now.' Courtney's smile was warm.

Tarryn nodded. 'We used to think you were a snob, but you're not really.'

'Thank you.' She shuffled, feeling uncomfortable and exposed. She closed the textbook. What was geography when there were people to get to know? What good did studying do Andy? It all went to waste. Only the things of eternal significance would last.

'Let's go for a walk,' she suggested, and the girls heartily agreed.

'Did you know I smoke?' Tarryn asked as they trudged down the dirt road.

Beth wondered if the question was a challenge. 'Not marijuana, I hope.'

Tarryn looked surprised. 'What do *you* know about drugs?'

'I've known a few people caught up in them.'

'Like who?'

'It doesn't matter. I just know it's a rough world out there.'

Tarryn looked affronted. 'You don't know the half of it.'

'True, but I'm learning fast.'

'I used to shoplift all the time,' Emily burst out, her eyes fixed on Beth, as though expecting a strong reaction.

'Why?'

'I had to. That's how I survived.'

'Were you ever caught?'

As they walked, the girls opened up in a way Beth never dreamed possible. The more she listened, the more she understood how tough their lives had been. A week ago, she would have been shocked and discomfited by their revelations, but now she knew how broken the world really was. She also knew how desperately they all needed God's help to survive.

IT WAS GETTING DARK, but Beth didn't want to go home. Mum was working late, and she hated the thought of being alone in the big house.

'You can stay here and use my desk to get some schoolwork done,' Phil offered.

She smiled. 'Thanks.' She was too tired to socialise, and she had an English essay to finish. Pulling out her laptop, she sat at Phil's desk and turned it on. Slowly, it began its startup routine. She really needed a new one.

Opening the file with her essay, she began to type. Ten minutes later, the screen froze. She could reboot, but she couldn't stand the thought of losing what she'd already done.

'Phil,' she called through the door. 'My laptop's frozen.'

He came up behind her. 'What happened?'

'It just stopped.'

He reached over her shoulder and tried a few keys. 'It has, hasn't it?'

'What should we do?'

'Ask Gus.'

She laughed. 'He's a builder.'

'By trade, yes, but there's a lot more to Gus than meets the eye.'

'Meaning?'

Phil smiled. 'Just ask him.'

She ventured out to the kitchen where he was washing up. Working as usual. Did he ever stop?

He put down the washing-up brush and came to help. She stood behind him as he settled into Phil's office chair and studied her laptop. If Phil couldn't fix it, she seriously doubted Gus could. He tapped away at the keys and a code appeared on the screen. He typed in some commands that led him to places Beth hadn't known existed.

'What's error 243?' she asked.

'I don't know.'

'You don't know?'

'Not exactly.' He kept typing.

'Then how do you know what to do?'

He mumbled something she didn't understand, obviously absorbed in his work.

'Do you mean you don't know?' Beth pressed, 'or do you just think I wouldn't understand the answer?'

He stopped and turned with a smile. 'Okay, it means the stereotypical ORM's in the computer's hard field are clashing with the tandem cycles of oreosurgical input caused by uniform traces of minor distinction.'

She stared at him then fell into the computer chair at Clare's desk. 'Oh.'

A spark of amusement played in Gus's eyes as he turned back

to her laptop. A few seconds later he moved out of the chair. 'Try it now.'

'Later.'

'No, now. I want to see if it freezes again.'

She plopped into the chair with a frown. 'You think it was my touch that did it?'

'No. I want to see how you go about opening your program.'

She hesitated, and he raised his eyebrows, waiting. Her shoulders slumped. 'I don't want you watching me,' she confessed.

'Why? Am I intimidating or something?'

Or something. She didn't know what was happening to her. Something about Gus's protective tenderness these last few days had thrown her. Yes, he was still irritating and abrupt, but he was so much more, too. Her fingers shook as she moved the laptop closer, then rested her finger on the touchpad. To her surprise, Gus's hand touched her arm briefly, warm and gentle.

'Beth, I was just teasing with all that technological jargon. I made it up. I'm just as human as you are.'

And she knew he'd put his finger on the issue before she'd even recognised it. He might be human, but she knew she could never match Gus Richards' intelligence, energy levels, honesty or genuine godliness. No wonder he never planned to get married. He'd never find a wife his equal.

Her respect for the man she once found so medium in every way had soared to new heights. He was a genius and she didn't know how to deal with that—Didn't know how to deal with the complex man that he was, nor her feelings toward him.

BETH COULDN'T BELIEVE it when she was finishing her English essay on her laptop at home the following afternoon and it froze again. The essay was due first thing in the morning. *Please God, make it work.*

After ten minutes with no success, she took out her phone and stared at the screen. Gus was the only one she knew who could fix it, but he would be working. Guilt warred with need, and finally she called his number.

Gus answered almost immediately. She spoke fast. 'Gus, my laptop has frozen again. I wondered if you have the time to come over and have a look?'

'Is your mother home?'

'No. Why?'

'I just don't think I should be in there if you're on your own.'

Hurt tightened her chest. 'You don't trust me?'

'It's not about trust, it's about wisdom and how it appears.'

Argh! She glowered into the phone. She never should have made herself vulnerable and called him. 'You've made it clear to everyone that you have the gift of being single, so no one's going to get the wrong impression whether they think I'm trustworthy or not, so ...'

'They have reason to think you're untrustworthy?'

'You're deliberately taking my words the wrong way. Oh, forget it!' She jabbed the phone to finish the call. Right now she'd rather get zero for her essay than deal with Gus.

She stared at the screen. *It's just you and me now, God. Please help me.* She scrabbled around in her school bag for a pen and began writing up the essay by hand. There was no way she'd risk using Mum's computer after the way hers had frozen on her.

The doorbell rang. With a sigh she heaved herself up to check the door viewer. It wouldn't be Andy and she couldn't think of anyone else she'd want to see.

'Hello Beth.' Gus's serious face looked into the camera.

She swung the door open, and stuttered, unable to get any words out. His lips twitched. 'Did you get your computer working?'

She glanced behind her. 'Mum's still not here.'

'I brought Brayden.'

'Oh. Hey, Brayden.' She opened the door wider to let them in. 'But you didn't have to come.'

'So is it working, or isn't it?' Gus took off his ragged hat and hung it on the hatstand as he came in the hallway. He was the only one she'd ever seen actually use that stand.

'It's still not working. Brayden, there's cake on the kitchen bench.' Mum had left it for her, but she wasn't hungry.

Brayden grinned and went into the kitchen while Beth led Gus into the office. He gazed around, taking in their extravagant house with all its extra trimmings. And he thought cushions were unnecessary …

'You've got some nice equipment here,' he said as he pulled out the computer chair. She didn't comment, but watched his skilful fingers begin their work. How many people were aware of his brilliant mind? She glanced at his face. His brow furrowed in concentration as his capable hands moved automatically across the keyboard.

He began a scan on the computer and let it finish while he sat back and looked at her. 'Bored?'

'Not really.'

'I wouldn't have thought this was a spectator sport.'

A smile escaped. 'Sport? It's not work to you?'

'I enjoy it.'

'Is there anything in life you don't enjoy?'

He didn't hesitate. 'Dressing up, being in crowds, being up front and on display. Yep, there's things I don't enjoy.'

'But not many?'

'No, I find most things easy. I guess my fast mind is a blessing.'

There it was again; his frank acceptance of his own brilliance that shut out any possibility of another human ever being his equal. But more than that, it shut out need for any help, and Beth liked being able to help. Or rescue, in Joel's words. But she had nothing to offer someone like Gus. She'd just have to swallow her pride and keep accepting his help with nothing to give in return.

He sat up, facing the screen again. 'Scan's done. Should be good now, but you need to look into getting a new laptop.' He stretched. 'And I better get back to work before someone thinks I'm doing something untrustworthy or inappropriate.'

Beth gave him her most disgusted look. 'Yes, you'd better. You can see yourself out. And collect Brayden on the way.'

He stopped in the doorway and turned back. 'Do you want to say thank you? I don't want you kicking yourself later when you realise you didn't.'

She didn't want to. But as irritating as he was, she knew she should. Everything within her rebelled, but she forced out a quiet 'thank you' between her teeth.

He laughed. 'No, thank *you*,' he said.

For what? She'd never understand Gus Richards.

CHAPTER TWENTY-EIGHT

Beth didn't expect to do well in the end of year exams. Brain fog and memory issues had plagued her since Andy's death. But maybe it was a mixed blessing. The last thing she wanted was to be awarded Dux when Andy was no longer around to compete for it.

It still happened.

'I know you've had a tough year,' Mrs. Hendon said when Beth questioned her results, 'but that makes it all the more commendable that you have done as well as you have. We used your earlier results and gave you a bereavement exemption for some of your later assignments.'

Beth closed her eyes as the now familiar sick feeling returned to her stomach. Mrs. Hendon touched her shoulder. 'You are here for a reason, Beth. Andy's death is not your fault.'

Beth knew she was right, but an intense, heavy sadness still weighed her down as she went up to receive the Dux award. The school clapped, but she couldn't smile. For the first time, Mum had found time to come and watch the ceremony, but Beth didn't want her there.

'Andy would be so proud of you,' Dara said when Beth tried to escape out the door. 'I bet he's looking down from the clouds, clapping louder than anyone.'

Beth increased her speed. 'I'd prefer not to talk about it.'

Dara kept pace with her. 'Everyone's saying you're only Dux because Andy's not here, but I told them that Andy doesn't care. Awards like that are meaningless in heaven.'

'Dara.' Beth spun to face her. 'Please. Just stop!'

Dara's eyes went wide, and Beth bolted before she said something she'd regret.

'You okay?' Clare asked at dinner that night when Beth found herself unable to get any food into her mouth. Mum was working late to make up for her time at the ceremony.

Beth met Clare's concerned eyes and knew she could confide in her. 'I can't handle the way Dara keeps talking about Andy. It's like a power game to her.'

'Do you think she knows how you felt about him?'

'She worked out I was in love with him, so she mentions him every chance she gets. I really didn't need her reminding me I was up there today receiving the award that should have been his.'

'Not his,' Clare gently corrected. 'God never intended for him to get it and you've worked hard for it.'

Beth stared at her plate. 'Andy never needed to study. He was more intelligent than anyone, and he didn't have to pretend to be. He understood almost everything, he was good at everything and he understood people so ... so ...'

'He was human, Beth.'

'I know.'

'Sometimes you seem to place him in the superhuman category. Like God.'

Beth frowned. 'I know he's not God.' But Clare's words made her think. Had she allowed Andy to take the place of God in her life? Andy was the first one she went to with any problems. He was the one who made the world exciting. Her relationship with him had been more important than any other. The realisation jarred her. Andy was only human. God was the only friend who would always be there. Her relationship with him should come before any other.

'But God can't talk to me like Andy could.'

She hadn't realised she'd spoken her thoughts aloud until Clare spoke. 'He can and does. We just have to learn to recognise His voice.'

Beth sighed. 'I try, Clare, but I honestly can't tell when it's God and when it's just my own crazy thoughts.'

'Yeah, I used to have that problem until Scott preached a sermon about it once. He said God's voice is the one that matches God's character. He told us that when he lost his fiancé, he had a voice telling him it was all his fault and it made him feel so guilty that he stopped going to church. If it had been God's voice, he would have known God's love and been so moved by it that he wanted to run into God's arms, ask for forgiveness and walk with Him again.'

Beth stared at her. Did she know what happened when Grandpa died? Had Gus or Dan told her?

'Scott said that God builds up and encourages, but Satan tears down. He said Satan tries to tell us we're unworthy, but God says we're worthy because of Jesus. Satan condemns, but God convicts and loves and forgives.'

Beth's eyes slid shut. She'd been listening to the wrong voices for too long—Satan's condemnation and her own mixed-up ideas.

At home that night, she took out her journal. It was time to pour her heart out to God and listen for the voice she knew matched His character.

> *It really is just you and I now, Lord, so I'll tell you everything I would have told Andy ... things like that I'm hurting so much I can hardly breathe, and that I don't want to keep going. I feel betrayed and so overwhelmed by my emotions. I'm so scared of losing the people I love.*

She poured out her heart like she never had before, and as she did, peace stole over her, and burdens she didn't even know she carried were left with the God who loved her.

DESPITE A DEEPER RELATIONSHIP WITH GOD, Beth still wrestled with her daily thoughts. It was overwhelming at times. She struggled to eat, and when she looked in the mirror she saw a thin, oval face with eyes more haunted and hollow than Anique's had been.

Gus tried to help in his own way.

'You're too thin and pale,' he said. 'You need to slow down and eat more.'

'You don't know what you're talking about.'

He frowned. 'I do, actually. When I was suffering at the hands of my father, I couldn't grow. That's what made it so easy for kids to pick on me. I was tiny.'

Compassion replaced her annoyance. 'What did they do?'

'I don't remember much. My psychiatrist says I blocked it out. It's a survival thing.'

'You don't remember any of it?'

He looked down. 'I get flashbacks occasionally. I know Dad hated that I was clever. He called me ... well, all sorts of things and would try to beat it out of me. I've never been good at knowing what to say and what not to.'

Beth remembered the photo Clare found on her verandah of

the small, thin little boy and she wanted to cry. But the strong man standing before her didn't seem to need or want pity.

'A counsellor could help you,' Gus said. 'And God, if you'll let Him.'

'Who says I need help?' She turned away, unable to cope with the knowing look he was giving her.

Next thing she knew, he was sitting close beside her, the sleeve of his dirty work shirt brushing against her arm. 'How can I help you be happy?'

'I don't think you can. I've never really been happy, Gus. I think it's just my personality.'

He gave her his steady, serious look. 'I've heard that many of the most brilliant, creative people in history suffered from depression. It's part of what made them brilliant.'

She sighed. 'Then I'd prefer to be boring.' She looked up to see a silly grin on his face. 'What?'

'You don't think you can be brilliant and boring?'

'Definitely not. Brilliance requires someone to be extraordinary. You can't be extraordinary *and* boring.'

'What about a computer technician who talks in a language no one else can understand, who spends all day staring at the computer screen?'

'He's not brilliant. He's just good at one particular thing. If he were brilliant he'd know how to impress people.'

'Like I do, you mean?' His lips twitched.

'Your brilliance doesn't impress people. It's your steady, loyal personality.'

He laughed. 'Exactly.'

'Exactly what?'

'If my personality impresses people, then I'm brilliant. You've caught yourself out in your own argument, Beth Bateman.'

She couldn't help the slow smile filling her face. 'I have, haven't I?'

He grinned back, and she felt a bit lighter. To her relief, he seemed lighter, too. She was so clouded with grief these days that she feared her depression would drag down everyone around her. And Gus had been through enough.

She left him to his work, deciding to go and find Tarryn, Courtney and Emily. Gus said they were supposed to be doing homework at the Cairns' farmhouse. She was almost there when she saw a strange sight. Rod was pushing his son Billy down the road in what appeared to be a billy kart.

She grinned as she reached him. 'Where'd you get that?'

'Gus made it. He said every Billy needs a billy kart. He made this long handle here to make it easier to push. It even folds down. Look.' He demonstrated, while little Billy chattered away in his baby language, grinning at her and pulling his toes to his mouth. Rod talked back to him as though he understood every word. Then he shot Beth a sheepish look and she wondered how she could ever have been afraid of him.

'How's he going?' she asked, looking at Billy.

He rocked the kart. 'Bill's great.'

'And Toni?'

'Andy's death really shook her and she's obviously still struggling with lots of things.'

'Is she still angry with you?'

He pulled a face. 'Angry enough to keep me at a distance and refuse to let me help her. I've never known her to be like this before. She used to be so full of life and energy, but apparently this depression is a chemical imbalance she's got. If she'd just accept medical help, she'd be right.'

'Why won't she accept help?'

'Toni's always been independent.' Beth heard the admiration in his voice before it saddened. 'But that's also what keeps her from seeing that she needs other people and that she needs God.'

She wondered if Rod was right. If Toni was anything like her, the refusal to accept help was not independence, but fear. Fear that people would find out she didn't have it all together after all and that in fact, she was falling apart.

SOMEONE in the church invited Gus out for dinner, so Beth felt comfortable accepting Clare's invitation to eat with her and Phil. She fiddled with her dinner as usual, but the way Phil watched her put her on edge. When she cleared her plate into the bin, he was still watching. She sat back down, discomfited by his scrutiny.

'Rod and I were talking this afternoon,' he said. 'He's such a different person to the Rod I used to know.'

Beth smiled and Phil smiled too, but his green eyes were shadowed. 'He notices things I don't even notice. For example, I hadn't noticed how thin you've become.'

Beth stiffened. 'I haven't been feeling good.' She hadn't meant to sound so defensive.

'I know.'

'I'll get over it,' she added quickly, then forced a chuckle. 'I talked to Rod today, too. It's so weird to see him pushing a baby around in a pram. Or kart, or whatever it is.'

'It does look strange,' Clare laughed. 'If anyone had told him a few years ago that he'd be doing that, he would've had a fit. It looks kind of odd, a big tough guy being so gentle with a baby.'

Beth and Clare continued their musings but Beth was aware of Phil's thoughtful gaze. She made an excuse and escaped outside. She was sitting on the step, looking up at the stars when the door opened and Phil sat down beside her.

He followed her gaze skyward. 'What are you thinking about?'

'Lots of things.'

'Anything you can share with me?'

She shrugged. 'I'm wondering if God really does change lives.'

'You're thinking of Toni?'

'And Dara. And Joel. And the other Guests.'

Phil shifted his gaze to meet hers. 'Don't forget Rod Green,' he said. 'God is a God of the impossible. I think He likes to amaze us.'

'In the past, maybe. He used you and Clare. But I'm tired of hearing about what God has done in the past. I want to see Him work *now*.'

'He's still working, Beth.'

Even in this? Tears stung her eyes. 'How? Where?'

'Slowly, bit by bit, quietly. We just have to stop and listen and look.'

'But I have been, and there's nothing. Andy died, Dara keeps attention seeking, Joel deceived me, Anique can't accept what Andy did for her, Toni won't accept God's or Rod's love, Tarryn thinks Christians are hypocrites, you're not well ... and my life is falling apart.'

His lips lifted in a small smile. 'The journey can be hard, I know. It wasn't all smooth sailing for Clare and I. We had times of despair— even agony—but God always lifted us up and the sun shone again.'

How she wanted to believe him.

'Beth, the sun will shine again. I promise.'

How could he say that? It was too late.

'When God seems silent it's usually before he's about to do something big.' Phil smiled. 'Like the four hundred silent years.'

'What silent years?'

'Between the Old and New Testaments in the Bible. There's nothing recorded for four hundred years because it seemed like God was silent. But He was preparing for the birth of the Saviour of the world–the biggest, best thing that's ever happened. He was working the whole time.'

Beth groaned. 'I can't wait four hundred years, Phil.'

He nodded and put his arm around her shoulder. 'I know Beth,' he said. 'I know.'

He stood with a sigh and headed back inside. He spoke to Clare, clearly unaware his bedroom window was open. 'Clare, I'm worried about Beth.' His tone was troubled. 'She's not eating and she's way too thin.'

Clare chuckled. 'Beth's always been petite, not chubby like me.'

Phil's tone turned tender. 'You're far from chubby. You're perfect, but Beth is ... well, if she loses much more weight she'll float away. I put my arm around her and I could feel her bones poking through her skin.'

There was silence before Clare's concerned voice floated through the window. 'I hadn't noticed with everything going on. Is she really that thin?'

'Yes.'

'I know she's having a tough time, but do you think she's, well, could she be anorexic or something?'

Phil sighed. 'Have a look in the bin.'

She heard Clare walk out of the room and tensed, knowing exactly what she'd find.

'It's all here. She didn't eat anything!' Clare sounded horrified.

'No, and I suspect she hasn't for a while.'

'What can we do?' Clare sounded close to tears.

'Pray, but I think we need to tell someone, too.'

'Who? Not Mum—she'll panic. She won't be any help.'

Too right she wouldn't. Beth hugged her arms across her chest, holding her breath.

Phil's voice came again. 'What about *my* mum?'

'That will work. But Joel's first hearing is two days away. Maybe we should wait until that's over.'

Beth let her head fall into her hands. She wasn't anorexic, but she doubted they'd take her word for it.

As if they don't have enough to worry about. I wish I wasn't such a burden—

She stopped mid-thought. *God, I know that was my own negative thought. I want to hear your voice, not mine.*

It didn't come at first, but as she gazed back up at the sky, she drew in a deep breath.

I made all this and I love you. I'm here. Even in this.

She had no doubt that was God. Warmth filled her very being.

CHAPTER TWENTY-NINE

Beth faced Joel. She felt no fear, only deep, consuming anger that scared her. Joel never loved her; he used her, and his accomplice killed Andy with no concern for his family, his friends, his life.

God, is this what hate feels like? Because I can't forgive him.

Her voice shook as she testified. The judge looked mild, bored even. He obviously didn't understand what Joel had done, whose life his actions stole. He hadn't seen Andy lying there in the dirt, gasping out his final breath.

The judge set a date for the trial. A year away. Joel hadn't gotten away with it, but she couldn't stand the fact that it would be so long before justice was served. She paced outside the courthouse, consumed by pain and anger. Someone called her name and she realised it was Gus. Clare had said he was coming as support but she hadn't noticed him until now.

'Beth,' he said again, and she forced herself to focus and look at him.

'I have to forgive him,' she said through clenched teeth. 'But how can I?'

Gus took her by the shoulders and looked into her eyes. 'By choice. My father pushed me around my whole childhood, and now, every time I think of him, I choose to let it go. I choose to forgive him, because God doesn't hold my sin against me anymore, either.'

Beth sank onto a low brick wall, overwhelmed by emotion. 'Oh, Gus, I can't be that nice. I'm not as nice as people think I am.' She covered her eyes, longing to block out the vision of Grandpa gasping out his last breaths. Of Anique running from Andy. Of Joel's hand closing over the gosling. Her body shook.

She was vaguely aware of Gus saying her name, of his gentle touch to her arm, but all she could see was Joel tying her to that tree. All she could hear were her screams of terror as Gus's knife cut the ropes. All she could feel was the icy hatred in Joel's expression as he left the courtroom. She swallowed down a scream and tried to breathe, but panic swelled in her chest, and she clutched her throat. Adrenaline surged, telling her to run, to hide, to get away.

Suddenly, strong arms wrapped around her, drawing her up to a standing position and holding her firm. She struggled, shoving against a firm chest. The arms released her and she stared up at Gus.

'Well, that worked,' he muttered.

'What ...' she gasped, firmly back in the present. 'What are you doing?'

'Distracting you.'

She blinked at him, wide-eyed and confused. 'You hugged me to distract me?'

He nodded, now looking sheepish. 'Yeah, maybe it wasn't the best idea, but it worked, didn't it? You needed a distraction and that's the first thing that came to mind.'

'Gus Richards!' she swatted his chest. 'You're the one who condemned Andy for hugging people. You said it's inappropriate.'

'I know, but you needed something drastic.'

'So, it's drastic to hug someone like me, is it?' She knew she was being unreasonable, but unexpected inner fury was surfacing. She needed to vent her feelings, and Gus was clearly offering himself. 'No one would hug someone like me because they have feelings for me, would they? Because they love me?' She poked him in the chest. 'No, I'm just here for everyone to use for their own purposes. Maybe you'd like to pretend to be my boyfriend so you can do drugs, too. Maybe you'd like to die so I can feel guilty about you, too. Or maybe you can tell me you're suicidal so I can feel compassion so strongly it hurts like death,' She was on a roll, now. 'And maybe—'

Gus pulled her back into his arms. Shocked, she fell silent as he placed a gentle, protective hand on her head, instantly calming her. His presence was warm and safe, exuding strength and kindness she desperately needed.

'I'm sorry,' he said quietly, his voice sounding deeper than usual with her ear against his chest. 'I don't mean anything romantic by it, and I'm not using you. I just care that you're in pain and thought it might help.'

She moved her head back to stare up at him, then turned as Clare and Phil came from the court house.

'Ready to go?' Clare asked.

Beth nodded, stepping away from Gus. She didn't want to see Joel come back out and be taken back to prison. She never wanted to see him again in her life. And she didn't want to deal with Gus right now. He was too confusing. Her emotions were too confusing. Getting away was the safest thing to do.

BETH WAS DETERMINED to find a way to live. She couldn't let Joel ruin her life. She began helping the farm Guests with their building assignment, not willing to admit that she liked being around Gus. His hug had affected her in ways she didn't understand.

She sighed and stepped back to survey the work she'd been doing in the new bathroom. Some of the tiles didn't look totally straight, but she'd removed and replaced them three times already. Tarryn insisted they didn't look crooked, but Beth wasn't convinced.

'Stopped working on us, have you?' Courtney asked with a playful grin, looking up from her less careful effort to tile the shower wall. 'Going back home to your palace while we sit here in our half-finished slum?'

Beth couldn't help laughing. 'You call this a slum?'

Courtney glanced around. 'Well, maybe not.'

'I'm never going to do tiling ever again,' Tarryn groaned, stretching her arms. 'If I ever build my own house, it's going to have tile-less bathrooms.'

'Now Tarryn, this *is* your home.' Courtney put on a formal air. 'Everybody needs to belong somewhere, and for now, this is where you belong.'

Tarryn screwed up her nose, trying to hide her amusement at Courtney's mimicry of Rod's words earlier today. 'When this looks like a home, I might consider calling it home. Until then it's a slum.'

Beth smiled. 'I think it's starting to look a bit less like a construction site and more like a home.'

'A home,' Tarryn muttered. 'It's like we're talking about an old people's home or an institution.'

Beth smiled wider. 'I don't think any of those types of homes look like this is going to. I love the design. If I ever build my own house it will look just like this.'

'You'll have to employ Gus, then.'

'Why?'

'Because he designed it. He based it on his grandfather's house. That's why it's got that heritage, cottage kind of look.'

Beth looked around at the huge building and laughed. 'I don't think cottage is the right word.'

A deep voice rumbled through the wall. 'Why not?'

Courtney's hand flew to her chest and she laughed, pointing to the hole in the wall Gus was listening through. 'Gus,' she chided. 'You shouldn't be eavesdropping on feminine conversations.'

His mouth tilted into something close to a smile as he poked his head further through the hole. 'Why? What's feminine about your conversation? I didn't think construction was a feminine topic.'

'Well, some things that go on in bathrooms are,' Emily argued as Gus pulled his head out and came around and into the room.

'Like what?'

'You'd be better off not asking.'

'Don't tell me then.' He glanced around at them, his eyes resting on Beth. 'Beth thinks I need to learn more about what is appropriate and what isn't.'

Her eyes widened. 'I've never said that.' What would Gus come out with next?

'Yes, you did. You said I have no idea about what to say and what not to. It's true, though. I'm uneducated in etiquette and all those girly things.'

'Etiquette is not girly. It's common decency. Sensitivity to social norms is also common decency.' Beth stopped at the look on the girls' faces. She'd lost them.

Gus leaned against the shower wall. 'So what would you classify as *girly*, then?'

'Things like fashion and hairstyles.'

Gus shook his head. 'Some guys are interested in that.'

'Well what *aren't* guys interested in then?'

'Weight.'

'Yes they are.' Tarryn's hands went to her hips. 'They all want to bulk up.'

'Not all.'

Beth rolled her eyes. He was being literal again.

'Well, maybe not you,' Courtney conceded with a giggle, eyeing his solid, muscled form. 'But if you were skinny you'd want to.'

'I doubt it.' Emily looked down at her own bigger build. 'Why would anyone *not* want to be skinny?'

Gus rested his serious brown eyes on her. 'People can be too skinny.'

'I doubt it.'

'They can. Take Beth for example. She'd be healthier if she put on a bit of weight.'

Beth shot him a fierce glare, grateful when the other girls cast each other looks and changed the subject. She'd thank them later. Gus really should stay out of their conversations. He was way too insensitive to navigate them safely. Did he think that one comforting hug gave him the right to judge what she did and didn't need? He had said there was nothing romantic in it, so he had no right to talk as though he knew her or what was best for her.

'I CAN'T BELIEVE he said that about you, Beth!' Courtney whispered when Gus returned to his work.

Beth sighed. 'He's just speaking his mind.'

'But still ...'

Braydon poked his head around the corner, saving her from the awkward topic. 'Beth, Maria's outside and she wants to talk to you.'

She waved at the girls. 'Sorry, got to go.'

'But Beth, you can't leave us alone here in our slum.'

She laughed at Courtney and raced out the door to where Maria stood rocking Billy in his pram.

'No billy kart today?' Beth smiled as Maria greeted her with a hug.

'No. It doesn't really suit me the way it suits Rod.'

Beth took comfort in her warm smile. Clare said Maria Cairn was the best mother-in-law in the world. Beth believed her. She bent down and said hello to the smiling, gurgling Billy.

'Walk with me for a bit, Beth,' Maria said. Beth raised her brows in question, but fell into step beside her.

'I've been wanting to check in on you; see how you're going,' Maria said in her friendly way. 'You've been through so much and no one can go through what you have without some effects.'

'Effects?' Ah. Phil and Clare had talked to her about their suspicions.

'I'm worried because you don't look well.' Beth wanted to feel annoyed, but there was a kindness in Maria's eyes that reminded her of Phil. 'I know your mother is busy and it wouldn't be good to worry her, so I'd like to take you to the doctor.'

'Maria, I'm not sick. I don't have anorexia.' Unwanted tears filled her eyes. 'I just … I'm just tired and sad.'

'I know you are.' Maria's voice was filled with compassion. 'But Beth, sometimes sadness can go so deep it affects us in ways we don't understand.'

Beth's shoulders slumped. Seeing a doctor would be a waste of time. Nothing could be done for her sadness, because no doctor could bring Andy back. And she knew what a doctor would say— it was all in her head and she needed to pull herself together.

'I really am okay,' she reassured Maria. 'I will be, anyway. I just need some time.'

'Beth, you need to get help.'

Beth gasped, struck by the words and the memory they triggered. Andy, lying on the shed floor, telling her to get help. She couldn't help Andy, so how did she think she could help herself? She held her chest, as intense waves of pain rolled over her.

'Beth? It's okay. Breath slowly. In … out …'

'I'm sorry. I hate being a burden.' She drew in deep breaths and raised tear-filled eyes to Maria.

Maria wrapped her arms around her. 'We all need a bit of help sometimes. We all have different strengths, and we're not meant to do everything on our own. God designed us to be relational, to love and support one another.'

Maria's eyes slid shut, and Beth wondered if she was praying. She swallowed back tears. Why was it so hard to accept help? Why was she so bound—so imprisoned? She was scared of giving everything to something that didn't work. She'd prefer to never try than to know that she was completely helpless and out of control and that nothing could be done about it.

Maria opened her eyes and her caring gaze rested on Beth. 'Sometimes our real strength lies in confessing our weaknesses and allowing God to work.' Her eyes implored Beth to take the words to heart.

Beth let out a resigned sigh, aware her hands were shaking and her heart was beating abnormally fast. 'I'll go to the doctor, but will you come with me?'

Maria nodded and wrapped her arms around her. 'I'll be there every step of the way.'

BETH'S HEART pounded and she wrung clammy hands together as she sat beside Maria in the waiting room, watching doctors come out and call patients in, one by one. She took a magazine, her eyes locking on the picture of the beautiful women on the cover. She was no thinner than the model there, and the woman was stunning.

But at what cost?

She flipped through the magazine and this time she saw beyond the outward beauty. Not one of the models looked genuinely happy. None of them had eyes that sparkled with life like Maria Cairn's. Like Phil's, Clare's.

God, I want to be like Maria. And Clare and Phil. Please fix me.

'Elizabeth Bateman,' the doctor called. Maria touched Beth's hand before they stood and followed the doctor down the hall. This was it.

The doctor fired question after question at Beth and she trembled, her mind a fog, until she glanced at Maria. The genuine love and compassion in her eyes calmed Beth's heart. It was like having God there with her. And He was, she realised. He'd promised He would always be with her.

'Can you tell them for me?' Beth whispered as they returned to the cottage. Maria nodded and gave her hand a quick squeeze. Beth couldn't thank God enough for this kind, understanding woman.

Clare and Phil sat side by side on the lounge, waiting expectantly as Beth and Maria took the lounge opposite.

'Beth's going to be okay, but the doctor believes she has depression and anxiety,' Maria said calmly, gently. 'It's triggered an eating disorder. She also has other health problems related to malnutrition. He did some tests because he believes her iron levels could be dangerously low.'

Clare reached to hold Phil's hand. He covered it with his own. 'What can we do to help?'

Beth couldn't answer for the lump in her throat. Maria spoke for her. 'Just be here. Help Beth make good choices about food ... and be there when she tells your mum.'

Clare's eyes flew to Beth's. 'Mum,' she said. 'Mum will have to know.'

Beth swallowed hard. Mum would be so ashamed. She wouldn't

understand. She would expect her to snap out of it. She'd been at Beth recently to wash her hair more, to eat better, to slow down. The doctor had explained the limpness of her hair was a result of malnutrition.

'Beth has been prescribed medication and referred to a psychiatrist, but there are also support groups,' Maria said. 'I've offered to go with Beth so she won't have to be alone.' She patted Beth's hand in a motherly way.

Beth bit her lip to stop it trembling. It was going to be an uphill battle and she was already so, so tired.

'We'll be there for you as much as we can,' Phil promised, but Clare sat there quietly, her face strained.

'I'm sorry,' Beth whispered, tears stinging her eyes. The last thing she wanted was to disappoint and hurt Clare.

Clare sprang to life, rushing to Beth and hugging her tight. Tears now ran unchecked down her face. 'Beth, don't die! I know you miss Andy, but we need you.'

Beth moved back to look her in the eye. 'I'm not trying to die. I don't intend to let this beat me. I didn't mean for it to happen.'

'I know. I know you didn't. I'm not blaming you, I'm ... I'm just scared.'

Beth nodded. 'So am I.' Her voice quavered. 'I need a miracle.' If God performed miracles anymore.

Mum's reaction didn't disappoint them. She fretted, she fussed, she tried to talk Beth out of eating so little, she blamed herself for being at work so much, and then she tried to reason that many girls Beth's age were emotional, thin and lost their appetite. Clare waited until she calmed down before speaking again.

'We think Beth should have her evening meals with Phil and I, starting tomorrow night.'

'But she can't ride home in the dark!'

'Phil can drop her home.'

'What about studying for exams?'

'She can do it at our place. But I hardly think schoolwork is as important as helping Beth get better.'

Mum frowned. 'But you're still newlyweds. You don't need extra work and another mouth to feed.'

Beth's heart sank. She didn't want to be a burden. But Clare was smiling. 'Mum, you forget what Phil and I are like. We don't have to get out the special dinnerware because Beth's coming over. In fact, we won't even be using a tablecloth. And I'll ask you to pay for her food once she eats enough to cost more than a few cents.'

Mum gave a bemused smile and finally nodded her consent, but Beth felt her disapproval.

I approve of you.

That voice, she recognised as God's. It didn't matter what Mum thought. God's approval was enough.

MUM HAD to go back to work almost as soon as Phil and Clare left. Beth paced the living room at Lydon Estate, praying desperately for God's help. She'd never meant for things to get so out of control. She'd thought she was coping, but the negative thoughts had developed a life of their own. She'd tried to control her eating, but it had became a monster controlling her. She couldn't bear the thought of being here alone.

God, where is that peace you gave me a few minutes ago?

How had her life come to this? She looked across at the empty lounge and saw such a clear vision of Andy sitting there that she gasped. Her mind was playing tricks again. Maybe she was going mad. She turned on the television to try to distract herself from her own thoughts.

To her relief, the doorbell rang. She peeked through the peep-hole to see Gus. What was he doing here?

'I heard you'd be home alone, so I thought I'd bring some tea for you,' he said, holding up a casserole dish.

Though she'd been desperate for company a few seconds ago, she now wanted to hide. Someone had obviously told Gus about her condition. She eased open the door. 'Did Clare tell you what the doctor said?'

'No, Phil did. He was worried about you being by yourself tonight, so I said I'd come over.'

'I thought you were worried about being alone in the house with a female.'

He grinned as he walked past her into the kitchen. 'Everyone knows I'm too old for you. Besides, you're trustworthy, remember?'

'Too old? You're only Phil's age.' She blushed. No need to shoot down his arguments against a relationship between them. It could give him the wrong impression.

'Well you're too young or I'm too unmarriageable then. I'm not available.' He put the casserole dish on the bench. 'Ready for dinner?'

'I'm not hungry.'

'You can't not eat for two whole days and not be hungry. It's not physically possible.' The gentleness in his eyes didn't match his gruff tone.

'I can.' She watched as he went to the microwave and placed the dish inside. He set it going, then turned to her, his gaze kind. 'You're not overweight, Beth.' His eyes begged her to believe him. 'You need to eat.'

She dropped her head in shame, her words coming out so quietly he leaned forward to hear. 'I know I'm not, Gus, but I just can't eat. I feel too sick inside.'

'With grief?'

She raised tear-filled eyes to his. 'And guilt.'

'Guilt over what?'

She was too ashamed to say. She didn't understand it herself.

He reached to take her too-thin face in his hands, a gesture she found surprisingly moving. Those work-roughened hands were unexpectedly gentle as his eyes caught and captured hers. 'Beth, you had nothing to do with Andy's death.'

'I know. Not directly anyway, but Anique and I were both praying he would be ours. It must have been like a tug-of-war to God. The easiest thing was to teach us both a lesson by taking him. And I'm the reason Joel knew about Anique's drug past.'

'God took Andy in his own good time. Don't give yourself so much credit.'

'But it's not just that.' She slumped against the kitchen bench and her voice quavered. 'Even if it was God's time for Grandpa to die, I was part of it. And the galah that died … I just felt so help-less … I couldn't do anything to stop any of it.'

Gus rubbed his forehead. 'Is this what all this is about? Taking control because everything else in life feels so out of control?'

He looked so concerned, as though he wanted to offer comfort but held back. And something about it undid her. She felt the tears coming, the cries welling up inside until her shoulders shook and uncontrollable sobs burst out. It didn't surprise her when his arms came around her. She cried out her anguish there in his embrace, then drew in deep breaths. The microwave beeped and he pulled back, looking awkward. Her tears had soaked his shirt.

'I think you should eat.' His voice was gruff, and she knew she'd embarrassed him with her display of emotion. Poor Gus. He was the last one she should be dumping her pain on. He was the least capable of dealing with it. And she'd made the poor guy hug her again, as inappropriate as he believed it was. If he had any inkling how his hug had affected her heart he'd be running the other way.

She wiped her eyes. 'Are *you* eating?'

He nodded as he stirred the dish and put it back in the microwave for a few more minutes.

She swallowed hard and took a tissue to blow her nose. 'Okay, I'll try.'

He looked amused as she washed her hands, then busied herself getting out a tablecloth. She pulled out some cutlery, her heart jarring as she touched the metal knives and remembered Joel and Andy. When she reached for the plates, Gus stopped her.

'I'll just eat out of the dish it's in.'

'What? The casserole dish? No, you can't do that.'

'I can.' He took the plates from her hands and put them back. 'In fact, we both can.'

'What? Share?'

He shrugged. 'Why not? It saves washing up. Why waste water and energy?' He laughed at her horrified expression. 'Here, use a plate if you want, but I'll use the dish.'

She watched as he placed his knife and fork back in the cutlery drawer. She didn't dare ask what he planned to use. He set the large plastic serving spoon in his place at the table, then took the casserole dish from the microwave, spooning half of it onto her plate.

'I'll say grace.' He bowed his head.

Beth watched him as he thanked God for life, for food and for good company. Then he asked God to help Beth eat and get better. She couldn't help smiling as he dug into his food with the serving spoon, then shovelled it into his mouth. It was no wonder his chest was so broad. He stopped, spoon mid-way to his mouth and looked at her. She swallowed, realising she was staring.

'Going to eat?'

Thankfully he ignored the blush filling her cheeks. She picked up her knife and fork, hoping he wasn't going to watch. There was no way she could eat if he did.

He waited patiently, studying his phone while she attempted

to eat. Then he took her plate and ate her leftovers without comment.

He filled the sink, and she washed while he dried. It was all done calmly, quietly, like they'd done it a thousand times before. After placing the final cup in the cupboard, he casually meandered into the living room and lowered himself into the chair Andy always claimed as his own. Even in clean jeans and t-shirt instead of his dirty overalls, he looked out of place in Andy's chair. He was so different. So silent, serious and broad. Less colourful, more … medium. Except she knew he wasn't. She made herself look away.

'You want a game of something?'

He leaned forward in the chair and Beth subconsciously moved back to keep a safe distance from him. 'Yeah.'

'What would you like to play?'

'We've mostly got word games. Like Scrabble or Boggle.'

He nodded. 'Both sound good. You pick one.'

'Which would you prefer?'

He frowned. 'I said you pick one.'

She hated his abrupt displeasure, but she still found herself trying to work out which one he might prefer. Scrabble seemed more his type of game and it was something she was good at. No one in her family could beat her.

He beat her easily. Was there nothing he wasn't good at? She felt inadequate and intimidated but he merely smiled as he helped her pack up. 'Thanks for the game, Beth. I'll see you tomorrow night.'

'No, I've got a Youth Group planning meeting with the Holmes'.'

'So have I.'

Her eyebrows shot up. 'You're a leader now?'

'Not yet. Just checking it out and praying about whether I should be.'

A thought struck her. What would the Holmes' think when

they heard her diagnosis? Was she even fit to be a leader? 'Maybe you should take my place.'

He looked hard at her. 'I'm not taking anybody's place.'

'They might ask you to take mine.'

'Why?'

'Because I have a mental illness. I'm not exactly a good role model.'

'Why not? Because you have a recognised medical condition? I think you're a bit harsh on yourself, Beth. Most people are sympathetic.'

She gave a watery smile. 'But I want to be respected, not pitied.'

He merely smiled as he stood and gathered his things. 'Have a good pray,' he said as he walked out the door. 'And listen to what God says about it.'

She didn't like being told what to do, but she had to admit it was a good idea. There were lots of things she needed to ask God about right now.

CHAPTER THIRTY

Beth walked out to the farm after school to find Phil sitting on the back step, his head in his hands. He looked up and smiled but weariness showed in the lines around his eyes. 'How's it going, Beth?'

She hated that question. Better not to think about it and avoid answering. 'How are *you*?'

'Tired. A bit worn out.'

She knew how that felt. She sat beside him. 'You look more than tired.'

He chuckled half-heartedly. 'Yeah. I'm not sure I can keep going with all this. It seems I'm not the man I thought I was.'

'What? You're a true man in every way that matters.' He was one of the best men she knew.

He laughed. 'I just mean I don't have the physical strength I used to. But I do know that true strength is about *being* rather than *doing*.'

She waited for him to explain. He plucked a leaf from the pot plant beside him and began picking little pieces off and dropping them on the ground. 'God doesn't want us to try to make ourselves worthy of Him. He's already done that. He cares more about our relationship with Him, and who we are. Thankfully, physical strength isn't necessary for a good relationship.' His fingers stilled and he smiled. 'Time with Him is. And being too tired to do farm work means I have more time to spend with Him and write more songs.'

Despite his weariness, expression and life still sparkled in his eyes. Beth didn't remember her father, but she liked to imagine he was something like Phil.

BETH WENT TO FIND GUS. She chuckled when she found him trying to work around the half-grown gosling which was dogging his every step. He spoke to it, and it gave a funny squeaking honk in return.

'It was getting desperate to get outside,' Gus said when he spotted Beth. 'It might be time I took it back to the pond. It's worked out how to climb out of its crate in the Cairns' laundry and it makes a horrible mess.'

Beth smiled at the image and sat on a spare sawhorse. She watched Gus work for a few minutes, then voiced her concerns about Phil. 'I don't know if you've noticed how tired Phil is these days, but it seems to be getting worse. He hasn't been the same since he caught that virus on the mission field a few years back.'

Gus kept working, using the nail gun to join framework together, but Beth knew he was listening.

'Maybe people don't fully recover from a sickness like that.' She shifted to a more comfortable position. 'Clare said his organs had started to shut down and it's a miracle the doctors were able to save him. I don't know … I just know it frustrates him that he can't help out with the program as much as he wants to.'

Gus put down the nail gun to bring two more pieces of wood together. 'That's the problem with modern medicine,' he said. 'It gives us quantity of life, but not quality of life. Living longer is not necessarily a good thing.'

Beth stared at him, shocked. Fury rose within. 'I'm sure Phil's happy to be alive thanks to the help of modern medicine.'

Gus didn't pick up on her ire. 'Maybe. Then again, maybe he'd like to be up there singing God's praises with Andy.'

'I doubt that.'

He put in another nail. 'Why? It's our destiny, isn't it? To be with God. I've been reading Revelation lately, and I can't wait to see God. The sooner I leave this earth the better.'

Beth clenched her teeth, holding in a growl. Jumping off the sawhorse, she slipped away, determined not to lash out the way she wanted to. He was just so comfortable with death, but why did he have to bring up the topic in such an insensitive way? She kicked a stone, but it didn't release pent up anger.

His ute was parked up ahead by the side of the road. It was as confusing as Gus himself with its filthy, dirty outside and spotless inside. How could he be so caring one minute and so blunt and offensive the next? One minute she wanted to hug him, the next she wanted to hit him. Right now, she wanted to kick him. His ute would have to do. She charged up to it and slammed her foot into the door. 'Take that, Gus.'

It hurt, but it was worth it. She stepped back and stared in horror at the dent now spoiling the vehicle's sleek lines. *Oh God, what have I done? How can I ever face him now? I can't bear the thought of losing his friendship.*

A strong, warm, inner voice interrupted the downward spiral of her mind. ***I will give you courage.***

Despite God's reassurance, it took Beth several hours to gather up the courage to approach Gus. When she finally returned to the building site, she forced one foot in front of the other, holding back nausea. She found him inside, working on the kitchen. The gosling pecked around in the sawdust at his feet.

Help me, God.

He turned with a smile and she felt awful that he seemed pleased to see her. He stopped work and settled himself on the kitchen bench, studying her with something akin to amusement. 'What's up, Beth?'

'What makes you think anything's up?'

His amusement grew into a full-blown smile. 'The furrows in your brow and your defensive posture.'

She looked down at her crossed arms and let them fall to her sides. 'I um, I've come to apologise.'

'For?'

'I've done something terrible and I'll understand if you are angry—and well, you will be angry but I deserve it ...'

His expression didn't change. He didn't look the least bit worried. If only she didn't have to tell him. She didn't want to wipe that curious, amused expression from his face.

'Tell me what's going on,' he said.

'I put a big dint in your ute.'

Still, his expression didn't change. She waited. Finally, he jumped off the bench and shrugged. 'Accidents happen.'

'But it didn't just happen!'

The amused smile faltered. 'You did it deliberately?'

'Not really,' Frustrated tears filled her eyes. 'I mean, I didn't think it would happen. I kicked it and ...' She shrugged helplessly. 'I've never done anything like that before so I thought it was strong and I might break my toes but not ... not damage your ute.'

'You wanted to hurt yourself?'

She hated the disapproval in his eyes. 'Not really.'

He moved back to the bench and swung himself back up. 'Then I don't understand.'

'I was angry... well, with you.'

He tilted his head. 'Then I guess I can be grateful you damaged my ute and not me.'

'Gus,' she moaned, exasperated by his calm tolerance. 'Why can't you be normal?'

His brows shot up. 'You want me to be angry?'

'No. Well yes ... I don't know.'

'Well I am.'

He was so confusing. He looked anything but angry as he sat on that bench, his calm brown eyes watching her.

'I'm angry that I hurt you badly enough to cause such a reaction. And I guess I'm disturbed that you didn't think you could just come and talk to me about it.'

She stomped her foot, aware she must look like a child having a tantrum, but unable to help it. The gosling gave a startled squeak, which somehow fuelled her anger. 'Why can't you be more expressive? How am I supposed to know what you're feeling if you just sit there like nothing's happened?'

He smiled and reached for his drink bottle, but she snatched it away. She didn't want him escaping behind a drink of water when they might finally be getting somewhere in their conversation.

Gus took the bottle from her fingers anyway, slowly unscrewed the lid then took a long sip before looking at her again. 'Beth, I'm not ruled by emotions. I had to learn to control them a long time ago, but that doesn't mean I don't feel anything.'

'What do you mean?'

'I had to hold in my emotions as a kid. Blanking my expressions was the only way I survived. We aren't victims of our feelings. They only consume us if we allow them to.'

She lifted her chin. 'Well, I can't help my emotions.'

'No, but you can choose whether to let them consume you, or

you can hand them over to God. You can live in them or live around them.'

She stared at him. Could she really let go of the intensity of these feelings? Did she want to? 'I didn't used to be like this,' she confessed. 'Before I met you I didn't lose control—and no, I'm not blaming you for it. I've just changed, that's all. I didn't used to get angry.'

'You didn't get angry, or you pretended you didn't?' He put down his water bottle. 'Did you deal with your feelings, or did you sweep them under the carpet? It's easy enough to do until something happens to make your feelings too painful or too strong to ignore.'

Her shoulders sagged. He was way too close to the truth. 'What, are you a psychologist, too?'

He chuckled. 'If I was a psychologist I'd know how to stop upsetting you, wouldn't I?' He moved over on the bench and patted the space beside him. 'Now come up here and tell your incompetent psychologist what he did to anger you.'

She stared at him, not moving.

'What did I do?' Gus asked again, this time more gently.

'You were talking about death.'

His brows shot to his hairline. 'So you kicked in my door?'

She gritted her teeth. 'It might have helped if you made an effort to mask your emotions right now, if you're so good at it. You make me want to kick in your other door.'

His mouth twitched as though he was fighting not to laugh. 'I guess we could both use some help with the fruit of the Spirit, couldn't we?'

All the air drained from her lungs. Love, joy, patience, goodness, self-control … they were all from God's Holy Spirit. No wonder she hadn't been able to show them. They were supernatural and she was only human. She could never do it on her own. Her eyes slid shut. *God, help me. Grow your fruit in me.*

Gus's warm hand settled on her arm, his touch playing havoc

with her runaway emotions. 'You're forgiven for denting my car,' he said quietly. 'Will you forgive *me*?'

She met his eyes and could only nod.

'Now let's go and assess this damage,' he said, his tone light again. Dreading his reaction, she followed him to the ute, amused by the gosling waddling at his heels. When he saw the ute, he stood looking at the door, touched the dent, then turned to her. 'Where is it?'

She gave him the strange look he deserved. 'That's it.'

'And where else?'

'That's all.'

He ran his sun-browned fingers over the dent. 'I thought you said it was big.'

'It is.'

'Compared to what?'

She laughed. She couldn't help it. 'Compared to an ant.'

'A regular ant or a giant man-eating ant?' He didn't smile, but it was in his voice and eyes.

'A green head.'

Those eyes bored into hers. 'Are you sure? Not just your average black ant?'

She took the challenge. 'Maybe a sugar ant.'

'Brown?'

'Reddish brown.'

'A large one?'

'Large for its age, but small for its type.'

Gus chuckled, then nodded. 'Good. I'm glad we've got that sorted.'

She laughed, liking his sense of humour, and that he was able to laugh at his tendency to enforce accuracy. She liked that he was serious but didn't take himself too seriously. And despite saying he'd learned to blank his expressions, there was an openness and warmth in his smile that brought his face to life.

PHIL'S FIRST CD RELEASED, showcasing fifteen of his own songs. Beth was as excited as the rest of the family. The church asked if he would sing at a concert they would arrange for the town and Phil agreed, but he wasn't as enthusiastic as Beth expected him to be.

'He's always been cautious about becoming famous,' Clare explained when Beth asked her about it. 'He's worried about pride.'

Beth laughed. 'Phil's never come across as proud.'

'I know, and that's probably because he's so conscious of the danger. He wants to make sure He always puts God first. I've never come across anyone so humble and focused on God.'

Clare wasn't merely speaking as a devoted wife. Beth agreed with her. Philip Cairn's heart for God was like Andy's. If only Andy was still here to see the concert. Maybe he would watch from heaven.

The night of the concert, Beth's skin prickled with goosebumps as Phil sang. It felt as though heaven had come to earth and she was bathing in the warmth of God's love.

Phil stepped forward, guitar still strapped to his shoulder, as he read out some of the words he had sung.

I ran the race so hard and fast
I could not catch my breath,
every moment making up
for Your untimely death.
But then You took my cross from me
and showed to me those scars
the plan to bear it all for me
created with the stars.
You do not ask the world from me
You owned it from the start,

all You ask is what I have,
my life, my love, my heart.

He looked up at the group gathered in the hall. 'I wrote this song one day when I was so sick I could hardly get out of bed. I was struggling, but God reminded me it's not about doing. It's about being.' A sheen of tears glistened in his eyes. 'The fact is, I can't do it any more—not all the things I thought I should be doing. I always dreamed of singing, but I thought God would want me to spend my time and days doing physical labour for Him instead. But through illness, God has forced me to do what I always dreamed of doing. I had thought it would be too easy and enjoyable for God to really want me to sing. Ironic, isn't it?'

Beth nodded. Ironic that God gave Phil the desires of his heart when he didn't even know what they were. Was it possible that *her* dreams could come true when she finally realised what they really were? Or would they come true to make her realise what they should be?

Phil read out the bridge.

Just sitting in Your presence, Lord
and resting at Your feet,
knowing You will show Your strength
when I concede defeat.

'It's not about trying,' he told the audience and Beth's throat burned. She'd tried so hard her whole life. And what for? What did it matter that she topped the class, achieved, looked good? Such temporary things. Andy's death proved that. She wanted to know God and rely on Him. To let Him be her strength, to learn to recognise His voice. To just be His child. That was what it was all about.

That night she wrote in her journal.

God's kept me on earth, so I'm determined that none of my life will go to waste. All the grief, the struggles, the tragedy, will be used for God. I will sit back and allow Him to do His healing work. I will give everything, broken though I am, to God who loved me enough to send Jesus to die for me.

CHAPTER THIRTY-ONE

Beth felt so much more relaxed. She was able to eat again. She had more energy. The medication had helped, and seeing a counsellor had helped too, but she realised what had really made the difference. Hope. Hope that God had a perfect plan, and relief that she could leave it all with Him. She could trust His character, trust His heart.

She headed to the accommodation building to see Gus. He'd become a good friend; someone she could talk to about anything.

She stopped just inside the door, watching as Gus lifted a plank of wood and sat it beside Braydon. Braydon nodded his thanks and began hammering in nails. Gus was wearing shorts today. It must be too hot for overalls. She remembered how much she'd wanted to teach him some dress sense not so long ago. Not now. He looked … attractive? She took a step back. She couldn't be thinking this way.

Gus spied her and turned with a wave and smile that set her heart dancing. Waving back, she headed over, soaking in the warmth of his expressive brown eyes.

She needed to pull herself together. She wasn't in one of her romance novels. This was real life. Gus wasn't marriage material. He was medium, brown and boring.

Only he wasn't. She forced herself to act normal. 'Working hard?'

'No more than usual.'

She frowned. 'You realise you've been blessed with a lot more energy than most people?'

He nodded casually. 'And strength.'

She wanted to laugh. Was it arrogance that drove Gus to be so frank about his abilities? No, it took true humility to be able to accept himself as he was and just appreciate it.

'You know, Phil used to be really strong,' she said, 'but for some reason God allowed him to lose some of his strength.' She was testing him and his look said he knew it.

'Perhaps to direct Phil to the singing talent God wants him to use.'

She silently agreed. Gus obviously recognised that physical strength and stamina weren't all-important. So, could he see enough in her to admire her strengths and gifts despite the fact he'd seen her at her worst? Somehow, she didn't think so.

'What are you up to?' he asked, stopping work to sit on a block of wood in front of her.

'Just seeing what you're up to ... and if you need any help.'

He grinned. 'Yeah, see that wheelbarrow? It needs to go to the woolshed.'

She turned to see the wheelbarrow full of bricks. He had to be teasing. Pride made her want to push that wheelbarrow all the way to the shed, but common sense told her it was impossible.

'You're considering it, aren't you?' He grinned. 'I can see it in your eyes.'

She pulled a face. 'I want to.'

His grin widened. 'I know you do. Tell you what, I'll take the wheelbarrow, you take the,' he glanced around, 'um. .. how about you come along for moral support?'

She looked around. 'Where's your support gosling today?'

'In the dam behind the Cairns' place.' He stuck out his lower lip. 'He abandoned me as soon as he saw that water. Should have seen him splash around in joy.'

'Looks like I'd better step in, then. I promise I won't abandon you to splash around in the dam.'

'Thank you.' His eyes twinkled at her.

As she walked along beside him, she told him what happened the night of Phil's concert. 'It's like I could finally let go,' she said. 'I was able to trust God with everything and give Him my whole life, even though it's a complete mess.'

Gus was a good listener and with those brown eyes resting on her, she found herself sharing her heart and soul.

'I still want to be more than I am, but I think I'm beginning to be content with who God made me to be. I think I'm starting to be more relaxed about the things that don't really matter.'

'So I could come to your place and we could eat from the same bowl and you wouldn't mind?'

She gave him a pained look.

'Sorry, I couldn't resist asking.'

She laughed and poked him in the arm, making absolutely no impact on his rock-hard muscles. 'The changes will take time. Ask me again in another year.'

'I might not be around in a year.'

'Where are you going?' Her stomach sank. She'd always known he would leave again, but she didn't like the idea of not seeing him every day.

'I don't know. Who knows what will happen in this life?'

She glared at him. 'You just always have to bring up death, don't you.'

'Saying I might not be around doesn't mean I expect to die. God could lead me to another town.'

'You were talking about death, and you know it.'

'What if I was?' He tilted his head, studying her. 'It's a natural part of life.'

'No, it's not. It's a direct consequence of sin and it's devastating to those who've ever lost someone close. It's decay and pain I don't even know how to explain it to you. But then, I don't know that I would ever want to understand it, because to understand it you'd have to personally experience it.'

Gus looked evenly back at her. 'Death or grief?'

'You know I mean grief.'

He smiled.

'What?' She found it hard to remain angry when he was looking at her like that.

Mischief played about his eyes. 'I think you need a big hug.'

She glanced at his filthy clothes. 'You said it's inappropriate.'

'Ah, but you gave a very convincing argument about why I was wrong. Besides, it would just be a caring, brotherly hug. And you're not part of the program so I'm not in a position of leadership over you. I'm just a family friend.'

She held still, glaring a challenge at him. Somewhere along the line that face and those eyes had softened. He always said the wrong thing, but he had a good heart. 'If you make me dirty, you're in trouble!'

He took a step closer. 'But you don't care anymore, remember?'

'Only if it's accidental.'

'So, what if I give you a brief, brotherly, *appropriate* hug and *accidentally* make you dirty?'

'I would know if it was accidental or not, and if it wasn't, I would have to deal with you severely.'

'What would you do?' He took another step.

'I would make you come to my place for tea wearing a tux and make you eat off Mum's best crockery and use all the right cutlery and be on your best behaviour.'

He grinned. 'I wouldn't mind seeing you in a tux.'

'Not me. You ... stop taking everything the wrong way!'

He grinned wider. 'Would I have to have a shave?'

'Definitely.'

He took that final step and pulled her into a quick, brotherly hug. And just to make sure she got dirty, he ran his filthy hand down her arm.

She tried to hide the way his touch flustered her. 'Right, that's it, Gus Richards. You're in for a three-course dinner.'

'When?'

'As soon as I convince Mum you aren't as bad as you seem.'

He chuckled, then began unloading the bricks onto the wool-shed floor. Beth watched, trying to ignore the feelings running through her. Gus was a *family friend* as he put it. She still loved Andy. So what was this feeling? Was she really that fickle? And more to the point, why Gus, the insensitive, unrefined bachelor who vowed marriage would be an inconvenience? Beth's dream had always been to be romanced, to be swept off her feet like in the novels she read. There was no way Gus Richards could ever do that. *God, give me strength and wisdom.*

She reached into the wheelbarrow and lifted a brick. Gus was taking five at a time, but at least she was helping. She lowered another brick beside the sheep pen rail, then winced as her finger scraped wood. She was aware of Gus's eyes on her as she pulled out an offending splinter.

'Got it all?'

She shook her finger. 'I think so. Most of it, anyway.'

'Show me.'

'It's okay.'

'It's not. If there's some left, you'll get an infection. Sheep pens are not the cleanest place in the world, you know.' He reached for her hand, and blushing, she obediently held out the finger for him to inspect. 'There's some still there.' He pointed to a seat left by the shearers and obediently she sat.

He went to the first aid kit on the shed wall and pulled out a needle. 'Do you trust me?'

'Yeah.' She knew he was trying to lighten the situation; make her relax. Still, the sight of sharp metal unnerved her.

He sat directly in front of her. 'So why are you shaking?'

She ignored his question. His closeness was having a strange effect on her.

'You know,' Gus ventured as he rested her hand on his knee and poked it with the needle, 'anyone might think you did this on purpose just to get close to me.'

She stiffened. He kept talking. 'It wouldn't be the first time a girl has done it.'

She tried to pull her hand away, wincing as the needle dug in deeper.

He kept her hand in his firm grip. 'Beth, I'm joking. I'm just trying to add some humour to the situation.'

She couldn't look at him, but she tried to relax. It was ironic that she was the one being too serious. She studied his nimble fingers holding the needle as he proficiently worked at removing the splinter.

Finally, he held it out for her to see. 'Want to keep it? In memory of the infection you never had?'

She dared to meet those teasing brown eyes and teased back. 'No, you can have it as a keepsake in memory of this moment of intimacy.' She blushed even as she said it, but he was asking for it.

A deep chuckle rumbled from him as he took it all in his stride. Did nothing ever embarrass him?

BETH COULDN'T SHAKE the image of Gus's hands. She had studied them to avoid looking into his eyes, and now they were ingrained in her memory. She found a piece of paper. In the past, she always had her sketchbook within reach, but she wasn't even sure where to find it now. She sat at Clare and Phil's unclothed table and allowed herself to become absorbed in the lines of Gus's hands. How could she express the strength and work-roughened texture whilst also showing their fine structure and gentleness?

'Whose hands are you drawing?'

She jumped at Clare's voice and flipped the paper over. 'No one special.'

Clare's mouth widened into a smirk. 'Are you sure?'

'Well, maybe I based them on some I saw.'

'Maybe? Or definitely?'

Beth couldn't help smiling. 'Okay, I did, but don't ask me who because it's irrelevant.'

'If it was irrelevant, you'd have no problem telling me.'

'Okay, they're Gus's. But don't tell anyone. They might misunderstand.'

'What's to misunderstand?'

'That it doesn't mean anything. I just captured a moment, that's all.'

Clare looked sideways at her. 'They're very manly, well-shaped hands, aren't they?'

Beth threw her pencil at Clare, who laughed before disappearing out the door. Beth picked up her sketch to study it. They were. But it was natural for an artist to capture anything of significance or beauty.

She let her head drop to the table with a groan. *God, help me. What is going on?*

CHAPTER THIRTY-TWO

Mr. and Mrs. Holmes came to see Beth after Youth Group on Friday night.

'We need to talk,' Mr. Holmes said, his expression serious. It was unusual for Mr. Holmes to be doing the talking, but his chattery wife couldn't seem to meet her eyes.

Mr. Holmes rubbed his hands down his face. 'Look Beth, we know you've had a hard time lately, and we think it would be wise for you to take a break from leading Youth Group. Don't worry, we have someone to take your place until you feel better.'

Beth tried to comprehend what they were saying. She bit her lip. 'Have I done something wrong?'

'We're just trying to help you.'

'I'm doing fine. I love doing Youth Group.'

'I know, but we need to consider the young people, too. We need leaders who are role models, not people with … well, disorders.'

Beth couldn't speak. She'd thought things were improving, but his words fell like a heavy weight, crushing her heart. Nausea swirled. Maybe they were right. Maybe she *was* still falling apart.

'We're doing this because we care,' Mr. Holmes said. 'We'll be praying for you.'

Mrs. Holmes remained silent, but as they walked away Beth heard her plaintive voice directed at her husband. 'It's the right thing, Barry. Yes, of course it's the right thing. The young people need a good example.'

'I'll take you home,' a voice said. She turned to find Gus standing there. Without a word, she charged to the refuge of his ute.

Neither of them spoke as Gus drove her to Lydon Estate. He pulled into the drive and Beth finally looked at him. 'I've been asked to step down.'

'I heard.' He tapped his fingers on the steering wheel.

'Because I have an eating disorder.'

He nodded, his mouth set in a grim line.

She shrugged. 'I guess it's the right thing, but I can't help feeling hurt.'

'I disagree.'

She opened the door and escaped. She wasn't sure what he disagreed with, but she couldn't deal with it right now. He called out goodnight but she didn't even wave.

BETH WAS surprised by a late-night visit. Mum was already home and was working on her computer.

Rod, Clare and Phil stood at the door, rugged up against the cold winter night.

Her heart pounded. 'Is everything okay?'

'Everything's fine,' Rod said, but his jaw was tight. 'We heard about Youth Group tonight and we thought we should see you straight away.'

Her cheeks flushed with shame. Clare led them all into the

living room where they took off their coats. Mum peeked out, saw who it was, and went back to work.

'What did you hear?' Beth asked, swallowing hard.

Rod's hands went to his hips. 'That the Holmes' asked you to step down.'

'They said it's to help me, but they're worried my condition might have a negative effect on others.'

Phil's eyes flashed fire. 'I can't believe they said that.'

Surprised by his uncharacteristic anger, yet appreciating the support, she shrugged. 'I can understand their point.'

'What point?' Clare demanded. 'That no one is allowed to lead unless they're perfect? You have a recognised medical condition, Beth. That doesn't mean you can't be a spiritual leader.'

'I don't know. It's a weakness that's pretty obvious.'

'Like my chronic fatigue?' Phil shook his head. 'Just because God hasn't healed us doesn't mean we've lost His favour or we've sinned. And Beth, I honestly believe you walk closer with God than most of those teenagers in that youth group. We're going to talk to the Holmes' about this.'

She soaked up the kindness in his eyes. 'It's okay. There's no need to.'

'It's not okay,' Rod growled. 'They can't make a decision like that without even checking all the facts. We'll have you back in there in no time.'

'I don't want to be back in there.' Not now. It would never be the same again. 'I've never really fit in there since Andy died, anyway. Maybe I never did *before* he died.'

Rod looked fierce. 'Well, whether or not you come back, we'll still talk to them about it.'

Phil rested a hand on her shoulder. 'Beth, you will find your place. Sometimes God lets us feel like we don't belong because He's leading us to a place where we do.'

'You think so?'

'I know. Hang in there.'

She watched as they put on their coats and headed back out into the cold winter's night. Their love and concern was touching, but she didn't want to be the cause of conflict.

SHE RODE out to the cottage the next morning, slowing when she saw the Holmes' car outside. She wanted to run away, but forced herself not to be a coward.

'Come in.' Phil opened the door and pulled a chair out from the table for her. 'I'm glad you're here. We've been talking about last night and there's something we need to clear up.'

Beth nodded, unable to look at the Holmes, and Rod and Clare who sat across from them. She knew everyone was looking at her.

Phil spoke gently. 'Apparently you told Dara you wish she died instead of Andy?'

Beth's head jerked up. 'What? I would never say that! No, I didn't say anything like that. I asked her to stop talking to me about him, but that was ages ago.'

Phil nodded. 'I thought so.' He looked to Mr. and Mrs. Holmes. 'Dara has a tendency to twist things.'

Mrs. Holmes still didn't meet Beth's eyes, but Mr. Holmes looked troubled. He blinked a couple of times, then reached a hand to Beth across the table. 'I'm sorry we didn't realise that. We'd like you to come back on board.'

She managed a gracious smile. 'Thank you, but I'd prefer not to. I have school exams coming up, anyway.'

'Of course, dear,' Mrs. Holmes cut in, finding her tongue again, 'but you were doing such a wonderful job and we have no one to take your place. Yes, yes we need you.'

'I thought you had someone. You could ask Gus to take my place.'

'He doesn't want to be involved. He rang us this morning.'

Still, Beth didn't budge. 'I'll pray for someone else.'

'Yes, yes that's a good idea,' Mrs. Holmes said, while her husband looked troubled.

Beth didn't want to be here. She stood. 'I'd better go and feed Gilbert.' She smiled around at them. 'I'll see you later.' She flew out the door, relieved that no one stopped her.

Gilbert could now fly from one end of the chook pen to the other. Other galahs had been hanging around, and Beth knew it would soon be time to let him go. It was a bittersweet feeling—one Gus would understand now that the gosling spent all of its time at the pond. Maybe he would help her release Gilbert.

BETH FOUND Gus watching an electrician install power points in the new building.

He looked up. 'Meeting over?'

He knew about it? She nodded.

'What's the verdict?'

'Clare, Phil and Rod must have convinced the Holmes' to take me back, but I don't think they really want me. And to be honest, I don't want to be a part of it anymore. I stepped down. '

He handed the electrician a power point cover, but his eyes were still on Beth.

She frowned. 'I don't know how Rod and Phil found out about the whole thing.'

'I told them.' There was no apology in his words. 'I was bothered by what the Holmes' did.'

'*You* told them?'

'Yes. I thought they needed to know.'

She was touched. Gus cared a whole lot more than he liked to show. 'You be careful,' she teased. 'You might actually end up becoming nice. Then you might *have* to get married.'

'No one *has* to get married, and no one will change my mind.'

He looked and sounded gruff, but Beth wasn't fooled. He might get a surprise one day and discover marriage wasn't such a curse after all. He'd make a good husband if he could find a wife who didn't care about his abrupt nature and dirty clothes.

She followed him into the next room where he picked up a roll of cable. She helped him unroll it, then playfully tapped his arm. 'We haven't got you into a tux for that three-course dinner yet.'

'I know, but you haven't named the date.'

'Tomorrow night?'

He glanced up. 'Fine. I'll be there in my tux.'

He was a good sport. What would he look like in a tux? The thought had her smiling.

BETH WAS NERVOUS. Not because Gus would be dressed up, but because she didn't know what would slip out of her mouth. It wasn't easy hiding unwanted feelings from someone.

She jumped at the sound of the doorbell, even though she'd been expecting it. She opened the door and swallowed hard, forcing herself to look away. 'Come in.'

He followed her inside, hung his suit jacket on the hat stand and threw off his shoes. She was tempted to tell him that was cheating but stayed quiet. He was fiddling with his top shirt button as though it was choking him. But his tux was a perfect fit. His clean-shaven face and combed hair highlighted his handsome, chiselled features and clear brown eyes.

Okay, so she had it bad.

'Make yourself comfortable. I'll just help Mum serve dinner.' She stayed long enough to watch him settle back into the lounge chair and pick up one of her school assignments. Not what she would have thought was interesting reading, but maybe he would realise how intelligent she was, even if she'd never reach his brilliance. Who would ever have thought she'd care so much what he thought?

Throughout the meal he chatted politely with Mum, though most of his responses were abrupt, as usual. He didn't offer any more information than he was forced to, and all his answers were closed. Beth had to hope Mum was impressed by his appearance, because he didn't give her much else. He was much more comfortable asking questions and listening to the answers. Didn't he understand that communication and friendship were two-way? She desperately wanted her friendship with him to develop, but that was impossible if he didn't trust her enough to share his heart.

Mum insisted on washing up after the meal, shooing them into the living room. With a big sigh, Gus stretched out his legs and undid his top button.

Beth smiled at him. 'Uncomfortable?'

'Not anymore.'

She forced her eyes away from his, and watched his nimble fingers shuffle the pack of cards he'd picked up from the coffee table shelf.

He put them back down. 'What do you want to do now?'

She managed to look directly at him. 'I want to find out more about you. It's time I stopped dumping everything on you and listened to you instead.'

'Why?'

She shrugged, trying to be casual. 'Because that's how friendships develop.'

His eyes narrowed. 'Develop into what? I hope you're not using me to fill the place Andy had in your life.'

Where had that come from? She couldn't be bothered feeling angry. Just hurt. 'Of course not. You're nothing like him.'

'But you still have that need for romance in your life.'

'When did I ever ask you for romance?'

He tilted his head to the side and just looked at her. Then he put down the cards. 'Clare suggested it's time I noticed you. She has this idea that we'd be a good match.'

Oh Clare, why? 'Well it wasn't me who put that idea in her head.'

'Really?'

Now she was angry and defensive. 'For your information, I've had enough of romance and drama in my life. I want to live in slow, quiet reality for a while—with people who are willing to be friends. Dreaming only causes pain when you finally wake up. Don't worry, if I wanted to get married someday it wouldn't be to someone like you who is so independent and self-centred it drives me crazy.'

She bit her lip. What was she saying?

'And I'm just not Andy,' Gus said quietly.

She nodded, throat tight.

'But you wish I was?'

She looked down, refusing to answer. Why wouldn't he let it go? She felt his gaze as he shuffled in his seat.

'You know I said I don't want to get married. I told you that from the start.'

'For goodness' sake, Gus, all I'm asking from you is friendship. Everyone needs special friends in their life.'

'I don't think it's appropriate for us to be *special* friends.'

Him and his views on what was appropriate. The mere word now made her want to scream.

His serious expression didn't waver. 'I would only want to be *special* friends with a girl if I intended to marry her.'

'And you don't intend to marry because it would be an incon-venience and you don't need anyone or anything. I get it.'

'I didn't say that. I need God and I like having normal friends just like everyone else.'

Beth leaned forward in the chair and glared at him. 'But you don't need me, and you don't really need anyone. You're healthy and capable and brilliant. Mr. Perfect.'

'I'm not perfect.'

'And yet you're not shy about telling people how good you are at everything. You've never needed anyone or anything in your life, have you? And I don't think I fit into the *normal* or *appropriate* category so it looks like I can't even be your friend.'

'I didn't say that.'

Exasperated, she slashed her hand downward. 'I know you didn't. Because you hardly ever say anything, do you? But I wish you'd actually like me for who I am, not just spend time with me because you feel sorry for me and think you should help me.'

'That's not why I spend time with you.'

'Then why do you?'

'Because I haven't found any better company.'

'Well, that makes me feel better, doesn't it? Knowing you put up with me because you've got no other options.'

'I didn't mean it like that.'

'It sure sounded like it.'

Gus huffed out a sigh, his serious brown eyes looking hard at her. 'I don't think this conversation is helpful. I think we're both tired and should get some sleep.' With that, he stood, collected his jacket and shoes, and left the house.

Beth stared at the closed door. Now look what she'd done. It wasn't Gus's fault she felt more for him than he wanted her to.

Oh, Lord, what should I do? What was this attraction she felt for Gus? How could it have happened when she was still grieving for Andy? It didn't make sense. Nothing made sense anymore.

'Where's Gus?' Mum asked, poking her head in the room.

'Went home.'

The house was large enough and the living room far enough from the kitchen that she hadn't heard the heated discussion.

'What did he think of the meal?'

'Probably thought he could do better.'

'He what?'

'He didn't say that, but he's one of those self-sufficient, always-capable and best-at-everything type of people.' Okay, so she might be a bit annoyed with him.

Mum looked surprised. 'He doesn't come across that way. I kind of thought you asked him because you were sweet on him.'

She almost smiled. 'It was actually just the result of a challenge he lost.'

'Oh.' Mum looked relieved. 'Well, he's handsome but his communication skills leave a lot to be desired.'

She had no idea.

BETH SPENT time with the Guests, helping with the building project, but tried to avoid Gus. She wanted him to know she'd got the message and wouldn't let herself feel for him in a way he couldn't return. She wouldn't share her heart with him. It was foolish to keep putting it out there for him to tread on. She doubted he'd even notice.

She was wrong.

His attempts at conversation were constant despite her trying not to be drawn in. She wasn't rude, but she certainly wasn't going to weep all over him like she had done in the past. She tried to make sure someone else was always around so conversation couldn't get personal.

'Beth, can you go and grab me the hammer I left out in my ute?' Gus asked. She looked up, annoyed. Couldn't he see she was busy with the carpet underlay? He could have asked Courtney. Still, she headed out to his ute. Then turned to find him following. Sneaky. Before she could call him out on it, he spoke.

'Are you angry with me for not being available?'

She laughed through gritted teeth. Hadn't they been through

this? 'You're available. You just pretend not to be. You hide behind your self-sufficiency and independence.'

'Beth, I do have needs you can meet.'

'What? Like going to get your hammer, which is still inside anyway?'

He flinched. 'No. Your friendship.'

'You don't need my friendship, Gus. You make friends easily wherever you go. People just like you without you even trying to impress them, remember? You told me that yourself.'

His face fell. 'I didn't realise I was coming across that way.'

'What way?"

'So totally arrogant.'

'Of course you did, Gus! You're forever making sure I know exactly where I stand and exactly who you are.' She didn't know why she was so angry except that she was hurt and confused. She hated that she couldn't control her feelings for him.

'Perhaps I did to some degree.' He tilted his head, brow furrowed. 'And perhaps I did it because I was scared.'

She waited, surprised by his confession.

'You want to know more about me?' He rubbed the back of his neck. 'Well, I had a rough childhood, but I have trouble talking about it. I was hurt, and so I was determined to do whatever I could so that nobody would ever hurt me again. My father didn't want me, and so I decided I didn't need him—or anybody else in the world. I've been determined to be strong, independent and capable. I never want to be humiliated and abused again. I guess I understand what Jesus went through, because I've been through it to some extent. That's why I appreciate Him so much. But at the same time, I forget to let Him be my strength and I use my own strength. I'm sorry that hurt you.'

He swallowed hard, looking unsure, and compassion filled Beth. She wanted to hug him, but it wouldn't be welcomed. 'Couldn't you just be satisfied with being ordinary?' she asked, her voice catching. 'Why do you have to strive to be extraordinary?'

His lips tilted in a crooked smile. 'I don't know that I try. It comes fairly easily.'

He was just telling it how it was. She knew he couldn't help being extraordinary. How could she deny him her friendship? Perhaps, if she tried hard enough, she could be satisfied with that.

'I do like you, Beth.' He swallowed hard. 'I like your sense of humour, your personality, your compassion. I just like you. I spend time with you because I want to.'

She didn't know what to say. Awkward silence filled the space between them. She hadn't wanted to force him to compliment her. Did he think this was what she needed?

He bit his lip. 'So, are we okay?'

She nodded and stepped forward to give him a quick hug. 'Yes. We're friends.'

God, help me to see him that way.

CHAPTER THIRTY-THREE

Beth stood on Clare's front verandah watching the gosling swim around in the pond. Gus had returned it there, saying it looked too lonely in the dam. She smiled as it pecked at the ducks, making sure they knew who was boss. It had certainly changed from the fragile, vulnerable creature Joel had tried to destroy.

And she had changed, too.

A car came down the road. Toni-Lee. She pulled up at the front gate and got out.

'Hi Toni. Clare and Phil aren't here.'

'That's fine. I was looking for you.'

She still looked weary and Beth's heart went out to her. She knew what it was like to be trying to hold it all together. 'What can I do for you?'

'I heard about you having depression and all and, well, there's something I want to ask you.'

'Me?'

'Yes. I know you'll understand.'

Beth blinked, waiting.

'I need your help,' Toni finally said, looking tortured.

Beth wanted to laugh, but only in sympathy. She knew how hard it was for her to ask. 'How can I help?'

She hesitated, then gave a sheepish smile. 'With Rod. I can't handle him.

'I thought he was nice to you.'

'Exactly. I was attracted to the tough Rod. I found him intriguing—the way nothing could affect him or influence him. But now he's ... well, he's soft.'

Beth laughed. 'Believe me, he's still tough. He can still intimidate me with a look.'

'He's so sympathetic, though. He's being so caring about my condition, and I don't want to be pitied.'

Ah, that she understood. But she'd also learned it was a mistake to hide struggles and not let others help. 'So what can I do for you?'

'Come with me as support when I tell him I'm going to get treatment so that when I'm well I can have baby William back.'

Beth bit her lip. *God, what should I do?* She didn't want to get caught between Rod and Toni-Lee. She couldn't carry Toni-Lee through this. *Only you can, God.*

She made a decision. 'I'll come if you let me stay in the background. I won't say anything. This is something you have to do yourself.'

Toni frowned. 'Well, haven't *you* changed? What happened to the timid little Beth Bateman I used to know?'

Beth smiled. 'She gave up trying on her own and surrendered everything to God.'

Could this be any more awkward? Beth stood by the Cairns' fence while Toni crept up behind Rod. He was hanging clothes on the line, and looked started to find her by his side.

'Okay Rod, this is the deal,' Toni said before he could open his mouth. 'I'm going to the doctor about my depression, but if you push me into anything ...'

He stepped back, hands raised. 'I wouldn't dare.'

'And I don't want you to tell William about my depression ... ever.' His mouth tilted and she glared at him. 'I'm serious, Rod.'

'I know.' He looked steadily back at her.

'Will you come with me?' All bravado was gone and her voice trembled.

Rod's amusement evaporated. 'Yes.'

His expression didn't change but Beth knew that deep down he was nursing hope. Toni hadn't asked for help before. She'd refused medical assistance, and refused to let anyone get close enough to show they cared.

'But I don't want you to say anything,' she said.

'To who?'

'The doctor.'

Rod nodded. 'Okay.'

Toni shook her head in frustration. 'Why do you have to be so agreeable? Why can't you at least ...?' Her shoulders sagged.

'Why can't I what?'

'Yell at me or something. Push me around. I don't even know who you are anymore.'

Rod's mouth twitched. He looked over at Beth, quirked a brow, then faced Toni again. 'You want me to push you around?'

Toni didn't answer. Rod pulled the washing basket off the chair and pushed Toni into a sitting position. Then he sat on the brick wall across from her.

'You know why I won't push you? Why I won't take over?' His voice was gruff again. 'It's because this is *your* life. You are in the position you are in by your own choices.'

'What?' Her tone revealed her hurt. 'It takes two to tango, Rod. I didn't conceive William on my own.'

'No, but it takes a stubborn, independent person with a free will that has gone wild to mess up their life and still refuse to get any help. I'm not going to force my way into your life, Toni. I've done that too many times. This time I want you to ask me, and until you do, I'll stay out of it.'

Toni spun to look at Beth. Beth wanted to jump in, but held back. It was obvious Toni was tired of holding herself together. She needed to let go.

Rod picked up the washing basket and headed toward the house. At the last moment Toni jumped up and chased him. She grabbed his arm. 'What changed you? Why are you a gentleman all of a sudden?'

He stopped, his eyes boring into hers. Then they softened. 'Because,' he said, 'God is a gentleman and I want to be like Him.'

ROD CAME to the cottage for dinner a few days later, Billy in tow. He beamed around at them. 'I don't know what changed Toni's mind about getting help, but man, I'm thanking God.' He jiggled Billy on his knee. 'Who would have thought?'

'So, we might have you back on the project again,' Phil said with a smile. 'You can marry Toni, and together you can care for Billy and have more time for ministry.'

Rod's face fell. 'I don't think so, mate. She's still not letting God in. I know from experience that God's not going to force His way into her life. He's waiting there to help when she asks, but until then He'll stay out. She wants to blame God and me for the mess she's made, instead of taking responsibility.'

Beth reached over to little Billy who gave a gummy grin and

grabbed her hand. She understood what made Toni desperate for help. Billy—or William, as she called him.

Billy's slobbery hand reached for Rod's chin and he moved his head away. 'It's all turned out so different to what we expected, hasn't it? I mean the whole project, our whole lives, really.'

'It has,' Phil agreed, 'but one thing I've learned is that God never stops amazing us with *wonder upon wonder,* as the Bible puts it.'

Rod frowned. 'I could do with a few wonders at the moment. Sometimes it feels like God's stopped working.'

Phil smiled. 'Yeah, that happens when we forget the wonder of the Gospel. Remember how it affected you—how you just kept pondering it until one day you amazed us all by giving your life to God? I'll never forget it. I use you as my constant encouragement and reminder that God is working whether or not we can see it. I keep telling Clare, 'Don't forget Rod Green.''

'Seriously?' Rod's eyes lit up.

'Seriously. You're our reminder that miracles still happen.'

Rod let out a sigh and a load seemed to roll from his shoulders. 'Thanks mate, I needed that.'

CHAPTER THIRTY-FOUR

Beth's strength was increasing every day, and Mum suggested she spend less time at the farm and more time studying for the final school exams. It made sense, but what about Gilbert? Deep down she knew what she needed to do. She needed to let him go.

'Why not wait until after your exams?' Gus suggested as they sat in the cottage lounge room. He'd seen her bike out the front and dropped in.

'Then who would feed him?'

'Me.'

She studied him. He was wearing jeans and a t-shirt today. What had happened to his overalls? 'You wouldn't mind?'

'No.'

'You don't think I'm just delaying the inevitable?'

'No, you're waiting until a better time for you emotionally, and giving Gilbert more time to get strong.'

She breathed out a sigh of relief. 'Thank you.'

'Not a problem.' He leaned back in the lounge. 'Actually, I've got an idea I want to run by you.'

She waited.

'I want to start a Bible study here at the farm. Not just a fun time like Youth Group, but something deeper. But I don't think it's appropriate for me to be running it on my own, and the girls need a female Christian influence. I'd like you to help.'

Her breath caught. 'Gus, I have a mental illness, remember?'

'And I am insensitive and abrupt, but I'm working on it and God still uses me.'

His gaze captured hers and she couldn't look away. He had confidence in her that she didn't have in herself. 'Okay,' she heard herself say. 'I'll help you. But if it doesn't work out—'

'It will.'

She couldn't help smiling. 'You're being abrupt again.'

'I prefer to think of it as straightforward.'

'Well I think it's *inappropriate*.'

His mouth tilted. 'Oh, and hugs are more appropriate?'

'Depends on why and how they're delivered.'

'Really? Well how's this for delivery?' He jumped up, charged across the space between them, threw his arms around her and tackled her onto the carpet.

Shocked speechless, she couldn't even retaliate. She found herself on the floor beside him, his arms still around her. Her indignation drained when her gaze connected with those brown eyes, so close, sparkling with merriment and challenge.

'Okay, okay,' she managed to say with a laugh. 'You've made your point. You can let me go, now.'

He broke into a smile, his face still so close she could feel his breath against her skin. She couldn't help noticing the manliness of the dark shadow around his chin, and the perfect formation of his mouth. With a quick intake of breath, she pulled back and he let her go.

'Um,' he said as he moved back to his chair, 'perhaps I shouldn't do that kind of thing. People might get the wrong idea and match-make again.'

'Yes.' Still flustered, she returned to her placed on the lounge across from him. 'Sorry about Clare's match-making.'

He chuckled, leaning forward, his elbows on his jean-clad knees. 'She didn't match-make. She told me point blank that I was an idiot for not seeing how special you are. She accused me of being blind and self-sufficient and … well, she pretty much told me off like you do sometimes.'

Beth covered her face with her hands and groaned. *Clare, you're not helping.*

'Sorry to make you so uncomfortable.' He sounded genuinely contrite.

She wasn't sure if he realised how his touch had affected her, or if he was apologising for what he'd said.

'It's fine.' Uncomfortable? He had no idea.

THE END of school formal was being planned. The class voted on a couples' dinner, but Beth didn't want to think about it. It hurt too much. For years she'd dreamed of being there with Andy, working out which Uni they'd go to together.

Cameron Oliver asked her to go with him, but she couldn't tell if he was serious or not. Even if he was, she didn't want to sit through a dinner with him by her side.

'I'm taking Brett,' Dara said. 'Who are you taking?'

Beth shrugged, her heart aching with thoughts of Andy. Gus was the only one she'd be comfortable taking, but she didn't dare risk a lecture about how he intended to stay single and that going to such an event as a couple would be deceptive and give people the wrong impression.

BETH ENJOYED the first Bible study with the Guests at the farm. The new common room in the accommodation building was set up in a relaxed circle with comfortable beanbags and chairs. Gus had prepared insightful, thought-provoking questions and it soon became clear that Tarryn was angry with God and not afraid to express it. Gus remained unfazed, patiently listening and answering her questions as she fired them at him. Beth's heart went out to her. *Please Lord, heal Tarryn and show her how much You love her.*

She glanced around and caught Emily watching Gus with wide-eyed, admiring glances. She understood why. Gus made an excellent study leader. Despite not talking much, he listened well and encouraged discussion in his calm, patient way. But Beth now understood Gus's wisdom in asking her to be a joint leader. It was so easy for hurt teenagers to become emotionally attached to a person of godly character rather than God Himself. How well she knew that.

She had just closed her Bible, ready to head home, when something hit her on the arm. She looked up. Gus had found a broken pen on the floor and was pulling it apart and pelting bits at her. A pen tip landed in her lap. She smiled and shook her head. 'And here I was thinking how mature you are.'

He grinned. 'Now that's one thing I've never claimed to be, so that's on you.'

He was changing, Beth realised. Or was it her? Somehow he didn't seem so serious, so abrupt or insensitive. His expression was softening, his eyes taking on a new light.

Beth said goodnight to everyone as they headed off to their new rooms, then headed out into the cool night.

'Beth?'

She turned. Gus had followed her. 'I hear your formal is coming up.'

'Yeah.'

He rubbed the back of his neck. 'Dara asked me to go with her.'

'You? Why did she ask you?'

He grinned, tilting his head. 'Oh, I don't know. Maybe I'm irresistible now I've bulked up and become a man.'

She laughed. 'So you're going with her?'

'No. I told her I didn't think it was a good idea ... especially since she's going out with Brett.'

'Maybe she thought someone else might ask you and she wanted to get in first.' Gus frowned and she wanted to snatch back her words. 'Dara is very competitive,' she tried to explain.

'I don't see why she has to take anyone.'

'We're all supposed to.'

Those brown eyes met hers. 'So who are you taking?'

'I don't know. I won't be good company for anyone because I'll be sad all evening. Cameron asked me to go with him, but I don't want to give him the wrong impression.' She winced. 'To be honest, it would be easier not to go at all.'

'You could just go on your own.'

'I could, but everyone will notice and I don't want to draw attention to myself.'

She waited for him to tell her she shouldn't care what people thought, but he didn't. He looked thoughtful. 'So take someone who won't mind you being sad and who won't read anything into it. Take someone who's like a brother to you, that they're not going to assume you have feelings for.'

'Like who? Phil?' Her eyes widened. 'Like *you*?'

He looked amused. 'Beth, I'm not going to blend into a crowd. I offend people, I don't have any dress sense and I have no idea about etiquette.'

'I don't mind. Will you come?'

He tilted his head, studying her, then shrugged. 'If that's what you want.'

She smiled. It was—more than she'd realised. 'Thank you.' She gave him an impulsive hug. 'You've saved me.'

'A bit drastic, but you're welcome.'

BETH WAS DISMAYED to find they had been placed at a table with Dara and Brett and Tina and Cameron.

'So this is the guy who stole your heart,' Cameron said to Beth as they took their seats.

She blushed. 'What?'

'Well, only true love could make you refuse me.' He gave a heavy sigh that was clearly put on. 'Dara told me you found someone better and I can only assume it's the man you've brought with you.'

Gus ignored Cameron and reached for the bowl of chips in the middle of the table. He looked magnificent in his tux, and he wasn't even pulling at his tie.

'We're just friends,' Beth said, looking between Cameron and Tina. Tina didn't appear bothered that her partner was flirting with someone else.

'What does he have that I don't?' Cameron groaned, his over-the-top theatrics drawing attention from other tables.

Beth rolled her eyes. 'The ability to behave well in social situations, for a start.' She glanced sideways at Gus and winked. 'Maybe you should watch Gus and learn.'

Gus gave her a questioning look that quickly turned mischievous. Snatching up the bowl of chips, he dumped it in front of him, between his cutlery.

'He's becoming so socially acceptable I hardly have to reprimand him for anything anymore,' Beth added pointedly.

He raised his brows at her, then spat the partly chewed chips from his mouth back into the bowl.

'Gus!' Now she'd done it. Everyone stared at him open-mouthed.

'What?' He gave her his most innocent look.

Dara reached to take the bowl from him. 'If you can't eat properly, you don't eat at all.' Beth couldn't believe her ridiculous, flirtatious expression.

Gus grabbed the bowl back off Dara, then shovelled the partly-chewed chips back into his mouth. Everyone at the table stared at him in disbelief, apart from Cameron who slapped his knee, laughing hysterically.

'You wait 'til I tell the Guests what you did,' Dara said.

Gus shrugged. 'They won't believe you.'

'Of course they will.' Dara's smile was coy. 'I'm not the only witness here.'

Beth hid her irritation behind an innocent look. 'Witness to what, Dara?'

Did Dara seriously think she'd play her game when she was so blatantly flirting with Gus right under her boyfriend's nose? At least Gus was ignoring her attempts, but that was Gus. He probably didn't even realise Dara was flirting.

Beth noticed several of her classmates looking at Gus, and knew they were wondering about him. He didn't even look at them, and she was grateful for the way he deliberately entertained her, keeping her mind off Andy and focused on his antics. Occasionally he pulled at his tie, but he resisted the temptation to remove it or undo his top button.

Then it hit her. He was doing this for her. And she knew she could never repay him. Or stop loving him. She was in serious trouble.

The night was over too soon, and Gus dropped her home. 'Thanks so much for coming with me,' she said. There was so much more she wanted to say, but now was not the time.

He smiled through his open ute window. 'I enjoyed it. It was a good night and good food. I even saw *you* eat something.'

She smiled. 'See you tomorrow.'

He drove off into the night while Beth stood and looked up at the stars. Tonight she'd begun to believe the world could be exciting again. There must be some way she could thank Gus; let him know how much it meant to have him by her side, turning a sad night into one of hope and joy.

HE DROPPED in the very next morning while she was studying, looking smart in his Sunday shirt and dress pants.

She gave him a teasing smile. 'What's gotten into you?'

'What do you mean?'

'The clothes.'

He shrugged. 'They're nothing out of the ordinary.'

'For you, they are. You must be going somewhere. You wouldn't bother dressing up unless you were.'

'I think you're jumping to conclusions, Beth.'

'I'm not. I'm just making observations from what I know of you.'

Gus turned warm, friendly eyes to her. 'Oh, and you know me well enough now to do that accurately, do you?'

How could she navigate that question safely? She sidestepped it. 'My first impressions of people are usually correct.'

He was quiet for a bit, then put his hands in his pockets. 'So, what were your first impressions of me? Or is that a dangerous question?'

She grinned cheekily. 'Probably.'

'What about your impressions now? Is that a dangerous question, too?'

Her face grew warm. How could she answer that question without revealing too much?

'I've caught you out, haven't I?' Gus laughed in triumph, misunderstanding her embarrassment. 'You've completely changed your first impressions of me.'

'My opinion, maybe, but not my observations of what you're like.'

'What's the difference?'

'I don't know ... maybe I've become accustomed to the way you take everything so literally. I don't mind it so much now, but it's still a fact that you take everything as literally as possible.'

'That's because it's the most sensible way. If I try to read between the lines, I usually get it wrong. I prefer people to be straight with me; tell me exactly what they're thinking and feeling. I'm not into the *guess what I'm thinking* game.'

And yet, every time she tried to tell him what she was feeling for him, things went badly. Maybe she was the one with the communication problem.

'You're right, though,' he said with a sheepish smile, glancing at his watch. 'I'm on my way into town to see the solicitor and surveyor. We have to arrange a final inspection of the accommodation block.'

Beth's heart sank. 'Does that mean you're finished with the program? Are you going to leave?'

'I'm not sure what God has for me, but I'm going to take some time off and visit my mum. And I'm applying for a job in the city, testing a few doors. I leave Friday. But don't worry, Phil and Clare said they'd look after Gilbert while I'm away, and Phil's happy to run the Bible study with you until I get back.'

So, he was coming back. But for how long? She'd been kidding herself that she could live happily with him as a friend—because mere friendship meant he could leave. Any time. Without her. And she couldn't bear the thought of not seeing him every day, talking with him, enjoying his steady, reliable presence.

When he left, she put aside her study books, pulled her journal out from under her mattress and began reading. To her surprise she found more and more mention of Gus and less of Andy. Gus was right. First impressions weren't always accurate.

CHAPTER THIRTY-FIVE

'What's up with you?' Clare asked as Beth sat quietly, poking at her dinner with a fork.

'Just thinking.'

Phil chuckled. 'Pretty serious thinking. Who are you thinking about?' She didn't answer and he grinned wickedly. 'It's Gus, isn't it? There's been a lot of talk going around about you two.'

'It's not like that. We're just friends. He doesn't want to get married and he's probably moving away.'

'He's just protecting himself,' Phil said. 'He's always been very careful and thoughtful.'

'I don't think so.' Beth put down her fork and sat back with a sigh. 'He's made it very clear where we stand.'

'But that's because you haven't told him how you really feel.'

'I don't have to. He knows.'

Clare raised an eyebrow. 'Are you sure?'

'You need to tell him, little sister.' Phil's green eyes shone with encouragement. 'That's what friendship is all about ... taking risks and being totally open even when it could mean being hurt or rejected. You need to show him your heart.'

Beth bit her lip. She'd been asking God for wisdom all after-noon. Was it time to tell Gus exactly how she felt? He'd throw it back in her face, but at least she'd be being straightforward and honest, not leaving him to read between the lines.

SHE COULDN'T CONCENTRATE during the Bible study Friday night. Her heart beat too fast, and she couldn't meet Gus's eyes. Instinc-tively, she knew it was the wrong time to reveal her heart. Still, she'd give him the picture she'd sketched of him walking down the farm road to the accommodation building, the gosling by his side. It had taken all afternoon, but she was happy with the way she'd managed to capture his kindness and strength.

'Where were you tonight, Beth?' Courtney teased as the study finished. 'I don't think you listened to a word we said.'

She smiled absently, watching as Gus stood and looked around at the group. 'Well, sorry guys, but I have to go,' he said cheer-fully. 'I told my mum I'd be home by morning.'

Beth found her tongue. 'You're not travelling alone through the night are you?'

He gave her a steady, knowing look. 'Nothing's going to happen to me, Beth. And even if it did, God would get you through it.'

Awful fear clutched her heart. She watched Courtney and Braydon give him a hug while the others milled around asking him questions, saying goodbye.

She was relieved when no one followed him out to his car. She ran after him. 'Gus!'

He turned with a smile. 'Beth, I nearly didn't say goodbye.'

This was her chance. She shoved the picture at him, her words running over each other. 'I just wanted to give you this before you go, I drew it for you this afternoon, and I tried to capture a moment in time that represents you, but I don't know how well I did, anyway, it's just a thanks for ... well, everything.'

He took the picture and studied it. She couldn't bring herself to look at him. Finally, unnerved by his silence, she looked up.

His eyes were warm, and his face crinkled into a smile. 'It's great. You're very talented.'

She smiled at his genuine delight, her heart dancing at the warmth expressed in his eyes. 'I wanted to do something more for you. But I didn't know, well, I'm not sure how to express myself properly to tell you what you mean to me. But you've seen me at my worst and still been there for me. I didn't used to be so moody, but you've put up with all my confusing mood swings, my struggles, my grief. God knew I needed someone who would listen and be steady, loyal, dependable and caring. I know He sent you to build for the program, but He sent you here for me as well.'

Gus studied the drawing again, and a sinking feeling started in Beth's chest. She knew that disapproving look. She edged away. 'Well, have a good trip.'

'Wait, Beth!'

She ignored him and raced back inside. It would crush her if he lectured her tonight. She didn't need to be reminded that dreaming of a future with him was hopeless. He could save whatever he had to say until he got back. If he came back.

BETH MISSED GUS, but life was so busy she managed to avoid thinking about him most of the time. Final exams came and went, and then Christmas. Toni continued to insist Beth come with her to see Rod. Then she asked her to deliver personal messages. Beth was embarrassed, but she did it.

'Ask her why she bothers to visit me and Billy when she could just do it all through you?' Rod growled at Beth.

She passed on the message.

'Tell him I don't want William to have a childhood like we had,' was Toni's quiet response.

Rod frowned when she delivered the message. 'Then ask her why she refused to marry me.'

'Rod, I can't ask her that.'

He shrugged. 'Then tell her whatever you like.'

Beth passed on the message. Toni frowned. 'His marriage offer was in the past—I was struggling then and I was still depressed.'

Depressed was putting it mildly. She was so different since she'd started medication and had counselling. She was the confident, independent Toni again. She was almost happy. 'So, what exactly do you want me to tell him?'

Toni stood. 'Nothing. I'm going to deal with him myself. He's so exasperating!'

Beth smirked, knowing there would be fireworks. The two of them could be entertaining when they got going.

'Come on,' Toni ordered.

Beth didn't like being told what to do, but she was too curious not to come along. A few minutes later, she informed Rod that Toni was in the lounge room and wanted to see him.

Rod passed Billy to Maria and wandered out. 'Decided to see me in person, did you?' His voice was gruff, but his jaw twitched and Beth knew he wanted to laugh.

Toni's hands went to her hips. 'I want to know why you won't propose or something.'

'I already did.'

'I know, and I made a mistake when I refused. Okay, see, I confessed. I made a mistake.'

He shrugged. 'I never thought anything would make me propose to a girl in the first place. Don't expect me to do it again. Once was humiliating enough.'

'Humiliating? And you think it was easy for me? How do you think it feels to be proposed to out of obligation? I don't want a man to marry me out of sympathy, or even out of love and concern for my son. I want to be loved.'

'You don't think sympathy is love? It's a love that you choose, Toni. It's not about romance.'

Beth rolled her eyes. He'd obviously spent too much time with Gus.

Toni's hands went to her hips. 'Well I don't want a man to have to force himself to love me. I want him to admire me, respect me, not be able to live without me.'

Rod shook his head, all amusement gone. 'I can't pretend to need you, Toni.'

To Beth's surprise, Toni burst into tears. Rod appeared unmoved. When Toni finally looked at him, the struggle was clear in her eyes. 'You're heartless, Rod Green. You haven't really changed. You're no gentleman.'

When he didn't respond she stood and left without another word. With a helpless shrug, Beth followed.

Toni wiped her eyes as they walked down the road back to Clare and Phil's. 'I didn't even get to see Billy,' she wailed. 'I really thought Rod would have a change of heart.'

Beth wrestled with her thoughts, then gathered up the courage to voice them. 'I don't think he needs a change of heart, Toni. I think you do.'

Her mouth dropped open and she stopped mid-step. 'What do you mean?'

'You won't let yourself be vulnerable around him. You keep putting up barriers to keep him out.'

'I burst into tears in front of the guy!'

'What kind of tears, though?'

'I don't know. Frustration, I guess.'

'Yes, and Rod saw that. He knows you're still fighting strong on your own.'

She spun around. 'I have to go back and see him again.' She grabbed Beth's hand.

I guess I'm coming too. Lord, please change Toni's hard, independent heart.

Rod's eyebrows shot up when they returned. 'What are you doing back here?'

Toni swallowed hard. 'I need you, Rod.'

'You don't.'

'I *do*. Come on, I just forced myself to come back here and humiliate myself by confessing my weakness. What do you want from me?'

He hesitated, then rubbed a hand along his square jaw. 'I want you to see that God is the only One you need. I want you to stop fighting Him and let Him back into your life. Just like you don't want to be married out of sympathy, I don't want to be married because you think you need me. It wouldn't work between us, Toni.'

Toni's chin quivered. 'Why? Aren't you attracted to me now that I've had your baby and put on so much weight?'

Rod stared at her, then with lightning reflexes, grabbed her and pulled her into his arms. She gasped as he bent his head and kissed her in a way that made Beth blush just watching. She looked away as Toni surrendered to his kiss, then jumped when the door banged. Rod had broken away from Toni and shut the door in her face.

And she'd thought Gus was confusing.

Toni stood staring at the door, breathing hard.

'I think that gives you your answer,' Beth said with a sheepish grin. 'He's still attracted to you, but until you have your heart right with God, he's not going to let you back into his life.'

They headed back to Phil and Clare's cottage. 'I just want this all to end,' Toni said bitterly. 'I feel like if Rod would take me back it would all be okay.'

'Having Rod wouldn't fix anything. I always thought everything would be okay once I had Andy, but people come and go. God is the only One who's always there.'

'Are you saying God is enough to make you happy?'

Beth pulled a face. 'I'd like to say that, but I'm human and I still have unfulfilled dreams. Life is better than I ever imagined it could be, though. The last few years have been pretty tough—in fact my whole life has been. But I feel like suddenly the rain has gone and the sun has come out. God has blessed me far more than I know how to thank Him for. And it's all because I stopped struggling to achieve and be someone impressive, and just let God take over. I still have problems, but I know He's in control and He's the only one who can get me through.'

'So, do you think God heals depression?'

'He can. I know that for sure. But if He can use you better with it, He won't take it away. He'll just give you the strength to live with it.'

Toni stopped, eyes riveted on her. 'So, you're saying I can be happy without Rod if I give up the fight and give it all to God.'

'Maybe not happy, but content. At peace. There's a difference.'

'I'm so tired of struggling, Beth,' she admitted with a sigh, 'I'm sick of trying to hold my life together when it's all such a mess.'

Beth smiled. 'Then why do it? God wants to do it for us and He can do it so much better than we can.'

'I can't.' Her eyes filled with tears. 'I don't want to be like Billy.'

Her baby? Beth waited until Toni drew in a deep breath and explained. 'I resented him. He just kept taking and taking and never gave anything back in return. It's all so one-sided. I've got nothing to give God.'

'You don't resent Billy now, though do you?'

She didn't hesitate. 'No.'

'So what changed?'

She looked thoughtful, then her eyes lit up. 'He smiles at me. He responds to me.'

'So smile at God. Let Him know you appreciate Him and all He's done for you.'

For a minute Beth thought Toni was going to laugh; that she didn't understand. Did she understand her own words? She remembered Grandpa. He never asked anything from her, but his eyes would light up when she entered a room. He was always waiting, ready to listen, to offer advice, to enjoy the beauty of the world with her. She was secure in Grandpa's love. There was no drive to achieve, and yet she always wanted to do things for him just because he loved her and she loved him. She remembered the first portrait she attempted of his friendly, wrinkled face. She ended up in tears of frustration at the way she simply couldn't capture the depth of love in his expression. Then her sleeve had smudged the charcoal. Yet Grandpa had loved that portrait. It hung in his room until the day he died.

Father God, You love me like Grandpa did, she realised with startling clarity. *You just love me because I'm Yours.*

Her thoughts were interrupted by Toni's voice. 'Okay,' she said. 'He can have it all.' She looked up. 'Hear me, God? It's yours. This whole mess. Sorry for the mess I've made of it but hopefully you've got enough miracles left to sort it out.'

Beth grinned. She was sure God never ran out of miracles. Toni's prayer of surrender was proof of that.

BETH FELT silly going back to Rod's with Toni a week later. He didn't look impressed when he saw her at the door, but then, he didn't know that Toni had surrendered her life to God—that she and Toni had spent the last several days talking about God, praying together, enjoying the fact that Jesus loved them so much.

'Rod, I know it's been a while,' Toni's voice quavered, 'but I've been spending a lot of time with Beth.'

His eyes bored into her. 'And she made you stay away from me and Billy?'

One side of Toni's mouth came up. 'No, not exactly, but she helped me see a lot of things more clearly ... and well, this is the last time I'll bring Beth with me to see you, because I've given up the fight. I'm letting down the walls and I promise I won't use her to keep the distance between us anymore. I can't guarantee I won't try to take my life back again sometimes, but I believe ... I know God will help me.'

Rod opened the door wider and motioned them inside. When they were seated, he sat forward, his penetrating gaze on Toni. 'What are you saying?'

'I'm saying I ran for a long time but I'm finally on the right road home. I've stopped fighting God and trying to do everything on my own. I've surrendered.'

Beth could tell Toni was nervous. *God, give her the words.*

Toni wrung her hands, then forced herself to look at Rod. 'I want to marry you. I admire and respect you. I don't want you to propose again because it's not about romance. It's about choices. I choose to commit my life to God, and I choose to love you as best I can with God's help ... if you will have me.'

Still Rod didn't speak.

Toni shuffled uncomfortably in her chair. 'Remember you said you wouldn't chase after me anymore? Well, I've stopped running,' She paused and when he still didn't speak, just gave her that intense look, her frustration showed. 'Do I have to chase *you*?'

A flash of amusement passed over his face. 'That might be fun.'

She bit her lip to stop her smile while Beth wished she could disappear.

'So, do you think we should get married?' Toni pressed.

'Yes.'

She smiled and moved toward him, but he jumped over the lounge, using it as a barrier between them. 'Things are different now, Toni. I don't want a long engagement—you know what we're like with self-control. But I want us to have pre-marriage counselling. There's a lot we need to talk about.'

'Like what?'

'Like if our goals are the same. If we would work together.'

Toni nodded, still smiling. 'It will work if we keep God at the centre. He will help us be good partners and good parents.' Then her face fell. 'I guess we won't be getting married today if we do counselling and everything.'

'No,' Rod said with a smile. 'But you need time to get a dress and everything, anyway.'

'I don't want a wedding dress. Besides I don't really have any family to come along. We won't even need a reception or anything.'

A sheepish look passed over Rod's face. 'I want a wedding dress.'

'Huh?'

'I mean I want you to wear one. And I want all our friends to be there. I want Scott Cairn to marry us.'

Toni smothered a laugh. 'Rod! What's happened to the tough guy I used to know?'

His eyes softened. 'He fell in love. First God changed him, then the love of a woman changed him a little bit more.'

'So, you do need me?'

'No, but maybe I want you a bit.'

She levelled him with a look. 'Want me a bit, meaning ...?'

'More than anything I've wanted in my life.'

Beth couldn't stop the laugh that bubbled up and burst out. Their married life certainly wouldn't be boring. They both spun to face her and Rod's eyes narrowed as he tried to look like the tough, unreachable Rod again. 'Do we still need our messenger?' he asked Toni pointedly.

With another laugh, Beth escaped out the door. They'd be fine without her. It was clear that even practical love made by choice could become romantic. In fact, she thought, it might be even more romantic than romance itself.

CHAPTER THIRTY-SIX

Clare and Phil beamed when Beth told them about her afternoon.

'See, God still gives people the desires of their heart, if they let their desires match His best plan for them,' Clare said. Her smile turned mischievous. 'Gus is coming home tomorrow.'

Beth shook her head. 'Please don't, Clare. I don't want to dream crazy dreams anymore.'

'I don't believe they're just dreams.' She laughed softly. 'How the tables have turned. Do you remember saying the same thing to me about Phil?'

'Every relationship is different, though. My dreams for Andy weren't God's plans. And it's the same with Gus. He doesn't want to get married and he's never given any indication that he feels anything special for me.'

'No?' Clare eyebrows shot up. 'You don't think seeking you out all the time is any indication? Beth, if you knew Gus before, you'd know he's a changed man since he met you. He's softened so much and he laughs more.'

'Laughs more? He must have been ridiculously serious before.'

'You have feelings for him, don't you?' Clare's eyes searched Beth's for the truth.

'You know I do, but I don't see how it could ever work—especially not now. When I saw him as a friend, I could be natural with him, but now I panic every time he looks at me.'

Clare laughed. 'Beth, if only you could see this from my point of view. It's all kind of amusing. You're going to look back on it all someday and understand what I mean.'

Beth smiled too, but she doubted it. It was all too confusing and painful to be amusing. But at least she'd learned to let go and trust God.

BETH WANDERED down the farm's dirt track, thinking and praying. She'd applied for an Environment and Wildlife Studies course at Uni. She needed to get on with living her life, and she wanted to do something she loved. Maybe someday she'd come back to the farm and work on the conservation land here, maybe teach the Guests how to care for wildlife.

A figure appeared in the distance, heading toward her. The boundless energy and strong, steady walk were familiar, but it was the gosling at his heels that gave him away. Gus was back.

It was ridiculous how hard her heart was pounding, either with excitement or nerves —she wasn't sure which. He sidestepped the gosling—which was more like a gander now—and she smiled as he came to a stop in front of her. His brown eyes were alive with warmth and delight, as though he'd missed her as much as she'd missed him. She wanted to throw her arms around him, but held herself back, so they just smiled at one another.

Beth finally came up with something sensible to say. 'Welcome home. How was your time away?'

'Good.'

'Did you apply for any jobs?'

'Yes.'

'Did you get one?'

'Not sure yet.'

She laughed at his usual one-word answers. They walked side by side, and she told him about the Uni course she'd applied for. 'I know people are more important than animals,' she said, trying to read his reaction to her news. 'But I love working with wildlife and the course seemed perfect.'

'It does seem perfect for you,' Gus agreed. 'And we're supposed to care for God's creation. It was the first job God gave Adam to do in the garden—as well as protecting Eve of course.' He looked sideways at her, the hint of a smile playing about his mouth. 'Helping people understand God's creation gives them a glimpse of the Creator. And I hear that you have helped Toni understand God's love for her?'

'Yes! She believes now.' Unable to contain her joy, she told him all about the drama she'd witnessed playing out between Rod and Toni. 'So God *does* make some people's dreams come true,' she said with a triumphant smile.

Gus faltered, then stopped walking. 'Remember when I was leaving and we were saying goodbye, you said that I'm special to you? That God sent me here for you? What made you say that?' His eyes held hers, demanding an honest answer.

She stiffened. She should have known she wouldn't get away with it. 'I was afraid I would never see you again,' she admitted, 'I just needed to make sure you knew. I guess I was scared God was going to take you.'

'Because God always takes the ones you love?'

His eyes were knowing, but she couldn't tell if he was pleased or displeased.

'Yes,' her voice came out in a whisper.

'But I'm here,' he said quietly. 'And you're here and you're healing.'

'Yes.' Was that it? She'd expected him to berate her for her feelings. She needed this sorted before she headed off to Uni. She took a deep breath. 'Gus, when I go to Uni, can we keep in touch? You know, email each other, maybe?'

He gave her his steady, appraising look. 'Long-distance relationships aren't my thing.'

She palmed her forehead in frustration. 'I'm not talking about that kind of relationship. I know you said you'd never go out with a girl unless you planned to marry her, and you don't plan to get married, so ...' She sighed. 'I think I know where we stand, but I hope someday you will come to realise woman was created as a helper, not a curse. We work well together.' She bit her lip, trying not to cry. 'It's just I will miss you so much, Gus. And I'm sorry I just can't seem to help loving you more than you want to be loved.'

With that, she turned and ran, unable to handle whatever he might say in return. She left him standing there on the roadway, looking after her, the gosling pecking at his heels. Why did he have to be so confusing? She swiped at unwanted tears.

Lord, show Gus if you want him to get married someday. And show him if that person is me. And if not, help me to survive the next few years at Uni without him.

She smiled through her tears. Whatever happened, God was her strength. He'd brought her through her worst nightmares; Grandpa dying. Andy dying. It was clear Gus was determined not to let her into his heart. It was also clear that all the time he'd ever spent with her was for her sake, not his own. He pitied her and wanted her to be what he expected everyone to be–strong and well.

Well, I'm well now, but it's not because of you, Gus Richards! It's because of God.

She forced herself to remember all the irritating things about him. His insistence upon logic, his independence and total lack of social grace. His blunt, contrary words, his lack of dress sense.

Yet those things only made her smile. She no longer cared if he put dirty marks all over the lounge ... just so long as he was there on the lounge talking with her. She didn't care if he hugged her and messed up her clothes or hair, just so long as his strong arms surrounded her. Yes, with God's help she would even accept that he didn't love her or want to marry her, just so long as he didn't disappear completely from her life.

And yet it seemed she had no say in it.

God, thank you that You are always with me. You will get me through whatever life brings. I trust You to be my comfort and refuge no matter what happens.

BETH NEEDED to talk to Clare. She wasn't at the house. She'd been landscaping at the accommodation building lately. Maybe she was there.

She wasn't. 'I think she went to the shed to get some more rose bushes to plant,' Courtney said.

Beth headed that way. There was the sound of someone moving around inside. Then the sound of something being dropped to the floor. She stepped inside and stopped short. It wasn't Clare. Gus was there, shirt off, arm muscles flexed as he lifted a heavy beam and moved it to the side. She backed out as fast as she could.

'Beth, don't go!'

Her face burned, but she stopped and turned. He dropped the piece of wood to the floor. She forced herself to look in his eyes and avoid his bare chest.

'Um, h... have you seen Clare?' she stammered.

'She's gone to buy some more plants.'

'Thanks.' She turned to leave, but he called her back.

'I want to talk to you.' He reached for his shirt and slid it over his well-toned chest. 'I just wanted to tell you I've changed my mind about marriage. I think it's a good thing for a man to marry. I've thought and prayed and I've been talking with Phil—and well, it's definitely not a curse.'

She stared at him, her heart pounding so hard she was sure he could hear it. 'There's good things about it,' she murmured, her face burning.

He grinned. 'I hear it's very good. And I admit it would be nice to hold a woman without having to second-guess whether or not it's appropriate. Thanks to you, I've discovered I quite enjoy hugging, and it would be nice to be free to do more of it without feeling guilty about it.'

Shocked speechless, she tried to swallow but it wasn't going smoothly. She couldn't think straight. Gus thought marriage was good? Well that was a complete turnaround—almost too much to take in. But she couldn't assume he wanted to marry *her*. She wasn't his only admirer, and once she left for Uni and others realised he was available … She couldn't stand to think about it. She needed to change the subject until she could pull her thoughts and emotions together.

'These look really good,' she said, touching the wooden rails he'd built.

His brown eyes studied her before he sat down on the pile of timber he'd been moving. 'That was an abrupt change of subject.'

Her face burned hotter and she still couldn't look at him. 'Sorry. What were you saying?'

He chuckled and bent to pick up a piece of rubbish on the floor, which he then threw at her before standing and returning to his work.

She left, her mind whirling. If only she'd had the courage to ask questions, but he'd flustered her. She returned to the cottage to wait for Clare, unable to focus on housework, although it clearly needed doing. Instead, she began sketching, deep in thought.

'How's it going?'

Her hand flew across the sketch before she flipped the pad over. 'Hey, Gus.'

'What are you doing?' He bent over her, his brown eyes soft and almost playful.

'Just scribbling.'

'Scribbling or sketching?'

She didn't answer. She didn't feel up to a debate about whether smudging the truth was actually lying.

'Are you going to tell me or do I have to have a look myself?'

'I was sketching a hat.'

A smile played about his mouth. 'Not my raggedy old one?'

'Why would I sketch that grubby old thing?'

'You avoided my question very neatly.'

Cornered. She considered sitting on the sketchpad, but doubted he'd snatch it from her anyway. She looked away from his laughing eyes, then squealed when a mouse shot out from behind the sideboard and across the lounge room.

Gus laughed, and she crossed her arms, feeling sheepish. 'I'm not tough like Clare when it comes to snakes and spiders and mice.'

'I can see that.'

'Did you know Clare cut up a snake once?' She knew she was babbling nervously, but couldn't seem to help it.

'I had heard, yes.'

'Mum and I always get Clare to get rid of any spiders or mice.'

Gus raised his brows. 'How does Clare dispose of them?'

She ignored his obvious urge to laugh. 'She hits them with a fly swat, or sprays them.'

He did laugh, then. 'I meant the mice.'

She looked back, face deadpan. 'So did I.'

His face screwed up in distaste and Beth let out a shout of laughter. Slowly, his mouth tipped into a smile. 'Think you're funny, do you?'

'Must be. I saw you trying not to laugh when I squealed.'

'It was a bit amusing.'

'What's funny about being scared of mice and spiders?'

'It's just such a girl thing.'

'Girl thing?' She smothered another squeal as the mouse did a lap of the room.

'Why don't you set a trap?' Gus stepped back and followed the mouse with his eyes. 'I presume that's what Clare really does.'

'Yeah, but I can't bring myself to do it.'

'Why not?'

'I don't want to kill them. I like them too much.'

'Traps?'

'Gus Richards! Why do you always have to take everything the wrong way? I meant the mice and you know it.'

His eyes twinkled. 'How could I know? You're terrified of mice, so it doesn't immediately correlate that you like them.'

'I don't like how fast and unexpected they are, that's all. I hate seeing them dead in the traps and knowing I've taken a life.'

He stood. 'Show me where the traps are, and I'll set one for you, then I'll come and check it later.'

Beth found a trap in the laundry, then set it on the bench in front of him. He took a knife from the cutlery drawer. 'Got some peanut butter? It sticks better and makes sure the critter doesn't run off with the bait.'

She placed the peanut butter jar on the bench and he began his careful work. She watched his nimble fingers and felt that confusing sensation she'd been trying to avoid. To distract herself, she read aloud the warning on the trap. 'Beware of fingers while setting trap.'

Gus stopped what he was doing and pinched her on the arm.

She jumped and rubbed the spot, staring at him. 'What was that for?'

A smile danced about his mouth. 'Well, you did read the warning, but you didn't watch out for fingers.'

That set her off into giggles and Gus just stood there grinning at her. 'You 'right there?' he asked when she regained control.

She nodded, and he carefully set the trap beside the sideboard. Then he nodded to the lounge. 'You got time to talk?'

Her heart began pounding, but before she could answer, a loud snap startled them. She looked at Gus in dismay. 'Already?'

He looked pleased. 'Sounds like it. I told you that peanut butter was good stuff.'

He headed toward the trap while Beth followed, a little way behind. As he bent over to check the trap, she acted on impulse.

'Beware of fingers while checking trap,' she said, reaching to nip him with her fingers. Before she could get him, he spun around so fast she jumped and squealed, wincing at the sight of the dead mouse in the trap. 'We got it.' She felt sad and triumphant at once.

'First go, too,' Gus said, moving the dead mouse into the kitchen, out of view.

Beth sighed. 'I hate taking a life, but it's so convenient.'

He glanced back at her. 'That's what Hitler said.'

She giggled, despite herself. 'Don't you dare compare me to Hitler!'

'Or what?'

'Or, I don't really know.'

He set the trap down and stretched his fingers toward her. 'Beware of fingers while making threats ...'

She turned to run, but found herself pulled back against his chest, locked in his strong embrace. She struggled and he loosened his hold so that she could turn in his arms. Slowly, she looked up into his face. Those warm brown eyes were smiling and his expression was tender. It took all the fight out of her. Silence, charged with something she'd never felt before, filled the space between them. When he spoke, his voice was deep and soft.

'Beth, I know I'm not Andy. I know I can never take his place. But I love you. It was just brotherly love at first—a caring love that made me want to protect and help you—but I feel much more than that now. I respect you and your amazing gifts. We work great as a team. I think it would be good to marry you. If you go to Uni, I'll find a job near you.'

She gasped, eyes wide. What about going out for a while—getting to know one another more? And yet Gus had always said he wouldn't commit himself to any girl unless he wanted to marry her. But was this a proposal? She had no idea.

'When you change your mind you do it quickly,' she finally stuttered.

A smile hovered about his mouth. 'Well, maybe I was thinking about it for longer than I cared to admit.'

He stepped back slightly, his arm still around her. She tried to read what was in his eyes. 'Are you sure you think marriage is a good thing?'

He frowned. 'I'm not the type to make a decision without a lot of thought and prayer.'

She knew he wasn't. She bit her lip. 'So, what now? Where do we stand?'

He released her. 'I thought I made that fairly clear.'

She saw through his abrupt answer. He was nervous. So much for romance. But it wasn't romance she wanted anymore. She wanted Gus, just the way he was.

He shuffled his feet. 'I was thinking we could get married after you finish your Uni degree.'

'That could be years away.'

'Well, maybe before then. We'll see. But I want children, too.'

Whoa. She wanted to tell him to slow down and stop being so businesslike. She held her tongue. He was as unsure as she was. This was new ground for both of them, and she doubted he'd read romance books, so how would he know the proper way to go about it? Besides, he probably wouldn't do it the conventional way even if he did.

Suddenly he released her and picked up the sketch she'd left on the table. He gazed silently at the portrayal of his ragged hat, then his eyes met hers. 'Can I have this?'

'Yes.'

He put it in his pocket and headed out the door, looking kind of dazed. There was no hug, no kiss, no promise he'd see her tomorrow … nothing. She watched him bounce down the back steps and head down the road. And she began to laugh. What could she expect if she wanted to spend her life with Gus Richards? Certainly not predictability.

Proof of that hit her when she turned to find the dead mouse still in its trap on the bench. With a shudder she dropped the whole trap in the outside bin. She'd prefer to buy a new trap than deal with the poor lifeless creature. As it hit the bottom of the bin with a thud, ripples of laughter overcame her. Gus certainly wasn't himself this afternoon. She would never have dreamed anything could make him absently leave a dead mouse on the kitchen bench. She doubted he'd ever done anything so vague or illogical before in his life.

CHAPTER THIRTY-SEVEN

Beth sat on the cottage verandah, swinging her legs, waiting for Clare to return from shopping. The Guests were digging a garden around the accommodation building and Clare had gone to the local nursery to choose some plants. Her car appeared around the corner, and Beth stood and paced as it crawled toward the driveway. Her impatient frown morphed into a smile when she saw the reason for Clare's speed. Green foliage pressed against the windows, filling the car and surrounding Clare as though she were driving in a mini jungle.

Beth bounced down the steps to meet her. 'I think I might be engaged.'

Clare laughed as she pushed aside leaves and got out of the car. 'Well I would hope you'd know.'

'Well I always hoped I'd know, too, but it's impossible to know anything with Gus.'

Clare stopped, her expression a mix of bewilderment and hope. 'What are you saying?'

'Gus wants to marry me.'

'He said that?'

'Yes, but he didn't ask me, and he didn't propose or anything. He just told me when would be a good time and where we should live.'

'You're kidding.'

'Nope.' Beth grinned. She understood Clare's disbelief. She found it hard to believe, too.

Clare shoved a waving palm leaf further into the car and shut the door, then settled her full attention on Beth. 'And you're saying you're okay with this?'

Laughter spilled over. 'Of course. It's a miracle that he even sees marriage as a God-given blessing rather than a curse that will hinder his ministry.'

'Beth, I don't understand.'

'What's to understand?'

'Well, you always wanted to be swept off your feet—you're more of a hopeless romantic than I am. And Gus, well, he irritates you like no one else I know.'

'You'd be surprised who irritates me, Clare. I just happen to be free to express my irritation with Gus.'

'Seriously?'

She nodded, joy bubbling up inside and coming out in another laugh.

Clare shook her head. 'Sometimes I wonder if I know you at all.' She glanced around. 'So where is Gus now?'

'Probably working as usual.'

'He proposed then went back to work?'

Beth's laugh was unrestrained, now. 'He didn't exactly propose, remember?'

Clare grabbed her wrist and dragged her to the chairs on the front verandah. She leaned forward, her gaze capturing Beth's. 'Are you sure this isn't a rebound thing? I mean, you're getting better and you're healing from grief over Andy, you've just finished school, and well, I'm worried you might just be taking Gus because all the other doors have closed.'

Poor Clare. Beth could see why she was worried, but there was no need. 'There's no one else like him, I agree with you there. I love him, Clare. I can't stand the thought of being with any other man, and to tell you the truth, I can't stand the thought of living without him.'

'But Beth, even his proposal—or lack of it—shows what sort of man he is. You can't expect flowers and chocolates and romantic walks under the stars.'

A serene smile widened Beth's mouth. 'I know, and I know you couldn't do without those things. That's why God gave you Phil. But Clare, I've dreamed about romance all my life and I don't want it anymore. I need reality. And Gus is real and he loves me and I love him. I'll still be romantic—I can't help it, really, but I don't need Gus to be.'

Clare's expression softened, and her eyes filled with tears. She reached over and pulled Beth into a hug. 'I've never met anyone quite like you Beth Bateman,' she said huskily, 'You are as mature as you are intelligent and beautiful.'

Instead of blushing awkwardly, Beth smiled graciously. 'Thanks, Clare. That means a lot.'

BETH WENT to find Gus first thing next morning. He was putting the finishing touches on the shed rail, but stopped the moment he saw her. 'I was hoping you'd come today.'

She smiled, suddenly shy. 'You could have called and asked me to.'

'I know, but I kind of expected you to come. We've got some unfinished business.'

She followed him to the workbench where he sat down, then reached to lift her up beside him. He turned to face her, and his expression turned sheepish. 'I talked to Phil and he said I should ask you to marry me and get you a ring. So, will you marry me?'

Amusement, along with affection for this man filled her and she felt as though her heart would burst with love for him. He was trying so hard to get it right. 'Would you prefer to wait, considering we'll probably not actually marry for a few more years?'

'I know my mind, Beth. I want to marry you, so I might as well ask you now. So will you marry me?'

She smiled. 'Yes.'

He smiled back. 'Good. Is this when we're supposed to kiss?'

Awkward. She chuckled. He really had no clue. 'Perhaps we should wait until it's more spontaneous?'

'Oh.' He actually looked disappointed. 'Well, I figured we should go ring shopping together because I have no idea what to get.'

H was still being practical, but she liked that. It made him so dependable.

'Are you free in half an hour?' he asked. 'I thought we could go then.'

'Sounds good to me.'

His smile drew her in with its overwhelming warmth, but it quickly faded. 'You know, I realised when I got home that I left that mouse somewhere.'

'On the kitchen bench.'

'Oops. Were you disgusted?'

'No, I was honoured. My presence actually made you do something illogical and impractical and well, downright disgusting.'

One side of his mouth lifted. 'I always do the disgusting bit. I wonder if your mother will have me.'

Beth hadn't told Mum. She jumped down from the bench. 'She has no choice.'

BETH AND GUS were coming out of the jewellery shop a few hours later when Dara stopped them.

'What are you doing here?' Her eyes moved from Beth to Gus.

'Ring shopping.'

'For who?'

Beth gave her best smile. 'Gus and I are engaged.'

She gaped. 'What do you mean?'

'Gus and I are getting married.'

Dara's eyes shot to Gus. 'I thought you hated the idea of marriage.' Her tone was accusing.

'I did. Until I met the right one.'

Her mouth opened and closed, then she gave a tight smile. 'Brett and I were discussing the same thing, but we think the mature thing is to go out for a while and wait until we're a bit older. I've heard that the older you are when you get married, the more likely it is to last.'

Gus gave Dara a challenging look. 'Where did you hear that?'

She shrugged. 'I don't remember.'

Beth saw his expression and knew he was about to challenge Dara about her honesty. She took Gus's hand and gently tugged it. 'We'll see you later, Dara.' She knew better than to add *Nice to see you.* Gus would question her sincerity.

'Now there's one more thing to do,' Gus said as they climbed in his ute.

'What's that?'

'Talk to your mum.'

Nerves immediately began a frantic flapping in her stomach. Mum could be fearsome when she disapproved of someone or something. She wasn't going to like Beth being distracted from her career by a relationship.

'Where is she?' Gus asked.

'You want to see her right now?'

'The sooner the better.'

'Why? Are you afraid you might change your mind?'

His brow furrowed. 'No. I just want to get it over with, and to know you are totally mine.'

MUM INVITED them into her office and offered them a seat. She was the picture of professionalism.

'So, it's happened,' she said, accepting the news with surprising calm. 'Clare warned me this was coming a long time ago, even before you two knew it.' She looked at Gus. 'To tell you the truth, I think Beth needs someone like you.'

Gus nodded confidently, while Beth stared at Mum in amazement. She sat there in all her CEO glory giving her away as though she'd always known it would happen.

'Of course, I've always had my dreams for Beth,' Mum said, straightening a notepad on her desk, 'but mostly I've always wanted my daughters to be happy. And I can see that your presence in her life has been healing.'

Of course, Gus denied it. 'Only God can heal a person, Mrs. Bateman.'

'Veronica,' she said, her eyes focusing on the ring on Beth's finger. 'Nice,' she smiled. 'I'm proud of you, Beth. You've come through so much. I never could have imagined what a truly compassionate, beautiful young woman you would become.'

Beth swallowed, holding back tears as she realised that all her mother really wanted was to see her become a mature, assertive young woman. For so long she'd tried to please her and failed. All it took to make Mum proud was to stop trying and let God be her strength.

BETH WANTED to tell everyone at the farm about her engagement, but storm clouds gathered and let loose a torrent of rain the moment they arrived at the accommodation building where Gus was now living. They ran from his ute onto the verandah, laughing as the gosling squawked and chased them, flapping his wings.

Gus looked down at the gosling, his eyes bright and alive. 'I know, it's exciting weather isn't it?'

Beth screwed up her nose. 'I much prefer sunshine.'

'Why?'

'It's all grey and gloomy and I never know what to do when its raining.'

Gus grinned. 'I wouldn't mind trying kissing. Except maybe this time you could respond a bit more positively.'

She blushed and instinctively stepped back. He was so *not* romantic. She stopped as her foot slid in a wet patch on the boards, totally soaking her shoe.

Gus laughed and took another step toward her. She pretended to glare at him and with a quick flick of her shoe in the puddle, spattered water all down his shirt.

'Do that again and I'll dump you in it,' he growled low in his throat, while Beth chuckled and flicked it at him again.

'I warned you.'

Quick as lightning he pounced, and she struggled in vain as he lifted her and gently lowered her into the puddle. She gasped as water soaked through her clothes and to her skin.

'Gus! I've got nothing else to wear!'

'So?'

'I can't talk to anyone looking like this. It looks like I wet myself.'

'You can explain.'

'What if they don't believe me?'

He reached a hand to help her from the puddle. 'We'll stay

here, then.' He grinned mischievously. 'I still like my original plan.'

'But I want to tell everyone.'

'Tell everyone what?'

'That I'm happier than I've ever been, and that you're mine.'

'You could always wear some of my overalls.' He smiled into her eyes and she couldn't help taking up his challenge.

'Okay.'

He got a pair out for her, then left his room so she could change. Chuckling to herself, she put them on. They swam on her. She emerged from the room, a belt tightened around her waist. Gus stared.

'Stylish?' she asked with a grin. She couldn't help laughing at his look.

He came to her like a magnet and her laugh muffled when he placed a kiss firmly on her mouth. 'I love you,' he breathed against her lips.

She swallowed hard. 'I love you, too. I have for a long time.'

Then he kissed her again, and this time she didn't feel awkward or embarrassed. His warm lips on hers felt so right, so natural. Her arms came up around his neck and she decided everyone would have to wait to hear their news.

CHAPTER THIRTY-EIGHT

The day Beth was accepted into Uni, Gus was offered a job in construction in the same city. Beth knew she could no longer put off releasing Gilbert.

'I'm going to miss you,' she told him. He raised his crest and ruffled his feathers, studying her out of his dark eyes. She slid the latch across the door. 'But you don't belong here anymore. It's time to fly free. Time to go home.'

She stepped back, leaving the door wide open. For a moment, Gilbert didn't move. Gus came up behind her, drawing her back against him and crossing his arms over her chest, offering his support.

'Lord, give him a long, happy life of freedom,' he prayed and at the sound of his voice, Gilbert let out a squawk and flapped his wings. Then in a smooth sweeping move, he flew out of the cage and soared up into the sky. Beth watched until he was out of sight.

She swallowed hard. 'Now he's where he's meant to be.'

Gus squeezed her tight. 'But you'll miss him.'

'Yes.'

'And that's okay.' He turned her to face him. 'And you're also allowed to miss Andy. I never wanted to replace him.'

She looked at him, heart filled with turmoil. 'You've never been a replacement for Andy, Gus. I just feel like I shouldn't be feeling sad when I have you. I've been so blessed!'

He drew her back into his arms. 'Grief is a funny thing. It hits when it wants to and for as long as it wants to. Please don't run from me when it hits. I want to share every part of your life.'

She smiled up at him, and a tear tracked down her cheek. Gus was the best thing to ever happen to her. 'It's his birthday tomorrow,' she confessed. 'I keep having dreams ... and I found something.'

He watched as she reached into the backpack hanging from her bike handlebars. She held out a notebook.

His brows rose. 'What's this?'

'My old journal. My dreams.'

He flipped through it, then looked at her with that quizzical, patient look she'd come to love.

She didn't want to tell him, but she needed to. 'I recorded everything—every conversation, every interaction with Andy. I thought I knew how it was going to end and that it would make a good story one day.'

'And it doesn't?'

'No. Life is not a storybook. Dreams don't come true like they do in romance novels. Sometimes the main character dies.'

'But Beth,' Gus said, handing it back to her, 'I think you're wrong. You were just writing with the wrong focus, the wrong characters. Andy was a major character for a while, but he wasn't the main character. He was meant to move off-stage for someone else.'

She smiled. 'You.'

'No, God,' He gave a lopsided smile. 'I don't mind having a major supporting role, though.'

'This journal shows how blind I was. How naive. I'm going to burn it.'

'No.' His hand stopped on hers, his eyes looking into her soul. 'Keep it. Rewrite the story God's way.'

'Gus, I can't.'

He reached over and pulled her close. 'Maybe not today, but someday—someday when it hurts less. Someday when you can look back and see that those who believe in God don't need to put their faith in dreams.'

A CHILLY BREEZE came with the sunrise at the farm. Beth leaned her bike against the gate to the accommodation building and gazed up beyond the hills and into the sky. Today was her last day here. She and Gus would leave this place she had grown to love. She'd be boarding with Gus's mother and step-family in the city while he rented a unit nearby.

But today was also Rod and Toni's wedding day. Who would have thought it would ever happen? And who would have thought she would fall in love with Gus Richards?

She shivered with the intensity of emotion. This was goodbye in so many ways, but also an exciting new beginning. She looked up into the sky, to the last place she'd seen Gilbert, his wings spread wide, embracing life and freedom. She knew God cared for all of His creation, and that included Gilbert. Gus reminded her often that God shared her love of all creatures. He cared when a single sparrow fell to the ground. And He cared even more for her.

The clouds shifted and Beth blinked into the light, watching as a shimmering form appeared, clearer and clearer before her eyes.

Andy.

She gasped. He was smiling down at her from heaven, and

she'd never seen him so full of life and joy. He didn't speak, but he waved to her, then turned back to the figure standing behind him. A man. Tall, with flowing white robes and warm, understanding eyes. Eyes that knew her. Eyes that loved her and delighted in her.

And she couldn't help smiling back in delight at the One who knew her, loved her, gave His life for her. 'I love you Jesus,' she whispered.

'Beth?'

She turned at the sound of Gus's voice, deep, warm and filled with concern. It was then that she felt the tears tracking down her face, dripping off her chin.

Gus came down the path and stood before her, his hair ruffled, morning stubble shadowing his cheekbones. He reached to push the hair from her eyes and wipe her tears with his fingers. 'Are you okay? I looked out the window and saw you here.'

'I saw Andy, Gus.'

'In a dream?'

'I don't know.' She waved up at the sky. 'He was just there. And he was so, so happy. He's free, where he's meant to be. But I also saw Jesus. And I just know He loves me.'

Gus smiled and looked up at the cloudless sky. 'He does. It's pretty amazing how much He loves us.' Then he pulled her close and kissed her with tenderness and passion that spoke of the kind of love, loyalty and commitment she could depend on. The kind that lasted because it was a gift from God.

And in that moment, Beth knew like she never had before; Jesus was more real than any story she'd ever read. He was more real than she was. And His plan was so much greater than any story she could ever have created. Life was just as God always planned it to be.

Jesus, You are the main character of this life story, she prayed as she leaned back against Gus's firm chest. *You're the centre of anything that ever existed, anything I ever needed. You give me joy deeper than happiness. Even when I was in pain, You were always there, giving me strength to go on. Whatever happens, Lord Jesus I am yours. Whether you let Gus outlive me or take him away tomorrow, I know You are always with me and I am Yours.*

She looked up at Gus as he smiled down at her. *But thank You for giving Gus to me now.*

Gus's warm brown eyes searched hers. She reached a hand up to his cheek and felt the morning stubble there. 'What are you thinking?'

'I was thanking God for you,' he said, and his smile broadened into a grin, 'and thinking I'm looking forward to proving that marriage is definitely not a curse.'

She wrinkled her nose at him and he laughed, then bent to kiss her again. That was Gus and she loved him despite the socially unacceptable things he said and did. Maybe even because of them.

Today was a day of new beginnings and the world, though broken, looked exciting again.

I am with you always, Beth. I love you.

She'd recognise that voice anywhere.

God, I love You, too. Thank You for saving me.

ABOUT THE AUTHOR

Jenny Glazebrook lives in a small country town in Australia. She and her husband Rob have four young adult children who fill their lives with joy.

They also have many pets and rescue animals including a sheep who thinks she's a dog, and a goose who thinks he's a human. Life in the Glazebrook household is never boring.

Jenny writes stories that capture what it means to know Jesus and live for Him in a broken world.

She has a Diploma of Theology, is a qualified chaplain and experienced inspirational speaker. She loves to encourage others to understand God's love, see His hand in their lives, and walk with Him each day.

www.jennyglazebrook.com

ACKNOWLEDGMENTS

I want to begin by thanking my husband Rob, the hero of this story. Without him, this story would not exist. Rob, God used you to show me that He wants to give me a life and love so much greater than my dreams. I love you!

Thanks also to:

Aunty Mel (Merilyn Baxter) for your encouragement, enthusiasm and insight. I always wait with great anticipation for your feedback on my manuscripts.

My fellow author, Michelle Dennis Evans, who once again made time to proofread and help me improve the story.

Erika-Lee Eksteen for her thorough and helpful edits. Erika-Lee, you went above and beyond, and I look forward to seeing how the Lord uses your gifts for His glory.

My teenage beta readers, Indi Bezant, Caitlin Miller, Nadia Broekman, Bethany Willersdorf, Cate Broekman, Merridy Glazebrook, Michaeli Broekman, and Joanna Shannon. You are priceless!

My original publisher, Elizabeth Chapman of Daughters of Love & Light. Liz, the way you believed in my stories and understood the heart of them gave me the courage to share them with the world. Thank you!

Above all, thank You Lord for the gift of creativity, Your inspiration, and the way You bring joy from brokenness and hope from despair. I love the way You weave redemption into the stories of our lives. Your story is always better than any I could have written or dreamed possible.

ALSO BY JENNY GLAZEBROOK

The Aussie Sky Series (YA fiction):

Blaze in the Storm

Heart of Thunder

Clouds of Prayer

Mist of the Morning

Clinging to Rainbows

Forgiving Sky

The Bateman Family Novels (YA/new adult fiction):

Daring Clare

Saving Beth

Framing Fleur

Seeing Jess

Living Melody

Loving Zoe

The Trinity Lakes Series (Christian romance)

Where Our Hearts Lie

In Truth and Love

Like Stars that Shine

Other books

How The World Turns

Molly the Dog-Sheep and other true pet parables (coming soon)

BATEMAN FAMILY NOVELS BOOK 3

What will it take for Dan and Fleur to trust the Father heart of God and accept His undying love for them?

Dan Bateman has been forced to move to the small town of Caldon to finish his apprenticeship, and he's not impressed.

But then he crosses paths with feisty Fleur Lester. Is she really the daughter of a millionairre?

What secret is she hiding?

Fleur instinctively fights against Dan. The abuse and betrayal she suffered as a child leave her unwilling to trust any-body, especially an insensitive tease like Dan.

Can such deep heart-wounds be healed?